Global Pandemic, Technology and Business

This book presents an exploration of a wide range of issues in law, regulation and legal rights in the sectors of information protection, the creative economy and business activities following COVID-19.

The debilitative effect of the global pandemic on information protection and creative and business activities is powerful, widespread and deeply influential, bringing a range of uncertainties to these sectors. The effects of the crisis challenge the fundamentals of the legal systems of most countries in their attempt to govern them. Written by international academics from a diversified background of law disciplines and legal systems, this book offers a global vision in exploring the wide range of legal issues caused by the COVID-19 crisis in these fields. The book is organised into three clear thematic parts: Part I looks at information protection and intellectual property rights and strategies; Part II examines contracts and mediation in the post-COVID-19 market arena; and Part III discusses issues pertaining to corporate governance and employment rights.

The book explores the unprecedented challenges posed by the pandemic crisis from a global perspective. It will provide invaluable information and guidance in this area to those in the fields of law, politics and economics whose interests are related to information, business and the creative industry, as well as providing indispensable reading to business practitioners and public servants.

Luo Li is Assistant Professor in Law at Coventry Law School, Coventry University.

Carlos Espaliú Berdud is Main Researcher of the Research Group on Security, Risks Management and Conflicts at the University of Nebrija, Madrid (Spain) and Full Professor.

Steve Foster has taught law at Coventry for over 40 years and was Head of Coventry Law School until 2017.

Ben Stanford is a Senior Lecturer in Law at Liverpool John Moores University.

Global Pandemic, Technology and Business

Comparative Explorations of COVID-19 and the Law

Edited by Luo Li, Carlos Espaliú
Berdud, Steve Foster and Ben Stanford

Routledge
Taylor & Francis Group

LONDON AND NEW YORK

First published 2022
by Routledge
2 Park Square, Milton Park, Abingdon, Oxon OX14 4RN

and by Routledge
605 Third Avenue, New York, NY 10158

Routledge is an imprint of the Taylor & Francis Group, an informa business

British Library Cataloguing-in-Publication Data
A catalogue record for this book is available from the British Library

Library of Congress Cataloging-in-Publication Data
Names: Li, Luo (Law teacher), editor. | Espaliú Berdud, Carlos, editor. |
    Foster, Steve, 1955– editor. | Stanford, Ben (Law teacher), editor.
Title: Global pandemic, technology and business : comparative
    explorations of Covid-19 and the law / edited by Luo Li, Carlos
    Espaliu Berdud, Steve Foster and Ben Stanford.
Description: Abingdon, Oxon ; New York, NY : Routledge, 2022. |
    Includes bibliographical references and index.
Identifiers: LCCN 2021033117 (print) | LCCN 2021033118
    (ebook) | ISBN 9781032010281 (hardback) | ISBN
    9781032010311 (paperback) | ISBN 9781003176848 (ebook)
Subjects: LCSH: COVID-19 (Disease)—Law and legislation. |
    COVID-19 Pandemic, 2020—Economic aspects.
Classification: LCC K3575.C68 G562 2022 (print) | LCC K3575.C68
    (ebook) | DDC 344.04/362414—dc23
LC record available at https://lccn.loc.gov/2021033117
LC ebook record available at https://lccn.loc.gov/2021033118

ISBN: 978-1-032-01028-1 (hbk)
ISBN: 978-1-032-01031-1 (pbk)
ISBN: 978-1-003-17684-8 (ebk)

DOI: 10.4324/9781003176848

Typeset in Galliard
by Apex CoVantage, LLC

Contents

Contributors

Carlos Espaliú Berdud received a scholarship from the Spanish Ministry of Education (1995–98) to complete a doctorate in International Law. He has been Lecturer in the University of Navarre (Spain) (1998–2000), Legal Officer of the International Court of Justice (2000–06), Ramón y Cajal Researcher in the University of Córdoba (Spain) (2007–12) and Associate Professor in Public International Law and European Union Law at the International University of Catalonia (UIC). At the latter university, he was also Director of the Charlemagne Institute of European Studies (2012–18) and Vice-Dean for Academic Affairs at the Faculty of Law. At present, he is the Main Researcher of the Research Group on Security, Risks Management and Conflicts at the University of Nebrija, Madrid (Spain) and Full Professor.

Andrés Jerónimo Arenas Falótico studied and graduated as a lawyer and a journalist. He has a Master of Business Administration, a Master in Education, and a doctoral degree in management. He is accredited as a 'Senior Fellow' by the Higher Education Academy in the UK. He has published several academic articles in different indexed scientific journals worldwide, as well as book chapters. Andrés has worked in multinational companies such as CEMEX, Bellsouth, Mack Trucks, and has been a senior consultant of several national and international companies. Andrés is currently working as professor and researcher at Nebrija University.

Steve Foster has taught law at Coventry for over 40 years and was Head of Coventry Law School until 2017. He specialises in human rights, prisoners' rights and legal writing. He has published widely in various journals on human rights, prisoners' rights, administrative law and freedom of expression. He is also the author of several textbooks including *Human Rights and Civil Liberties* (Pearson 2011) and (with Mark Ryan) *Unlocking Constitutional and Administrative Law* (Routledge 2018). In 2007, he was awarded a PhD by portfolio for his writing on prisoners' rights. He is also editor in chief of the *Coventry Law Journal*.

Johanna Gibson is Herchel Smith Professor of Intellectual Property Law at Queen Mary, University of London, where she teaches and does research on intellectual property, legal theory and philosophy. Gibson's most recent book is *Owned, An Ethological Jurisprudence of Property* (2020), in which she develops a theory of ethological jurisprudence in relation to property and intellectual property. Gibson is also the author of *Community Resources* (2005), *Creating Selves* (2006), *Intellectual Property, Medicine and Health* (2009/2017 2nd ed) and *The Logic of Innovation* (2014), as well as editor of the collection *Patenting Lives: Life Patents, Culture and Development* (2008).

Juha Karhu is Professor (emeritus) at Law Faculty of University of Lapland, Finland, where he worked as Professor of Contract Law and Tort Law 1993–2017. He was also Dean of Law Faculty 2013–17 and acted as the Vice Rector of the University of Lapland 1999–2004. His research focuses on the foundations of commercial law, including themes such as the role of legal principles in dynamic contractual networks, the legal protection of business assets in cooperation projects, and the role of fundamental and human rights in the new global economy. His research has a strong emphasis on comparative perspectives.

Olga Kokoulina is a Carlsberg Foundation Postdoctoral Fellow. Her primary research interests lie at the intersection of Law and Technology. Olga holds a PhD in law from the University of Copenhagen, and MSc and LLM degrees from the University of Oxford (Oxford Internet Institute) and Lund University. Her postdoctoral research, conducted at the Centre for Information and Innovation Law (CIIR), addresses the topic of algorithmic decision-making. Examining the limits of algorithmic accountability, the project focuses on issues of intellectual property rights, competition and data governance.

Luo Li is Assistant Professor in Law at Coventry Law School, Coventry University. She teaches and does research on intellectual property, cultural heritages and digital transformation. Prior to joining Coventry University, Luo had worked at the Law and Legislative Advice Division of the World Intellectual Property Organization in 2013. She was Associate Editor of *Queen Mary Journal of Intellectual Property* (2015–17) and currently, she is a journal article reviewer for *QMJIP* and the *International Journal of Cultural Policy*. She is also a grant reviewer for the National Social Science Academy in Poland. She was a visiting scholar at the University of Copenhagen in Denmark.

Anja Møller Pedersen LLM is a research assistant working with human rights and technology, particularly privacy and data protection, at the Center for Information and Innovation Law (CIIR), University of Copenhagen, and the Danish Institute for Human Rights.

Jessica Bayón Pérez is a professor at Nebrija University and a doctor of social sciences with a specialty in direction and people management. Her professional career focused on human resources in the socio-sanitary field. She is also the author of book chapters for prestigious publishers and relevant working experience as a Lecturer in different national and international universities in the legal and human resources fields. She is an author in more than ten international indexed publications. She is a member of the advisory committee of the indexed journal *Ethos* and of the editorial committee for the indexed Panamá University journal *Revista Colón Ciencias, Tecnología y Negocios*.

Geraldine Bethencourt Rodríguez has a PhD in law and economics from the CEU San Pablo University with international doctorate mention. Her research work and teaching activity is carried out mainly in the fields of commercial law and alternative conflict resolution systems. Currently, she is the Director of the Degree in Law (distance modality) at Nebrija University. She works as a mediator and facilitator. Her contribution to the promotion of mediation in Spain was recognised with the Professional Merit Medal awarded by the Spanish School of Mediation and Conflict Resolution and Mediation Journal in 2017.

Neshat Safari is a lecturer and researcher at Coventry University. She is a specialist in comparative corporate law and corporate governance and corporate social responsibility. Her current research concerns the issue of corporate social responsibility with particular focus on a company's responsibility toward its employees' rights and interests and the tension between labour and capital.

Jens Schovsbo LLD, PhD is a professor of intellectual property law at the Center for Information and Innovation Law (CIIR), University of Copenhagen. He is and has been writing on a broad variety of topics within the fields of intellectual property and information law and has focused lately on the relationship to contract and competition law. He is, amongst other things, President of the International Association for the Advancement of Teaching and Research in Intellectual Property (ATRIP) (2019–22).

Alex Simmonds holds a degree in law from the University of Sheffield (2005) and was called to the Bar of England and Wales at the Honourable Society of the Inner Temple in 2008. He is presently a PhD candidate in employment law at Coventry University. In addition to employment law, he also researches space law and has published articles in both the *Coventry Law Journal* and the *Wolters-Kluwer Journal of Air and Space Law*. Before coming to academia he worked as a trade union representative for seven years in warehousing and further education, representing union members in disciplinary and investigatory hearings.

Ben Stanford completed his PhD in 2017 which examined counter-terrorism executive orders and the right to a fair trial. His current research focuses on democracy and political rights, in particular free speech, protest and the right to vote. Ben is an editor for the *Asian Yearbook of Human Rights and Humanitarian Law* and a fellow of the Higher Education Academy. Ben was recently appointed as a lay observer to monitor the welfare and access to justice of people held in court custody. He has previously worked for Rights Watch (UK), Peace Brigades International (UK) and the Human Rights Lawyers Association.

Figures

Introduction

1 The pandemic crisis and its global legal impact on information protection, creative economy and business activities

Luo Li, Carlos Espaliú Berdud, Steve Foster and Ben Stanford

Introduction

Since January 2020, this new coronavirus – COVID-19 – has infected more than 200 countries and territories, with millions of confirmed cases and a massive loss of life. The pandemic disease is not only an unprecedented crisis for global public health and safety, but also threatens the global economy and presents the potential to disrupt all global business and its surrounding sectors. This virus has been described by many people as World War III – a war in which human beings fight against the virus,[1] its short-term impact on the economy and the uncertainties over a longer period of time. In other words, a global economic war by humans fighting against chain reactions followed by a public health and economic crisis. With contingency policies including closing borders, lockdown of cities and minimising business activities in many countries with the purpose of restricting people's movement and reducing infection speed, the global economy hangs in the balance with so many uncertainties. Creativity, innovation and commercial and business-related activities that require the active engagement of social members are fundamentally challenged, at present and in the future. These challenges are a result of the pandemic itself, the related government responses and their policies and, more generally, the potential and uncertain changes reflecting future emergent situations.

This text is a monographic research book aimed at bringing together a diverse range of chapters on the contributing authors' specific areas of expertise under the broad and ambitious banner of information, the creative economy and business activities. It will explore the theoretical and practical impact of the pandemic

---

1 Farrokh Habibzadeh, 'World War III' (2020)11(3) *The International Journal of Occupational and Environmental Medicine* 117–18; Abhishek Kumar, 'World War III: Humans vs Corona' (*Biotechticle*, 11 April 2020) <https://biotechticle.com/world-war-iii-humans-vs-corona/> accessed 10 November 2020; Raghu Krishnan, 'View: Coronavirus Conflict Is World War 3' (*The Economic Times*, 17 May 2020) <https://economictimes.indiatimes.com/news/international/world-news/view-coronavirus-conflict-is-world-war-3/articleshow/75792202.cms> accessed 10 November 2020.

DOI: 10.4324/9781003176848-2

crisis with respect to information, business and the creative economy, broadly defined, by addressing a variety of legal issues and fields. To achieve this aim, the book firstly explores the impact of COVID-19 upon the use of intangible assets by examining both the theoretical framework and practical application of rights of information and privacy, and the public interest in the copyright context and how the pandemic re-shapes fashion industry, one of the most active creative economies, and relevant intellectual property concerns. It then reflects how this global pandemic challenges methods of dealing with various legal issues in commercial activities, including the substantial impact of relevant doctrines, principles and approaches in contract law and dispute resolutions. Finally, the book explores the rights of different legal parties in the business environment and how they will be impacted by relevant developments. This book offers timely guidance for scholars, students and practitioners to better understand and map the uncertainties caused by COVID-19 in the sectors of information, creative economy and business. The book also aims to strengthen the dialogue of scholars in both the legal field and in other disciplines – both nationally and internationally. This will establish an inter-disciplinary dialogue to promote a better understanding of the global COVID-19 crisis and its impact and possible responses to a wide variety of commercial and business sectors from both a global and local perspective.

COVID-19: the pandemic crisis

On 11 March 2020, the widespread COVID-19 was defined as a "pandemic" by the World Health Organization (WHO). The term pandemic refers to 'an epidemic occurring worldwide, or over a very wide area, crossing international boundaries and usually affecting a large number of people'.[2] Nevertheless, this classic definition does not cover population immunity, virology or disease severity but seems to cover seasonal epidemics not normally considered as pandemics.[3] The WHO's official website defines pandemic as 'the worldwide spread of a new disease. An influenza pandemic occurs when a new influenza virus emerges and spreads around the world, and most people do not have immunity.'[4] The WHO's definition was described by Peter Doshi as elusive,[5] and in May 2009, just before the declaration of the H1N1 pandemic, the WHO changed its definition and removed the words 'resulting in several simultaneous epidemics

2   Miquel Porta (ed), *A Dictionary of Epidemiology* (5th edn, New York, OUP 2008) 179.
3   Heath Kelly, 'The Classical Definition of a Pandemic Is Not Elusive' (2011) 89 *Bulletin of the World Health Organization* <www.who.int/bulletin/volumes/89/7/11-088815/en/> accessed 16 March 2021.
4   'What Is a Pandemic?' (*World Health Organisation*, 24 February 2010) <www.who.int/csr/disease/swineflu/frequently_asked_questions/pandemic/en/> accessed 16 March 2021.
5   Peter Doshi, 'The Elusive Definition of Pandemic Influenza' (2011) 89 *Bulletin of the World Health Organization* <www.who.int/bulletin/volumes/89/7/11–086173/en/> accessed 16 March 2021.

worldwide with enormous numbers of deaths and illness' from the definition.[6] The Council of Europe had concerns whether H1N1 influenza should be labelled as pandemic influenza as this revised definition would result it in declaring a pandemic 'without having to demonstrate the intensity of the disease caused by the H1N1 virus'.[7] The pandemic preparedness guidelines provided by the WHO only contains a definition of the pandemic phase, instead of pandemic influenza, and its determinations 'do not correlate with clinical severity but rather with the likelihood of disease occurrence'.[8] Therefore, such a definition received massive attention and criticism.[9] There is an argument that 'simultaneous worldwide transmission of influenza is sufficient to define an influenza pandemic and is consistent with the classical definition of "an epidemic occurring worldwide"'.[10] There is, therefore, a need to redefine the term "pandemic" for the purpose of describing the potential severity range of future pandemics.[11] While the discussion about the definition of pandemics continues, there is no issue in defining the widespread COVID-19 as a pandemic. On 11 March 2020, when the WHO declared COVID-19 as a pandemic, there were more than 110 countries and over 118,000 cases of illness in the world. Until 16 March 2021, there were more than 100 million confirmed cases and more than 2.5 million confirmed deaths reported on the WHO's website. When looking at the determinative factors of disease severity, population or simultaneous worldwide transmission, COVID-19 is indeed a pandemic.

In the WHO's declaration, Dr Tedros Adhanom Ghebreyesus, WHO Director General, said the pandemic 'is not just a public health crisis, it is a crisis that will touch every sector – so every sector and every individual must be involved in the fight.'[12] This indicates the spread of the COVID-19 epidemic is not a simple

---

6   'Pandemic Preparedness' (*World Health Organization*, 2 February 2003) <http://web.archive.org/web/20030202145905/www.who.int/csr/disease/influenza/pandemic/en/> accessed 16 March 2021.

7   Kelly (n 3).

8   Doshi (n 5). See also 'Swine Flu of 1976: Lessons from the Past' (2009) 87 *Bulletin of the World Health Organization* <www.who.int/bulletin/volumes/87/6/09-040609/en/> accessed 16 March 2021.

9   ibid. See also 'The Handling of the H1N1 Pandemic: More Transparency Needed' (*Parliamentary Assembly, Council of Europe*, 7 June 2010) <https://pace.coe.int/en/files/12463/html> accessed 16 March 2021; Elizabeth Cohen, 'When a Pandemic isn't a Pandemic' (*CNN*, 4 May 2009) <http://edition.cnn.com/2009/HEALTH/05/04/swine.flu.pandemic/index.html> accessed 16 March 2021; Donald G McNeil, 'WHO to Rewrite Its Pandemic Rules' (*The New York Times*, 22 May 2009) <www.nytimes.com/2009/05/23/health/policy/23who.html> accessed 14 March 2021; Lisa Schnirring, 'WHO Foresees Problems with Pandemic Severity Index' (*Center for Infectious Disease Research & Policy*, 13 May 2009) <www.cidrap.umn.edu/cidrap/content/influenza/panflu/news/may1309severity-br.html> accessed 16 March 2021.

10 Kelly (n 3).

11 ibid.

12 'WHO Director-General's Opening Remarks at the Media Briefing on COVID-19' (*World Health Organisation*, 11 March 2020) <www.who.int/director-general/

pandemic disease or a health issue, but that such a pandemic would result in an emergency in wider sectors of society, including the public health sector. The term "crisis" is commonly used in the areas of politics, finance, the economy, management and the natural environment to describe a negative and complex situation. In the Cambridge Dictionary, the term "crisis" is defined as 'a time of great disagreement, confusion, or suffering'.[13] The WHO defines the term "crisis" by referencing the Oxford Pocket Dictionary, and the term embraces two meanings: the first refers to

> A situation that is perceived as difficult. Its greatest value is that it implies the possibility of an insidious process that cannot be defined in time, and that even spatially can recognize different layers/levels of intensity. A crisis may not be evident, and it demands analysis to be recognized. Conceptually, it can cover both preparedness and response.
>
> ("crisis management")[14]

The second aspect focuses on the 'time of danger or greater difficulty, decisive turning point'.[15] The common features of a crisis include 'the perception of threat arising from extreme discrepancy between desired and existing states',[16] un-anticipated event with a lot of uncertainties,[17] and short response time,[18] but requiring 'a rapid and highly structured response'.[19] Normally, the causes of the crisis may vary or be unknown and not possible to identify in a short time. Most crises that human beings face in history are made by humans themselves, except some public health crises, such as economic, financial and organisational crises. Sometimes, even if these crises are unpredictable, it might be because humans do not recognise such a crisis before it has developed towards extreme danger. In contrast, a natural crisis possesses an inherent un-anticipated nature, such as an earthquake.

When the term "crisis" is applied in the public health sector, it normally means a certain disease significantly affecting community health and resulting in a loss of life. Its severity is determined by the number of infections and the affected

---

speeches/detail/who-director-general-s-opening-remarks-at-the-media-briefing-on-covid-19-11-march-2020> accessed 16 March 2021.

13   'Definition of Crisis' (*Cambridge Dictionary*) <https://dictionary.cambridge.org/dictionary/english/crisis> accessed 1 October 2020.

14   'Definitions: Emergencies' (*World Health Organisation*) <www.who.int/hac/about/definitions/en/> accessed 19 March 2021.

15   ibid.

16   Matthew Seeger and others, 'Communication, Organization, and Crisis' (1998)21(1) *Annals of the International Communication Association* 233.

17   ibid 235.

18   ibid 234–35.

19   Edward Borodzicz, *Risk, Crisis and Security Management* (West Sussex, John Wiley & Sons 2005) 79.

geographical areas or the death rate.[20] If an existing epidemic is ignored by the public, and its research and knowledge lags far behind, such an epidemic will result in a forthcoming public health crisis. An example is the unknown widespread of hepatitis C virus (HCV). 'Hepatitis C is just as deadly as HIV – both kill about 10,000–15,000 people per year in the United States'.[21] Its infection is five times the size of the HIV epidemic, but relevant diagnosis, research and public awareness is lagging far behind.[22] Accordingly, Lauren Gravitz describes HCV as a smouldering public-health crisis.[23] Some scholars use the terms "public health crisis" and "public health emergency" interchangeably, explaining that both terms refer to 'a state of affairs in which the health of a substantial portion of a community's members is either compromised or in imminent danger because of the inability of existing mechanisms for safeguarding the public's health to cope with an emergent health threat'.[24]

There is no doubt that the COVID-19 pandemic crisis has similar features to a natural crisis, in that the crisis is inherently unprecedented; although many epidemiologists warn that pandemic viruses like COVID-19 may outbreak at some point.[25] Since COVID-19 is a virus infecting human bodies and places human life in danger, this pandemic also absorbs features of a normal public health crisis, meaning that a substantial number of people in the world will be affected and their health would be in danger. Furthermore, the COVID-19 pandemic is worse than other virus-resulted public health crisis such as HIV and HCV, due to its wide geographical spread in a short time and easy infection and transmission. Meanwhile, this pandemic crisis has common features of a crisis, such as a short response time and with many of the uncertainties in a foreseen future.

However, the pandemic crisis not only absorbs features from different types of crisis but shows its special characteristics; its effects are unpredictable, rapid and widespread (pandemic), possessing the potential to affect all business sectors and humans' work and lifestyles in a short period of time. The COVID-19 pandemic results in many deaths or significant effect on their health in a very short period of time, and humans know little or nothing of this new virus, let alone its treatment and vaccination. From this point of view, an outbreak of an unknown disease

20 Lauren Gravitz, 'Introduction: A Smouldering Public-Health Crisis' (*Nature*, 8 June 2011) <www.nature.com/articles/474S2a> accessed 19 March 2021.
21 ibid.
22 ibid.
23 ibid.
24 Alex John, 'Research in a Public Health Crisis: The Integrative Approach to Managing the Moral Tensions' in Jennings B (ed), *Emergency Ethics: Public Health Preparedness and Response* (New York, OUP 2016) <https://oxfordmedicine.com/view/10.1093/med/9780190270742.001.0001/med-9780190270742-chapter-7> accessed 19 March 2021.
25 George Gao and others, 'Prevalent Eurasian Avian-Like H1N1 Swine Influenza Virus with 2009 Pandemic Viral Genes Facilitating Human Infection' (2020)117(29) *Proceedings of the National Academy of Sciences of the United States of America* 17204–210 (*PNAS*, 21 July 2020) <www.pnas.org/content/117/29/17204> accessed 19 March 2021.

alone is a crisis in the public health sector, and this has not happened in recent human history. Furthermore, since this is an unknown virus outbreak, without any vaccination and any appropriate medicines to treat this disease, the oldest but most effective approach to prevent virus spread in a short time is to quarantine the infected from the non-infected and to restrict human movement. As a result, a series of policies including quarantine, lockdown, travel bans and other restrictions have been implemented in a number of countries in the world.[26] Nevertheless, these measures significantly disrupt globalisation progress developed in the past decades.

> [G]lobalisation may be described as the ever closer economic integration of all the countries of the world resulting from the liberalisation and consequent increase in both the volume and the variety of international trade in goods and services, the falling cost of transport, the growing intensity of the international penetration of capital, the immense growth in the global labour force, and the accelerated worldwide diffusion of technology, particularly communications.[27]

Because of COVID-19 and its response policies, the whole world's economy suffered a great deal. In 2020, '[T]he baseline forecast envisions a 5.2 percent contraction in global GDP . . . using market exchange rate weights – the deepest global recession in decades, despite the extraordinary efforts of governments to counter the downturn with fiscal and monetary policy support.'[28] The longer-term impact seems even worse. In the Global Economic Prospects produced by the World Bank Group in January 2021, it was predicted that the pandemic crisis would result in lasting investment losses,[29] a negative effect on human capital accumulation because of pandemic disrupted education,[30] and fragmentation of global trade and economic links.[31] From this point of view, the COVID-19 pandemic is not a simple public health crisis anymore, but would bring 'the deepest global recession in decades',[32] a forthcoming economic crisis that will have long-term effects on all countries and at all sectors in the world. Both a worldwide

---

26   Hannah Ritchie and others, 'Policy Responses to the Coronavirus Pandemic' (*Our World in Data*) <https://ourworldindata.org/policy-responses-covid> accessed 29 March 2021.
27   Parliamentary Assembly, 'Realising Both Economic Growth and Social Protection in Europe in an Era of Globalisation' (*Parliamentary Assembly Council of Europe*, 3 October 2007) <http://assembly.coe.int/nw/xml/XRef/Xref-XML2HTML-en.asp?fileid=17580&lang=en> accessed 22 March 2021.
28   The World Bank, 'The Global Economic Outlook During the COVID-19 Pandemic: A Changed World' (*The World Bank*, 8 June 2020) <www.worldbank.org/en/news/feature/2020/06/08/the-global-economic-outlook-during-the-covid-19-pandemic-a-changed-world> accessed 22 March 2021.
29   World Bank Group, *Global Economic Prospects* (Washington, World Bank Group 2021) 128–30 <www.worldbank.org/en/publication/global-economic-prospects> accessed 22 March 2021.
30   ibid 134.
31   ibid 71.
32   The World Bank (n 28).

public health crisis and an economic crisis – the two most important factors in maintaining a stable society – are triggered by the COVID-19 pandemic. This means the pandemic crisis will be much more serious than originally envisaged and it is predicted that this would trigger or accelerate more issues and conflicts with respect to international politics and relationships, and societal, legal, ethical and human values. To some extent, the COVID-19 pandemic crisis has created a chain reaction and has resulted in a crisis of human society. Through the COVID-19 crisis, humans need to reflect on its existing economic and social frameworks, its value in individual and public interests, and its rights and responsibilities to avoid or minimise COVID-19 damage in the future.

Legal concerns of the impact of COVID-19 on information protection, creativity and business

COVID-19 has undoubtedly affected human health, the economy, business and different sectors in the whole world to a significant degree. While many countries use the oldest approach of restricting human movement to spread the COVID-19 pandemic, modern technologies and approaches are also applied to support to prevent the spread of the virus. 'Mounting evidence demonstrates that the collection, use, sharing and further processing of data can help limit the spread of the virus and aid in accelerating recovery, especially through digital contact tracing.'[33] Digital contact tracing refers to a process that is able to identify people who have had contact with a COVID-19 patient in the previous two weeks.[34] Contact tracing has its own issues, such as being time-consuming to identify. This is because the virus can transmit between human without manifesting symptoms. In this case, if someone has contact with an infected person without yet showing symptoms, that person will not be treated as the one who has contacted an infected person unless and until that infected person has been confirmed positive.[35] Other issues such as individual incentives of contact tracing are discussed in the world as well.[36] However, the question that raises most concern around digital contact tracing is privacy and data security.[37]

---

33 'Joint Statement on Data Protection and Privacy in the COVID-19 Response' (*World Health Organisation*, 19 November 2020) <www.who.int/news/item/19-11-2020-joint-statement-on-data-protection-and-privacy-in-the-covid-19-response> accessed 23 March 2021.

34 'Tracking COVID-19: Contact Tracing in the Digital Age' (*World Health Organisation*, 9 September 2020) <www.who.int/news-room/feature-stories/detail/tracking-covid-19-contact-tracing-in-the-digital-age> accessed 23 March 2021.

35 ibid.

36 Manuel Cebrian, 'The Past, Present and Future of Digital Contact Tracing' (2021)4 *Nature Electronics* 2–4 <www.nature.com/articles/s41928-020-00535-z> accessed 23 March 2021. Cebrian concerns to what extent people would follow the recommendations of the contact tracing apps requiring stay at home and quarantine considering doing so may affect their mental health or loss of income.

37 Emanuele Ventrella, 'Privacy in Emergency Circumstances: Data Protection and the COVID-19 Pandemic' (2020)21 *ERA Forum* 379–93; Magdalena Kędzior, 'The Right to Data Protection and the COVID-19 Pandemic: The European Approach' (2021)21 *ERA Forum* 533–43.

On the one hand, individual privacy is a fundamental right, and collecting personal data must follow strict legal rules and regulations in case any infringement is committed. On the other hand, data collection and processing for tracing COVID-19 is an effective approach to prevent virus spread and is carried out in the public interest. Hence, the question is how to balance individual privacy with this public interest. Article 5 of the General Data Protection Regulation (GDPR) provides some guiding principles about processing personal data: personal data must be 'collected for specific, explicit and legitimate purposes',[38] and limited to 'what is necessary in relation to the purposes for which they are processed ('data minimisation')'.[39] While the GDPR is regarded as 'the most consequential regulatory development in information policy in a generation',[40] there is concern as to whether GDPR would hinder the effectiveness of COVID-19 tracing in being beneficial for the overall interests of society.[41] In fact, the issues on data collection and processing due to COVID-19 extend far further than to simple rights of privacy. From an information law perspective, individual rights holders are granted exclusive rights in information rights, but the purpose is to further a larger interest of the public in innovation and personal integrity. There are also concerns on the ownership of resulting data and the intersection with data privacy regulation. This means data-related activities and issues are covered – both in areas of information law and intellectual property law – and an activity of data collection, processing, using and securing affect various groups of creators, users and data subjects in these laws. Therefore, a series of questions and uncertainties are exposed as a result of these data-related activities carried out under the emergency. Without well-prepared laws in information law, and its relationship with intellectual property law, the circumstances where information may be shared and used and how the interests of relevant parties in data-related activities are balanced, must be addressed. From this point of view, the pandemic crisis brings a re-consideration of how to use intangible assets from a legal perspective.

In fact, such re-consideration is not limited to information protection, but also in wider creative sectors. On the one hand, there is no doubt that a large amount of people and enterprises in the creative industry have suffered income or profit loss, and even subsequent financial crisis, because of social-distance policies

---

38   Regulation 2016/679 of the European Parliament and of the Council of 27 April 2016 on the Protection of Natural Persons with regard to the Processing of Personal Data and on the Free Movement of Such Data, and Repealing Directive 95/46/EC (General Data Protection Regulation), OJ 2016 L 119/1, art 5(1b).

39   ibid art 5(1c).

40   Chris Jay Hoofnagle and others, 'The European Union General Data Protection Regulation: What It Is and What It Means' (2019)28 *Information & Communications Technology Law* 1 <www.tandfonline.com/doi/full/10.1080/13600834.2019.1573501> accessed 23 March 2021.

41   Deloitte, 'Privacy and Data Protection in the Age of COVID-19' <https://www2.deloitte.com/content/dam/Deloitte/be/Documents/risk/be-risk_privacy-and-data-protection-in-the-age-of-covid-19.pdf> accessed 23 March 2021.

carried out during the pandemic. In its report, the Organisation for Economic Co-operation and Development (OECD) warns those creative sectors, including arts, entertainment and recreation, that they are at risk from job loss, reduction of investment in creative sectors and a reduction of creative production and consumption.[42] Further, such risk is uneven across regions because of the pandemic crisis.[43] The European Parliament in its crisis effects and policy recommendation report, also raises concerns over the direct economic effects in Europe, including loss of income and business opportunities in the creative sectors.[44] While many people working in creative industries are low-wage, non-standing workers, they are significantly affected by the cancellation of their jobs or commissions due to lockdown or social distancing policies.[45] Oxford Economics released a report about the economic impact of COVID-19 on the UK creative industry,[46] stating that 'The Creative Industries (CIs) are projecting a combined £77 billion turnover loss over the course of 2020 compared to 2019 (-31%). This is expected to translate into a GVA[47] shortfall of £29 billion in 2020 compared to 2019 (-26%).'[48] A report provided by the House of Commons in the UK Parliament shows the COVID-19 outbreak resulted in a significant reduction of creative productions, income loss and/or permanent closure of creative entities and a risk to creative workforce.[49] The fashion industry, one of the most active creativity sectors, was one of the hardest hit because of the pandemic crisis. Like many other creative industries, the fashion industry is 'still almost entirely dependent

---

42 OECD, 'Culture Shock: COVID-19 and the Cultural and Creative Sectors' (*OECD*, 7 September 2020) <www.oecd.org/coronavirus/policy-responses/culture-shock-covid-19-and-the-cultural-and-creative-sectors-08da9e0e/> accessed 26 March 2021.

43 ibid.

44 Isabelle De Voldere and others, 'Cultural and Creative Sectors in Post COVID-19 Europe – Crisis Effects and Policy Recommendations' (2021) 31–34. <www.europarl.europa.eu/RegData/etudes/STUD/2021/652242/IPOL_STU(2021)652242_EN.pdf> accessed 26 March 2021.

45 OECD (n 42).

46 The Oxford Economics is a famous independent global advisory firm providing global economic and industry forecasting service and quantitative analysis service.

47 In economics, GVA means gross value added. The GVA is used to 'measure the contribution to the economy of each individual producer, industry or sector'. National Statistics, 'DCMS Economic Estimates 2019: Gross Value Added – Technical and Quality Assurance Report' (*Gov.UK Department for Digital, Cultural, Media & Sport*, 19 February 2021) <www.gov.uk/government/statistics/dcms-economic-estimates-2019-gross-value-added/dcms-economic-estimates-2019-gross-value-added-technical-and-quality-assurance-report> accessed 26 March 2021.

48 The Oxford Economics, 'The Projected Economic Impact of COVID-19 on the UK Creative Industries' (16 July 2020) 20 <www.oxfordeconomics.com/recent-releases/The-Projected-Economic-Impact-of-COVID-19-on-the-UK-Creative-Industries> accessed 26 March 2021.

49 Digital, Culture, Media and Sport Committee, 'Impact of COVID-19 on DCMS Sectors: First Report' (20 July 2020) 20–40 <https://committees.parliament.uk/publications/2022/documents/19516/default/> accessed 26 March 2021.

on physical retail and more than 80% of transactions in the fashion industry still happen in physical stores'.[50]

On the other hand, the pandemic containment policy not only results in the disappearance of millions of industry jobs and loss of revenue for fashion brands,[51] but also brings new changes to the fashion industry as a whole. In an interview by McKinsey, Maximilian Bittner, the chief executive officer of Vestiaire Collective claims that the pandemic crisis brings sustainable and ethical fashion to the forefront.[52] The European Parliament's report also notes wider social effects and new cultural consumer behaviours or habits that impact on the creative industry, including arts, music and entertainment, in the post-COVID age.[53] This is because the pandemic crisis substantially accelerates digital innovation and solutions in the creative industry. The previously mentioned changes will result in new challenges on how to use intellectual assets in this changing world. Therefore, it is necessary to map the changes in the creative industries like fashion industry, to re-consider the value of intangible assets and re-structure appropriate strategies in the creative sectors in response to changes arising from the pandemic crisis. Moreover, the pandemic crisis also raises concerns as to the relationship between the public interest and an individual's rights to intangible assets in the creative sector. While the entire creative industry is struggling with the loss caused by the pandemic and its containment policy, public users are also struggling with what intangible resources they can use. Digital innovation and solutions during the pandemic resolve the issue of alternative approaches of obtaining knowledge and information, but the law does not tell us clearly how to resolve subsequent legal issues because of these approaches. Legislators were not able to forecast a widely affected situation such as the pandemic, and therefore our laws dealing with intangible assets do not fully or effectively consider this aspect. As a result it is necessary to fill this gap and consider a well-prepared law in responding to future extreme situation like the COVID-19 crisis.

As mentioned earlier, the COVID-19 pandemic is a crisis that hits nearly every business sector, impacting significantly on both business enterprises and workers. The world economy is as a result struggling: most economies are in recession, suffering a decreasing of jobs and the risk of unemployment.[54] As the pandemic

50 Steven McIntosh, 'Coronavirus: Why the Fashion Industry Faces an "Existential Crisis"' (*BBC*, 30 April 2020) <www.bbc.co.uk/news/entertainment-arts-52394504> accessed 26 March 2021.
51 Vogue Business Team, 'Fashion Industry Crisis Deepens Amid Covid-19 Chaos' (*Vogue Business*, 6 April 2020) <www.voguebusiness.com/companies/fashion-industry-crisis-deepens-amid-covid-19-chaos> accessed 26 March 2021.
52 Achim Berg and others, 'A Perfect Storm for Fashion Marketplaces' (*McKinsey & Company*, 8 June 2020) <www.mckinsey.com/industries/retail/our-insights/a-perfect-storm-for-fashion-marketplaces> accessed 26 March 2021.
53 Voldere and others (n 44) 39–40.
54 Lora Jones and others, 'Coronavirus: How the Pandemic Has Changed the World Economy' (*BBC News*, 24 January 2021) <www.bbc.co.uk/news/business-51706225> accessed 29 March 2021.

rapidly and radically attacks the economy, the long-term impact is still uncertain. Consequently, a variety of commercial activities in the business context have been, or will be, affected, influenced and adjusted during and after the pandemic. Commercial contracts play an important role at any stage of the business activity in binding both parties legally. The pandemic containment policies bring legal concerns on rights and responsibilities in commercial dealings since the pandemic results in a significant delay of completion of business contracts. Moreover, the uncertain situation will result in a considerable increase in legal disputes in a commercial context. In this case, the question is how to make sure the legal system can respond to such conflicts. Whether an alternative dispute resolution such as mediation would be an effective way to settle disputes in extreme situations like the COVID-19 is worthy of consideration. If these concerns relate to legal issues arising from a business entity's outside activities, the following issues relate to its internal activities. The pandemic crisis will lead the direction of the economy and the business framework must accommodate some changes. Therefore, a business entity has to take measures to respond to such changes in order to survive. However, these measures will affect relevant key parties in the business entity and individuals working for them. In this case, how to deal with a relationship between employees and employers, and what kind of rights and responsibilities are owed to them during the extreme situation, will become a substantial concern of corporate governance, employment law and labour rights.

Although we have witnessed some short-term pandemic impacts on a variety of sectors, we still know little about their impact on the law, regulation and legal rights in the longer term. There is an urgent need to develop an understanding of the possible legal challenges and research-based guidance in adopting effective strategic responses to a crisis that threatens the business and creative endeavours of the whole human society. Therefore, this book presents some of the most prominent legal challenges and issues facing a wide range of sectors caused by the pandemic, including information protection, the creative economy and business activities, as well as the most pressing needs for research and action in order to respond to extreme situations such as COVID-19.

The volume in brief

This book (Volume 2) is presented in conjunction with (Volume 1) – *Global Pandemic, Security and Human Rights: Comparative Explorations of COVID-19 and the Law* – as the two collectively form part of a common research project. Volume 1 seeks to explore the theoretical and practical impact of the COVID-19 global pandemic on human rights and security. Measures taken to combat the pandemic by states worldwide have brought into question not only the legality and proportionality of restrictions to civil liberties (e.g. freedom of speech, assembly, privacy and movement), and the states' obligations to ensure the safety of individuals, but has also exposed the problems of a securitised approach to public health and how this can impact on personal, collective and global security. Volume 2 seeks to explore the theoretical and practical impact of the COVID-19 global pandemic with respect to rights of information, and intellectual property concerns in the creative economy. It also examines various legal issues in business activities, including the substantial impact of relevant doctrines, principles and approaches in the area of commercial law, in addition to how the rights of different legal parties in the business environment will be impacted. It is envisaged that readers will be able to best align their interests with one particular book, but should readers wish to broaden their horizons and gain a fuller and more comprehensive understanding of the crisis, this can best be achieved by reading both books in conjunction.

Since this public health crisis is a global incident, whose influence is no longer limited to certain countries, regions or sectors, but is widely linked and interactively impacted together, an approach with a global perspective has been adopted. The global perspective of the book is demonstrated in a number of ways. The widespread COVID-19 has been defined as a "pandemic" by WHO. As mentioned previously, COVID-19 is not only a threat to all humans' health and safety, but also significantly impacts on the economy, business and different sectors in the whole world, challenging existing legal systems with respect to the economy, business and different sectors. The book explores the legal challenges and implications resulting from the COVID-19 pandemic, adopts inherently a global perspective. Furthermore, some chapters in the book explore in general the impact of COVID-19 in the areas of information protection, creative industry and business, while other chapters focus on the impact and challenges in different jurisdictions, including China, the United States of America, the United Kingdom, Germany, Finland, Denmark, Spain, Switzerland, Brazil and New Zealand. This involves examining the different legal frameworks applied in the world: civil law legal systems, common law legal systems, socialist legal systems and Nordic legal systems. The Chinese legal system is identified as a socialist legal system; its framework reflecting the influence of the continental European legal system (civil law systems), but with Chinese characteristics. In the United States of America, the legal framework embraces a federal system of government, a codified constitution and a common law legal system, whereas New Zealand operates a common law legal system embracing customary law where appropriate. Selected countries in Europe (the United Kingdom, Germany, Finland, Denmark, Spain and Switzerland) adopt either a civil law or a common law legal system, or the Nordic legal system. In addition, Brazil is also a civil law country, but its current legal system also brings some elements of common law. In addition, selected countries/regions in the book are representative of both their regional area and/or the world in aspects of active economy and politics. Therefore, the book explores the legal challenges in these countries by approaching a variety of representative legal systems, thus reflecting a global view. It will also provide some common reference to other countries with similar systems in responding COVID-19 challenges. The book thus explores the theoretical and practical impact of the pandemic upon laws, regulations and rights worldwide, using national and international perspectives. It brings together experts in different areas of law from around the world to address a variety of legal issues and fields from both a national and international perspective, giving the project a global appeal. In addition, some chapters explore these issues and implications of COVID-19 from both legal and non-legal perspectives.

The book covers a variety of sub disciplines within law and the volume is divided into four parts.

Part I of the book deals with the implications of the pandemic crisis upon the use of intangible assets, including information, data and intellectual property, and from an intellectual property or intellectual property-related information rights/data protection perspective. The chapters in this Part map the impact of the pandemic upon information rights, the ways in which personal data is used during COVID-19, how the pandemic re-shapes the creative industry such as fashion, as well as considering the future relationship between public interests and monopoly copyrights after experiencing COVID-19. Olga Kokoulina, Anja Møller Pedersen and Jens Schovsbo investigate the impact of the COVID-19 pandemic on the process of balances and counterbalances in information rights by assessing regulations in both EU and Denmark and explore the question of what happens if we fail to achieve this balance. Johanna Gibson examines how the fashion industry, one of the creative sectors featured with the most creative activities, is significantly re-shaped by the pandemic crisis together with relevant concerns on use of trade marks in the changed fashion industry. Luo Li calls for the rebuilding of a Chinese copyright exception framework: advising a compulsory license for the public interest in the creative sector by examining the balance between public interest and exclusive rights, and regulation of use of copyrightable works during the pandemic crisis from a comparative perspective.

In Part II, authors explore the legal impact of the pandemic crisis on key commercial acts – contractual obligations and dispute resolutions from different aspects and in a wider commercial law context. In a commercial environment, commercial contracts are vital for both parties to effectively operate their business and clarify their rights and liabilities during commercial activities. However, the pandemic crisis unpredictably and significantly affects the implementation of commercial contracts. Juha Karhu examines how two common clauses – *force majeure* and changed circumstances (*clausula rebus sic stantibus*) – in contracts referring to the parties' obligations are influenced by the pandemic. This is achieved by assessing Germany's legal system, the Chinese legal system and the Nordic legal system. While Juha Karhu focuses on legal challenges and issues to key commercial act during the pandemic crisis, Geraldine Bethencourt Rodríguez examines what we can do at post-COVID-19 period to achieve more flexible methods of conflict resolution. Rodríguez explores the possible solution of online mediation for commercial dispute resolution at present and for the future.

Part III of the book focuses on two key parties: employers and employees, and addresses legal rights, obligations and the employment relationship in general during the pandemic crisis. This is achieved through the perspectives of company law and corporate governance, employment law and labour rights. After comparing the enforcement mechanisms of New Zealand with that of the United Kingdom, Neshat Safari argues that the crisis calls for re-thinking the traditional view of corporate governance. This is because the survival of companies demands that all stakeholders work together as a team, and that all the parties in the company, including both employees and shareholders, should share the burden in the firm's crisis. Alex Simmonds examines the impact of the pandemic on the enforceability and effectiveness of essential provisions in employment law and focuses on interference with employees' rights protection because of employers' acts during COVID-19. Part III ends with Andrés Jerónimo Arenas Falótico and Jessica Bayón Pérez, providing an investigation based on research on how employees' labour rights, legal rights relating to labour relations between employers and employees, and entrepreneur's activities are connected and impacted during and after the pandemic crisis.

Part IV provides the conclusion to the volume, offering some final reflections on COVID-19. In this part, we give the audience a general perception through gathering the research findings by chapter contributors, explain why these findings, and perhaps solutions, are helpful for the rest of the world. The chapter also considers the future direction of laws in responding to the pandemic in the area of information protection, the creative industry and business.

Acknowledgements

We very much appreciate many people that we have collaborated with during the pandemic period. Many thanks go to their contributions during this challenging time to make our book happen. Especially, we would like to thank Dr Lorenzo Pasculli, Associate Head of Research at the Coventry Law School at Coventry University, for his full support and fruitful advice to our book during the entire process. Also, many thanks to Alison Kirk and Emily Summers of Routledge Publishers for their kind support during the whole process of this book.

Bibliography

Berg A and others, 'A Perfect Storm for Fashion Marketplaces' (*McKinsey & Company*, 8 June 2020) <www.mckinsey.com/industries/retail/our-insights/a-perfect-storm-for-fashion-marketplaces> accessed 26 March 2021.
Borodzicz E, *Risk, Crisis and Security Management* (West Sussex, John Wiley & Sons, 2005) 79.
Cebrian M, 'The Past, Present and Future of Digital Contact Tracing' (2021)4 *Nature Electronics* 2–4 <www.nature.com/articles/s41928-020-00535-z> accessed 23 March 2021.
Cohen E, 'When a Pandemic isn't a Pandemic' (*CNN*, 4 May 2009) <http://edition.cnn.com/2009/HEALTH/05/04/swine.flu.pandemic/index.html> accessed 16 March 2021.
'Definition of Crisis' (*Cambridge Dictionary*) <https://dictionary.cambridge.org/dictionary/english/crisis> accessed 1 October 2020.
'Definitions: Emergencies' (*World Health Organisation*) <www.who.int/hac/about/definitions/en/> accessed 19 March 2021.

Deloitte, 'Privacy and Data Protection in the Age of COVID-19' <https://www2.deloitte.com/content/dam/Deloitte/be/Documents/risk/be-risk_privacy-and-data-protection-in-the-age-of-covid-19.pdf> accessed 23 March 2021.

Digital, Culture, Media and Sport Committee, 'Impact of COVID-19 on DCMS Sectors: First Report' (20 July 2020) 20–40 <https://committees.parliament.uk/publications/2022/documents/19516/default/> accessed 26 March 2021.

Doshi P, 'The Elusive Definition of Pandemic Influenza' (2011)89 *Bulletin of the World Health Organization* <www.who.int/bulletin/volumes/89/7/11-086173/en/> accessed 16 March 2021.

Gao G and others, 'Prevalent Eurasian Avian-like H1N1 Swine Influenza Virus with 2009 Pandemic Viral Genes Facilitating Human Infection' (2020)117(29) *Proceedings of the National Academy of Sciences of the United States of America* 17204–210 (*PNAS*, 21 July 2020) <www.pnas.org/content/117/29/17204> accessed 19 March 2021.

Gravitz L, 'Introduction: A Smouldering Public-Health Crisis' (*Nature*, 8 June 2011) <www.nature.com/articles/474S2a> accessed 19 March 2021.

Habibzadeh F, 'World War III' (2020)11(3) *The International Journal of Occupational and Environmental Medicine* 117–18.

'The Handling of the H1N1 Pandemic: More Transparency Needed' (*Parliamentary Assembly, Council of Europe*, 7 June 2010) <https://pace.coe.int/en/files/12463/html> accessed 16 March 2021.

Hoofnagle JC and others, 'The European Union General Data Protection Regulation: What It Is and What It Means' (2019)28 *Information & Communications Technology Law* 1 <www.tandfonline.com/doi/full/10.1080/13600834.2019.1573501> accessed 23 March 2021.

John A, 'Research in a Public Health Crisis: The Integrative Approach to Managing the Moral Tensions' in Jennings B (ed), *Emergency Ethics: Public Health Preparedness and Response* (New York, OUP 2016) <https://oxfordmedicine.com/view/10.1093/med/9780190270742.001.0001/med-9780190270742-chapter-7> accessed 19 March 2021.

'Joint Statement on Data Protection and Privacy in the COVID-19 Response' (*World Health Organisation*, 19 November 2020) <www.who.int/news/item/19-11-2020-joint-statement-on-data-protection-and-privacy-in-the-covid-19-response> accessed 23 March 2021.

Jones L and others, 'Coronavirus: How the Pandemic Has Changed the World Economy' (*BBC News*, 24 January 2021) <www.bbc.co.uk/news/business-51706225> accessed 29 March 2021.

Kędzior M, 'The Right to Data Protection and the COVID-19 Pandemic: The European Approach' (2021)21 *ERA Forum* 533–43.

Kelly H, 'The Classical Definition of a Pandemic Is Not Elusive' (2011)89 *Bulletin of the World Health Organization* <www.who.int/bulletin/volumes/89/7/11-088815/en/> accessed 16 March 2021.

Krishnan R, 'View: Coronavirus Conflict Is World War 3' (*The Economic Times*, 17 May 2020) <https://economictimes.indiatimes.com/news/international/world-news/view-coronavirus-conflict-is-world-war-3/articleshow/75792202.cms> accessed 10 November 2020.

Kumar A, 'World War III: Humans vs Corona' (*Biotechticle*, 11 April 2020) <https://biotechticle.com/world-war-iii-humans-vs-corona/> accessed 10 November 2020.

McIntosh S, 'Coronavirus: Why the Fashion Industry Faces an "Existential Crisis"' (*BBC*, 30 April 2020) <www.bbc.co.uk/news/entertainment-arts-52394504> accessed 26 March 2021.

McNeil GD, 'WHO to Rewrite Its Pandemic Rules' (*The New York Times*, 22 May 2009) <www.nytimes.com/2009/05/23/health/policy/23who.html> accessed 14 March 2021.

National Statistics, 'DCMS Economic Estimates 2019: Gross Value Added – Technical and Quality Assurance Report' (*Gov.UK Department for Digital, Cultural, Media & Sport*, 19 February 2021) <www.gov.uk/government/statistics/dcms-economic-estimates-2019-gross-value-added/dcms-economic-estimates-2019-gross-value-added-technical-and-quality-assurance-report> accessed 26 March 2021.

OECD, 'Culture Shock: COVID-19 and the Cultural and Creative Sectors' (*OECD*, 7 September 2020) <www.oecd.org/coronavirus/policy-responses/culture-shock-covid-19-and-the-cultural-and-creative-sectors-08da9e0e/> accessed 26 March 2021.

The Oxford Economics, 'The Projected Economic Impact of COVID-19 on the UK Creative Industries' (16 July 2020) 20 <www.oxfordeconomics.com/recent-releases/The-Projected-Economic-Impact-of-COVID-19-on-the-UK-Creative-Industries> accessed 26 March 2021.

'Pandemic Preparedness' (*World Health Organization*, 2 February 2003) <http://web.archive.org/web/20030202145905/www.who.int/csr/disease/influenza/pandemic/en/> accessed 16 March 2021.

Parliamentary Assembly, 'Realising both Economic Growth and Social Protection in Europe in an Era of Globalisation' (*Parliamentary Assembly Council of Europe*, 3 October 2007) <http://assembly.coe.int/nw/xml/XRef/Xref-XML2HTML-en.asp?fileid=17580&lang=en> accessed 22 March 2021.

Porta M (ed), *A Dictionary of Epidemiology* (5th edn, New York, OUP 2008) 179.

Regulation 2016/679 of the European Parliament and of the Council of 27 April 2016 on the Protection of Natural Persons with Regard to the Processing of Personal Data and on the Free Movement of Such Data, and Repealing Directive 95/46/EC (General Data Protection Regulation), OJ 2016 L 119/1.

Ritchie H and others, 'Policy Responses to the Coronavirus Pandemic' (*Our World in Data*) <https://ourworldindata.org/policy-responses-covid> accessed 29 March 2021.

Schnirring L, 'WHO Foresees Problems with Pandemic Severity Index' (*Center for Infectious Disease Research & Policy*, 13 May 2009) <www.cidrap.umn.edu/cidrap/content/influenza/panflu/news/may1309severity-br.html> accessed 16 March 2021.

Seeger M and others, 'Communication, Organization, and Crisis' (1998)21(1) *Annals of the International Communication Association* 233.

'Swine Flu of 1976: Lessons from the Past' (2009)87 *Bulletin of the World Health Organization* <www.who.int/bulletin/volumes/87/6/09-040609/en/> accessed 16 March 2021.

'Tracking COVID-19: Contact Tracing in the Digital Age' (*World Health Organisation*, 9 September 2020) <www.who.int/news-room/feature-stories/detail/tracking-covid-19-contact-tracing-in-the-digital-age> accessed 23 March 2021.

Ventrella E, 'Privacy in Emergency Circumstances: Data Protection and the COVID-19 Pandemic' (2020)21 *ERA Forum* 379–93.

Vogue Business Team, 'Fashion Industry Crisis Deepens Amid Covid-19 Chaos' (*Vogue Business*, 6 April 2020) <www.voguebusiness.com/companies/fashion-industry-crisis-deepens-amid-covid-19-chaos> accessed 26 March 2021.

Voldere DI and others, 'Cultural and Creative Sectors in Post COVID-19 Europe – Crisis Effects and Policy Recommendations' (2021)31–34 <www.europarl.europa.eu/RegData/etudes/STUD/2021/652242/IPOL_STU(2021)652242_EN.pdf> accessed 26 March 2021.

'What Is a Pandemic?' (*World Health Organisation*, 24 February 2010) <www.who.int/csr/disease/swineflu/frequently_asked_questions/pandemic/en/> accessed 16 March 2021.

'WHO Director-General's Opening Remarks at the Media Briefing on COVID-19' (*World Health Organisation*, 11 March 2020) <www.who.int/director-general/speeches/detail/who-director-general-s-opening-remarks-at-the-media-briefing-on-covid-19-11-march-2020> accessed 16 March 2021.

The World Bank, 'The Global Economic Outlook During the COVID-19 Pandemic: A Changed World' (*The World Bank*, 8 June 2020) <www.worldbank.org/en/news/feature/2020/06/08/the-global-economic-outlook-during-the-covid-19-pandemic-a-changed-world> accessed 22 March 2021.

World Bank Group, 'Global Economic Prospects' (*World Bank Group*, 2021) 128–30 <www.worldbank.org/en/publication/global-economic-prospects> accessed 22 March 2021.

Part I

Information protection and intellectual property rights and strategies

2 Mapping the legal landscape of information law in times of crisis

Olga Kokoulina, Anja Møller Pedersen and Jens Schovsbo

Introduction

The ongoing pandemic has touched nearly every corner of the world, bringing communities to a state of a prolonged health and humanitarian crisis. While reshaping the daily routines of individuals, the crisis has also provided challenges for national governments. Struggling to offer a rapid and effective response, they resorted to a range of long-established policy tools and mechanisms in a bid to stop the spread of the disease. As the number of cases ebbs and flows throughout the course of the pandemic, the expectations that data-driven and technology-aided solutions can, and should, be available to overcome the crisis have stood uniformly high. In stark contrast with fighting the plague in the Middle Ages, there is no principal shortage of statistical knowledge, data processing capacity or predictive modelling potential. Consequently, respective public health decisions – such as home confinements, border closures, curfews and the like – need not be universally contingent on the exertion of the "disciplinary power of the state". Instead, humanity should have been benefitting from data-powered decision-making, democratisation of technology, advancement of "open science" and collaborative innovative practices. Combined, these measures and initiatives should have ensured that we fared through the pandemic and managed health crises, if not better, then at least differently.[1] Despite the unprecedented theoretical potential, however, the promises of a data-powered crisis governance have yet to be delivered. While the communities throughout the globe are still at a crossroads with the pandemic, there is no better time to take stock of what the legal landscape of information law looks like. In finding out the lie of the land in this area, the present contribution pursues two goals. It first seeks to unpack the complexity of overlapping data landscape structures that moderate the flow of data in times of crisis. It then identifies some normative connections and

---

1 Cf. Foucauldian plague governance model in Michel Foucault, *Discipline and Punish: The Birth of the Prison* (Paris, Gallimard 1975) vis-à-vis his later developed "smallpox" governance model in Michel Foucault, *Security, Territory, Population: Lectures at the Collège de France* (London, Palgrave Macmillan 2009).

DOI: 10.4324/9781003176848-4

"flexibility conduits" that could be used to bridge the gap between the expectations of data-driven crisis management and the reality of going forward.

We start by briefly introducing information law as a primary field of enquiry. Focusing on attributes of "information" and "crisis", in Section 2 we explore the potential data needs that the state of health pandemic poses. We then, in Section 3, describe the patterns and configurations of the legal landscape through the categories of distinct legal regimes such as data protection law, copyright, database and patent law. In presenting this catalogue of rights, we focus, first and foremost, on their afforded scope of protection and embedded legal "flex" mechanisms that could be utilised to bolster and improve the data-powered crisis management. Lastly, we discuss the identified communalities and differences across the surveyed protection models and offer some concluding remarks.

Information law

The ongoing crisis placed a spotlight on the intricate landscape of overlapping, curbing patterns of legal protection regimes modulating the access and use of information. As an object of regulation, "information" itself is notoriously difficult to define. It has myriad meanings in various disciplines and contexts, so that its conceptual contours often appear fluid and unstable.[2] In statutory provisions, for example, its basic properties such as "data" and "information" are routinely referred to, albeit rarely comprehensively – if at all – defined.[3] The respective choice of certainty has evident advantages and costs. Thus, on the one hand, the lack of analytical clarity and precision necessarily obscures the boundaries of protected subject matter.[4] Admittedly, a more calibrated and comprehensive articulation of the terms in legislation would have reinforced its instructive authority and contributed to legal certainty.[5] On the other hand, a legislative preference for not providing exhaustive definitions and interpretations of existing legal categories is also a manifestation of pragmatic flexibility. In other words, it is not necessarily

---

2   See, e.g. Mark Burgin, *Theory of Information. Fundamentality, Diversity and Unification* (Los Angeles, World Scientific Publishing 2010); Luciano Floridi, 'Philosophical Conceptions of Information' in Giovanni Sommaruga (ed), *Formal Theories of Information: From Shannon to Semantic Information Theory and General Concepts of Information* (Cham, Switzerland, Springer 2009); Max Boisot and Canals Agustí, 'Data, Information and Knowledge: Have We Got It Right?' (2004) 14(1) *Journal of Evolutionary Economics* 43.

3   Regulation (EU) 2016/679 of the European Parliament and of the Council of 27 April 2016 on the protection of natural persons with regard to the processing of personal data and on the free movement of such data, and repealing Directive 95/46/EC [2016] OJ L 119 (General Data Protection Regulation – GDPR) and see also Directive 96/9/EC of the European Parliament and of the Council of 11 March 1996 on the legal protection of databases, [1996] OJ L 77 (Database Directive – DBdir).

4   Lee A Bygrave, 'Information Concepts in Law: Generic Dreams and Definitional Daylight' (2015) 35(1) *Oxford Journal of Legal Studies* 91.

5   Nadezhda Purtova, 'The Law of Everything: Broad Concept of Personal Data and Future of EU Data Protection Law' (2018) 10(1) *Law, Innovation and Technology* 40.

an indication of regulatory deficiency, and can also be approached as an intended legislative choice for introducing an optimal and "futureproof" solution.[6]

Thus, the "information law" space is surrounded by flexible and reconfigurable walls. Their adjustable design stems from the interplay of factors related, but not limited, to the philosophical underpinnings,[7] the political dynamics in existence[8] and economic qualities of information as such.[9] Further, within these regulatory walls, one is met with a complex topography of distinct legal protection regimes. Their boundaries and positioning are by no means fixed, owing to the ongoing discussion and negotiation on how to strike a balance between the interests of distinct stakeholders involved in the dilemma. The time of the crisis brings its own dynamics to this tussle by questioning, revisiting and ultimately reconfiguring the contours of protection models. Above all, the crisis is an opposite of normalcy. It further requires immediate actions to be taken due to its potential to be a serious and direct danger to the health of the human population.[10] Naturally, this perspective brings to the fore the "population" as a focal point of actions and concerns. This focus is grounded on recognition that "population strategy" helps to address the underlying causes in a mobilised and more efficient way. It proposes a convenient vantage point to explore the synergy potential to enable tackling the crisis at the broadest community level.

Apart from the policy and resource distribution angle, it also resonates with the staple methods of the scientific inquiry – epidemiology and biostatistics – that largely define the logic and *modus operandi* of public health measures.[11] As a strategy orientation, it requires gaining knowledge of the distribution and determinants of the disease incidence found in the population. This knowledge then cascades through a series of measures that could lower the mean level of risk factors and render the distribution of exposure in a favourable direction.[12]

---

6   Commission's commentary with respect to its amended proposal for a data protection Directive of 15 October 1992: COM (92) 422 final – SYN 287, 9.
7   On distinction between "data" and "information in the context of Artificial Intelligence ("AI") in Mireille Hildebrandt, 'Law As Computation in the Era of Artificial Legal Intelligence: Speaking Law to The Power of Statistics' (2018)68(supplement 1) *University of Toronto Law Journal* 12.
8   On political and legal preferences related to statutory vis-à-vis judiciary-driven interpretation, see Lyria Bennett Moses, 'Adapting the Law to Technological Change: A Comparison of Common Law and Legislation' (2003)26 *U New South Wales LJ* 394, 400.
9   On economic dimension of information and its ubiquitous and non-rivalry qualities Carl Shapiro and Hal R Varian, *Information Rules: A Strategic Guide to the Network Economy* (Boston, Harvard Business Press 1998) 6.
10   A definition of "public health emergency of international concern" by the World Health Organisation ("WHO"). World Health Organisation, 'WHO International Health Regulations (2005)' (*World Health Organisation*, 1 January 2008) <www.who.int/publications/i/item/9789241580410> accessed 30 March 2021.
11   Lawrence O Gostin and Lindsay F Wiley, *Public Health Law: Power, Duty, Restraint* (3rd edn, Oakland, CA, California UP 2016) 13.
12   Geoffrey Rose, 'Sick Individuals and Sick Populations' (2001)30(3) *International Journal of Epidemiology* 427, 431.

The default mechanics of the health crisis has distinct implications on finding balance among the interests of stakeholders in information law. Next we briefly address two key dimensions of such an impact. First, the health crisis highlights the essential role information of different kinds and origins plays in controlling and eradicating the disease. Data is critical for public health surveillance. It is an integral component supporting the identification of cases through primary testing, contact tracing, and in quarantining infected individuals and monitoring disease trends.[13] Secondly, beyond detecting and monitoring, data is also essential at the stage of devising, evaluating and adjusting interventions and treatments in minimising the risk and scale of the population's exposure. Thus, in many ways, data plays an enabling and virtually infrastructural role, and depending on the purpose of its use, various sources of data and distinct technologies might be utilised.

For example, location data could be beneficial in supporting contact tracing efforts and monitoring the spread of the pandemic. It could be obtained, in principle, from mobile service providers (e.g. Sprint, Vodafone, Tele2) or providers of handsets' operating systems (e.g. Apple, Google).[14] Apart from location data, it is also possible to use data relating to the proximity of mobile phones' users to achieve the same purposes of tracking potential cases of transmission.[15] By the same token, statistical data used for monitoring the pandemic and managing health resources might come from different sources. Public health authorities routinely process and make this kind of information available for public health services.[16] However, national health systems are not the only source of relevant statistical data. Potential epidemic intelligence could also be sourced from beyond the traditional bounds of health institutions, through the application of advanced computational techniques by private companies.[17] Finally, providing medical interventions and assessing their effectiveness requires immense scientific

---

13   World Health Organisation, 'Public Health Surveillance for COVID-19: Interim Guidance' (*World Health Organisation*, 16 December 2020) <www.who.int/publications/i/item/who-2019-nCoV-surveillanceguidance-2020.8> accessed 30 March 2021.

14   Article 29 Working Party, 'Opinion 13/2011 of 16 May 2011 on Geolocation Services on Smart Mobile Devices' (WP29, 16 May 2011).

15   European Data Protection Board, 'Guidelines 04/2020 of 21 April 2020 on the Use of Location Data and Contact Tracing Tools in the Context of the COVID-19 Outbreak' (*EDPB*, 21 April 2020).

16   European Centre for Disease Prevention and Control, 'Epidemic Intelligence Information System (EPIS)' (*ecdc.europa.eu*, 2021) <www.ecdc.europa.eu/en/publications-data/epidemic-intelligence-information-system-epis> accessed 30 March 2021; Klaus Hoeyer, 'Denmark at a Crossroad? Intensified Data Sourcing in a Research Radical Country' in Mittelstadt BD and Floridi L (eds), *The Ethics of Biomedical Big Data* (Cham, Switzerland, Springer 2016) 73.

17   Hyunyoung Choi and Hal Varian, 'Predicting the Present with Google Trends' (2012)88(1) *Economic Record* 2; see also on research limitations in Donald R Olson and others, 'Reassessing Google Flu Trends Data for Detection of Seasonal and Pandemic Influenza: A Comparative Epidemiological Study at Three Geographic Scales' (2013)9(10) *PLoS Computational Biology* e1003256.

data-powered research efforts. These research undertakings increasingly rely on heterogeneous data sources. The example of medical research is a case in point. Typically conducted through two general modes – clinical trials and observational studies – the respective research seeks to establish evidentiary bases for making clinical decisions.[18] Encompassing a wide range of diagnostic and monitoring procedures, clinical randomised trials essentially seek to establish the safety and efficacy of health interventions through a hypothesis-driven trial and error practice. Observational studies, by contrast, rely more heavily on already available clinical datasets. Often performed where experimentation may be unnecessary, inappropriate, inadequate and even impossible, observational studies are principally grounded in the analysis of existent information. It could be collected, for example, as a result of previously conducted clinical trials ("protocol-oriented" research databases) as well as in the course of digitalisation of patients' information for medical practice in general "practice-oriented" medical record database such as Electronic Health Records (EHRs) datasets.[19] On the face of it, the two outlined techniques of research appear to be antipodal as far as the data sources are concerned. Clinical trials mostly rely on structured data that is not available in large quantities. Observational studies, by contrast, presuppose the availability of a large volume of data recorded in various formats and originated from a wide range of sources. The big data trend, in its effect, somewhat blurs this traditional distinction. As a fairly recent but consistent trend, clinical trials increasingly involve the 'unstructured data from many different, real-world data sources'.[20] The current pandemic, with its resource-stretching effects, a pressing timeline for taking real-time decisions and an undeniable push for optimising designs and input of scientific research, not only confirmed, but also amplified, the value of data access and sharing for tackling the global crisis.[21]

---

18 Ravi Thadhani, 'Formal Trials Versus Observational Studies' in Mehta A and others (eds), *FABRY Disease: Perspectives from 5 Years of FOS* (Oxford, Oxford: PharmaGenesis 2006) ch14.

19 Rachel Richesson, Monica M Horvath and Shelley A Rusincovitch, 'Clinical Research Informatics and Electronic Health Record Data' (2014)9(1) *Yearbook of Medical Informatics* 215; Nick Black, 'Why We Need Observational Studies to Evaluate the Effectiveness of Health Care' (1996)312(7040) *BMJ: British Medical Journal* 1215; For an example of observational studies during the COVID-19 pandemic, see Mark W Tenforde, Kiva A Fisher and Manish M Patel, 'Identifying COVID-19 Risk Through Observational Studies to Inform Control Measures' (2021)325(14) *The Journal of the American Medical Association* 1464.

20 James Streeter, 'The Role of Big Data in Clinical Trials' (2016)25(12) *Applied Clinical Trials* <www.appliedclinicaltrialsonline.com/role-big-data-clinical-trials> accessed 30 March 2021; Niklas Morton and David Blackman, 'The Growing Availability of Wearable Devices: A Perspective on Current Applications in Clinical Trials' (2016) *Applied Clinical Trials* <www. appliedclinicaltrialsonline.com/growing-availability-wearable-devices-perspective-current-applications-clinical-trials> accessed 30 March 2021; Karen K Mestan and others, 'Genomic Sequencing in Clinical Trials' (2011)9(1) *Journal of Translational Medicine* 1.

21 Guillaume Taglang and David B Jackson, 'Use of "Big Data" in Drug Discovery and Clinical Trials' (2016)14(1) *Gynecologic Oncology* 17; Chunhua Weng and Michael G Kahn,

This point brings us to a second, related, observation about the interest and power distribution in the context of the health crisis. As was noted earlier, the crisis has given prominence to "population" and "societal needs" as an unrivalled figure in a fragile equilibrium of rights' holders. Furthermore, the innate characteristics of the pandemic, such as urgency, unpredictability and its extraordinary nature, suggest a distinct purpose and timeline for revisiting the boundaries of rights protection regimes. That is to say that since the crisis, by its very nature, epitomises a "departure from normalcy", such a deviation should be deemed temporary and exceptional. At the same time, the exact scope of this deviation might not be sufficiently clear at the time of proposing an action roadmap. Nevertheless, that in itself does not justify non-action. Conversely, sensible modulation of the risk includes immediate mobilisation of required resources in order to respond to different public health scenarios.[22]

Considered together, these properties and effects of the health crisis suggest a distinct analytical orientation of the discussion that follows. Thus, we explore data categories and the needs posed by the crisis primarily through the scope of legal protection of a given right. Furthermore, we internalise the crisis "*modus operandi*" in its urgency for action in conditions of uncertainty as a push for a normative perspective. In other words, we internalise the crisis perspective as a mandate to ask a pressing question: How could we use the available regulatory tools to overcome the crisis? We attempt to answer this question by examining particular parcels of information law in the discussion to follow.

Rights in information

As expounded, "information law" presents a puzzling landscape of distinct legal protection regimes. The underlying interests and rationales for protection are diverse. Thus, "rights in information" might be granted to protect human dignity and autonomy (e.g. personal data law), further societal interests in creativity and innovation (e.g. copyright and patent law), and even to safeguard and encourage investments in information processing system (e.g. database protection). Conceding that information, in principle, might be regulated through a variety of

---

'Clinical Research Informatics for Big Data and Precision Medicine' (2016)1 *Yearbook of Medical Informatics* 211; Mary Mallappallil and others, 'A Review of Big Data and Medical Research' (2020)8 *Sage Open Medicine* 1. See also examples of design and data sources of clinical trials in the context of COVID-19 at US National Library of Medicine, 'COVID-19 Studies from the World Health Organization Database' (*ClinicalTrials.gov*, 2021) <https://clinicaltrials.gov/ct2/who_table> accessed 30 March 2021.

22 World Health Organisation, 'Critical Preparedness, Readiness and Response Actions for COVID-19' (*WHO*, 4 November 2020) <www.who.int/publications/i/item/critical-preparedness-readiness-and-response-actions-for-covid-19> accessed 30 March 2021; On a risk-based approach in public health law: Snezhanna Chichevalieva, 'Developing a Framework for Public Health Law in Europe' (*WHO*, 2011) <www.euro.who.int/__data/assets/pdf_file/0004/151375/e95783.pdf> accessed 30 March 2021.

additional mechanisms and contexts, the present contribution limits itself to the consideration of a limited number of legal areas.

EU data protection

Pursuant to article 4(1) of the General Data Protection Regulation (GDPR), personal data is defined as any information relating to an identified or identifiable natural person. Article 2(1) shows that GDPR applies to processing of such personal data wholly or partly by automated means and to manual processing of data that forms part, or intended to form part, of a filing system. While anonymised data falls outside the scope of the GDPR, as the natural person is no longer identifiable, pseudonomised data falls within it.[23] The notion of "personal data", as a threshold for the GDPR application, has been conceived and subsequently interpreted in a broad and flexible way.[24] Furthermore, the ever-growing amount of data, and increasing sophistication of algorithms for analysing it, challenge the very potential of anonymisation to deliver a "permanent as erasure" inability of identification of individuals.[25] This high standard for exclusion from the scope of the GDPR implies that a myriad of data types needed for crisis management potentially belongs to a category of "personal data". From data-powered contact-tracing efforts, to statistical and research data, the requirements and guarantees of the European data protection law should be regarded as practically default considerations for data access and use.[26]

23 GDPR, rec 26.
24 Article 29 Working Party, 'Opinion 4/2007 on the Concept of Personal Data' (01248/07/EN WP 136, 2007); Article 29 Working Party, 'Advice Paper on Special Categories of Data ("sensitive data")' (WP29, 4 April 2011) 6; European Data Protection Board, 'Guidelines 03/2020 on the Processing of Data Concerning Health for the Purpose of Scientific Research in the Context of the COVID-19 Outbreak' (EDPB, 21 April 2021) 5 on "health data" in particular.
25 Article 29 Working Party, ' Opinion 05/2014 on Anonymisation Techniques' (WP29, 10 April 2014); Latanya Sweeney, 'Simple Demographics Often Identify People Uniquely' (2000)671(2000) *Health (San Francisco)* 1; John Bohannon, 'Genealogy Databases Enable Naming of Anonymous DNA Donors' (2013)339(6117) *Science* 262; Yves-Alexandre de Montjoye and others, 'Unique in the Crowd: The Privacy Bounds of Human Mobility' (2013)3(1) *Scientific Reports* 1 <www.nature.com/articles/srep01376.pdf> accessed 30 March 2021; Ann Cavoukian and Daniel Castro, 'Big Data and Innovation, Setting the Record Straight: De-Identification Does Work' (*Office of the Information and Privacy Commissioner, Ontario,* 2014) <https://ecfsapi.fcc.gov/file/102058078475/2014-big-data-deidentification.pdf> accessed 30 March 2021.
26 For the sake of accuracy, however, it should be noted that the GDPR is not the only "default" consideration and its application is commonly supplemented with provisions of other instruments such as Directive 2002/58/EC of the European Parliament and of the Council of 12 July 2002 concerning the processing of personal data and the protection of privacy in the electronic communications sector [2002] OJ L 201; Regulation (EU) 2018/1807 of the European Parliament and of the Council of 14 November 2018 on a framework for the free flow of non-personal data in the European Union [2018] OJ L 303; Regulation (EU) No 536/2014 of the European Parliament and of the Council of 16 April 2014 on clinical trials on medicinal products for human use, and repealing Directive 2001/20/EC Text with EEA relevance [2014] OJ L 158.

The GDPR, and its predecessor the Data Protection Directive, is underpinned by the dual objectives of protecting fundamental rights – in particular the rights to the protection of personal data and privacy (in articles 7 and 8 of the Charter of Fundamental Rights of the European Union (CFREU)),[27] and ensuring the free movement of data (in article 1 of the GDPR). Despite strong fundamental rights underpinnings, the market integration objective implies that exclusivity in data access is not an option. Instead, personal data must flow unimpededly, and the data protection scheme offers some flexibility in enabling its access and use. The protection afforded to personal data is structured around a set of procedural guarantees requiring respect for fundamental data protection principles. The examples of these guarantees can be seen in various categories and requirements of the GDPR, related to, for instance, the obligation of a data controller to ensure and demonstrate compliance with the GDPR,[28] as well as a requirement for *independent* control by supervisory authorities (under article 8(3) of the CFREU, article 16(2) of the TFEU, and article 51 and the rest of the GDPR). Data subjects, too, have the leverage of making use of a number of information and access rights allowing them, *inter alia*, to exercise *individual* control, and thus self-determination, over their personal data, contained in articles 13–22.

Pursuant to article 6(1) of the GDPR, all processing must be based on the data subject's consent or one or more of the legitimate grounds for processing, exhaustively listed therein.[29] With regard to special categories of data, such as health data, aside from one of the grounds listed in article 6(1) of the GDPR, the controller must ensure that processing is covered by one of the exemptions listed in article 9(2) of the GDPR – relating to the prohibition against processing such *sensitive data* otherwise stipulated in article 9(1) of the GDPR.[30] In the context of the pandemic crisis, this involves processing that is, for example, necessary for reasons of substantial public interest,[31] for the purposes of preventive or occupational medicine,[32] or for reasons of public interest in the area of public health, such as protecting against serious cross-border threats to health.[33] In these cases, this data enjoys more intense protection than ordinary personal data, as its legitimate processing necessitates the application of further requirements and safeguards.

27   Charter of Fundamental Rights of the European Union (Consolidated version) (CFREU) [2016] OJ 2016/C 202/391.
28   GDPR, art 24 and art 5.
29   CFREU, art 8(2).
30   Article 29 Working Party, 'Opinion 06/2014 on the Notion of Legitimate Interests of the Data Controller under Article 7 of Directive 95/46/EC' (844/14/EN WP 217, 9 April 2014) 15. Moreover, article 9(4) of the GDPR allows for the member states to introduce further conditions, including limitations, regarding genetic data, biometric data and health data.
31   GDPR, art (2)(g).
32   GDPR, art 9(2)(h).
33   GDPR, art 9(2)(i).

The embedded procedural guarantees and distinct governance regime afforded to certain categories of data enable and moderate the flow of personal data. In doing so, they create a form of information highways, intersecting and embracing the entirety of the legal landscape of information law.[34] However, although these procedural guarantees provide for general structure, there are certain additional constructions that could be used to alter the data traffic. We elaborate on two examples that follow.

The first concerns a "research exception", while the second relates to restrictions to data subjects' rights or to the obligations of the controllers and processors based on Union or Member State law.[35] Both of these regulatory mechanisms are essential components of data processing in times of crisis. As for the former, the respective rules aim to provide a special, "privileged" regime for data processing in the course of the research undertaking. Construed broadly, such research includes technological development, fundamental and applied research, and privately funded research and 'studies conducted in the public interest in the area of public health'.[36] As a way of facilitating and advancing research, the GDPR provides for special arrangement with regard to the principles and lawful grounds for processing,[37] rights of data subjects,[38] and the potential for Member States to introduce derogations from data controller's obligations,[39] (provided that the strict conditions for that are met[40] and appropriate safeguards are implemented).[41]

---

34   Relatedly, see Christopher Docksey, 'Four Fundamental Rights: Finding the Balance' (2016)6(3) *International Data Privacy Law* 195 on the interplay of the DP and privacy with an insightful analogy of the DP and the "Highway Code".

35   GDPR, art 23.

36   GDPR, Rec 159.

37   See article 5(1)(b) on presumption of compatibility for research proposes, article 5(1)(e) on storage limitation, article 9(2)(j) with regard to processing of special categories of data for archiving purposes in the public interest, scientific or historical research purposes or statistical purposes. Application of previously mentioned provisions is further conditioned on meeting requirements of article 89(1).

38   See article 14(5)(b) with regard to the right to information, article 17(3)(b) – research exception with regard to the right to erasure.

39   Article 15 on the right of access by the data subject; article 16 on the right to rectification; Article 18 on the right to restriction of the processing; and article 21 on the right to object.

40   Article 89 (2) with references to "in so far as" the rights to be derogated from are 'likely to render impossible or seriously impair the achievement of the specific purposes, and such derogations are necessary for the fulfilment of those purposes'. Notably, these conditions have been interpreted as setting a high standard for derogation, see, e.g. European Data Protection Supervisor, 'Opinion 10/2017 EDPS Opinion of 20 November 2017 on Safeguards and Derogations Under Article 89 GDPR in the Context of a Proposal for a Regulation on Integrated Farm Statistics' (*EDPS*, 20 November 2017).

41   Article 9 (j). See also Article 29 Working Party, 'Opinion 03/2013 on Purpose Limitation' (2 April 2013), highlighting the concern related to profiling at p. 28.

The second example relates to possible restrictions based on Union or Member State law.[42] These restrictions involve limitation of the scope of obligations and rights provided for in articles 12–22 and 34 of the GDPR, as well as corresponding provisions in article 5. These limitations should be interpreted narrowly and applied only in explicitly provided circumstances laid out in article 23.[43] Thus, restrictions could be introduced to safeguard, for example, national and public security,[44] as well as objectives of general public interest of the EU or of a Member State, including public health.[45] For restrictions to be lawful, they must meet the criteria of articles 8(2) – (3) and section 52(1) of the CFREU. Thus, they shall be provided by law, respect the essence of the right, and be necessary and proportionate.

The ongoing health crisis has offered a litmus test for the European data protection regime and its innate mechanisms by challenging their operational might, scope and potential. While Member States have been exploring various legal venues in search for data-driven and technology-aided solutions,[46] the European Data Protection Board (EDPB), European Data Protection Supervisor (EDPS) and the EU Commission and Parliament, have been supplementing these efforts with timely issued Guidelines, opinions and clarifications on the application of the GDPR. This includes their use in, for instance, contact tracing,[47] processing of health data for research purposes[48] and in the scope and interpretation of restrictions under article 23.[49] This practical exercise has convincingly demonstrated that the internal logic of data protection law, as expressed in its procedural guarantees, principles, exceptions and derogations, provides for a sufficient and flexible framework for dealing with the crisis. That is not to say there have not been any bumps in the road, but, if nothing else, these challenges, could be internalised as areas for potential improvement,[50] or heightened public scrutiny.[51]

---

42   GDPR, art 23.
43   On strict interpretation of the restriction, see European Data Protection Board, 'Guidelines 10/2020 on Restrictions Under Article 23 GDPR' (*EDPB*, 15 December 2020).
44   GDPR, art (23(1)(a) and (c).
45   GDPR, art 23(1)(e).
46   Importantly, the Treaty on the Functioning of the EU (TFEU) assigns limited responsibilities to the EU for the area of human health, see article 6 and 168 of the TFEU.
47   European Data Protection Board, 'Guidelines 04/2020 on the Use of Location Data and Contact Tracing Tools in the Context of the COVID-19 Outbreak' (*EDPB*, 21 April 2020).
48   European Data Protection Board, 'Guidelines 03/2020 on the Processing of Data Concerning Health for the Purpose of Scientific Research in the Context of the COVID-19 Outbreak' (*EDPB*, 21 April 2020).
49   European Data Protection Board, 'Guidelines 10/2020 of 15 December 2020 on Restrictions Under Article 23 GDPR' (*EDPB*, 15 December 2020).
50   European Data Protection Supervisor, 'Preliminary Opinion 8/2020 on the European Health Data Space' (*EDPS*, 17 November 2020).
51   European Data Protection Board, 'Statement of 2 June 2020 on Restrictions on Data Subject Rights in Connection to the State of Emergency in Member States' (*EDPB*, 2 June 2020).

Copyright

In the EU, copyright law offers protection to literary and artistic works which are "original". However, it also extends its reach to non-original databases. According to the case law of the Court of Justice of the European Union (CJEU), to be considered as a(n) "(original) work" a text/picture/computer program/ football match/taste of a cheese etc. etc. must be: (i) the result of the author's free and creative choices; (ii) not determined by technical constraints or by following rules; (iii) stamped with the author's "personal touch" and (iv) identifiable with sufficient precision and objectivity.[52] Following this test, copyright protection is not available to texts containing pure information about COVID-19, for example, to spreadsheets containing data or to simple illustrations.

For protected information, the Infosoc Directive[53] contains limitations and exceptions allowing uses for, *inter alia*, the purposes of news reporting, quotations, public security uses and uses in administrative and judicial proceedings. The CJEU has stated that the provision in article 5(3)(e) – which allows Member States to provide for an exception or limitation for "*use for the purposes of public security*" – gives Member States a wide margin of appreciation in deciding which situations fit within that provision.[54] This freedom is subject to the general principles of EU law, and, for example, national discrimination or acts that harm the effective exercise of the system of EU law (*effet util*), are not permitted. Furthermore, Member States must interpret the provisions in the light of the general aim of the Directive (including securing the protection at a high level),[55] and the three-step-test that has been implemented via the Directive's article 5(5). According to this test, exception and limitations shall 'only be applied in certain special cases, which do not conflict with a normal exploitation of the work or other subject-matter and do not unreasonably prejudice the legitimate interests of the right holder'.[56] In this way, the freedom of Member States is circumscribed.[57]

---

52 See most notably C-5/08, *Infopaq International A/S v Danske Dagblades Forening*, ECLI:EU:C:2009:465 (on newspapers and parts thereof); C-403/08 and C-429/08 *Football Association Premier League Ltd and Others v QC Leisure and Others*, ECLI:EU:C:2011:631 (on football matches); C-145/10, *Eva-Maria Painer v Standard Verlags GmbH and Others*, ECLI:EU:C:2011:798 (on photographs) – "C-145/10 Painer"; C-393/09 *Bezpečnostní softwarová asociace – Svaz softwarové ochrany v Ministerstvo kultury*, ECLI:EU:C:2010:816 (on computer programs); C-406/10 *SAS Institute Inc. v World Programming Ltd.*, ECLI:EU:C:2012:259 (on computer programs); C-469/17 *Funke Medien NRW GmbH mod Bundesrepublik Deutschland*, ECLI:EU:C:2019:623 (on military status reports) – "C-469/17 Funke Medien"; and C-310/17, *Levola Hengelo BV v Smilde Foods BV*, ECLI:EU:C:2018:899 (the taste of a cheese).
53 Directive 2001/29/EC of the European Parliament and of the Council of 22 May 2001 on the harmonisation of certain aspects of copyright and related rights in the information society OJ L 167, 22.6.2001, 10–19 (Infosoc Directive).
54 C-145/10 Painer, paras 100 ff.
55 Infosoc-Directive, rec 4 and 9.
56 Infosoc-Directive, art5(5).
57 C-469/17 Funke Medien, para 2 45 ff.

At the same time, however, the Court has also held, that the specific limitations and exceptions in Infosoc should be interpreted in the light of the CFREU.[58] This includes the general principles of freedom of expression and information, in CFREU article 11. For this reason, it seems likely that information related to the general public enjoy a privileged position.

As can be seen, the Infosoc Directive does not contain any specific carve out for a health or other "crisis", as it is not explicitly mentioned in an exhaustive list of optional exceptions and limitations to the rights of copyright holders. The CJEU has been traditionally proactive in constructing and interpreting their scope, and in reinforcing the harmonisation potential of the Directive. The central outcome of these efforts has been a decreasing flexibility for Member States to deviate from their uniform interpretation,[59] or to expand on the catalogue of limitations and exceptions found in the Infosoc Directive.[60]

To illustrate the use of copyright exceptions in times of the ongoing pandemic, two particular examples are worth noting. The first concerns access to online materials in a broader sense, while the second relates to access to, and analysis of, data specifically for research purposes. The ongoing COVID-19 pandemic has led to closing of schools, workplaces and public institutions such as libraries. This has put enormous pressure on online access to copyright protected material in a broader sense. Such needs have been addressed in different ways. By way of example, the Danish association for rights holders and users have relied on the rules of extended collective licenses in the Danish Copyright Act to increase access to the use of teaching material for online teaching and off-site use of material in public libraries.[61] Furthermore, a recently adopted Copyright in the Digital Single Market Directive (DSM Directive)[62] provides for a mandatory exception supporting digital and cross-border teaching activities.[63] However, the actual effectiveness

---

58   C-469/17 Funke Medien, para 38 and C-516/17 *Spiegel Online* EU:C:2019:625, para 59.
59   Eleonora Rosati, *Copyright and the Court of Justice of the European Union* (Oxford, OUP 2019).
60   Case C-476/17, *Pelham GmbH and Others v Ralf Hütter and Florian Schneider-Esleben*, ECLI:EU:C:2019:624 para 65.
61   Copydan Text and Node, 'Clarifications on a Special Copyright Arrangement for Education Purposes High Schools' (*ERKLÆRING: COVID-19*, 29 January 2021) <https://privateskoler.dk/images/2021/Nyheder/Erkl%C3%A6ring-VUC%20og%20de%20gymnasiale%20uddannelser-2021.pdf> accessed 17 May 2021; Copydan Tekst & Node, *Godkendelse af Copydan Tekst & Node i henhold til ophavsretsloven § 50, stk. 4, jf. § 50, stk. 2 – tillæg til aftale om tilgængeliggørelse af ophavsretligt beskyttet avismateriale mellem Det Kgl. Bibliotek og Copydan Tekst og Node og VISDA* (Approval of Copydan Text & Node by way of the Copyright Act § 50(4), cf. § 50(2) – Addendum to Agreement on the Making Available of Copyright Protected Newspaper-material between the Royal Library and Copydan Tekst & Node and VISDA) (23 December 2020) <https://kum.dk/fileadmin/user_upload/Godkendelse_-_Covid-tillaeg_til_aftale_om_avisdigitalisering__december_2020.pdf> accessed 17 May 2021.
62   Directive (EU) 2019/790 of the European Parliament and of the Council of 17 April 2019 on copyright and related rights in the Digital Single Market OJ L 130.
63   DSM Directive, art 5.

of this exception remains to be seen following national implementation of the provision.

The second access-enabling mechanism is provided by the text and data-mining exception (TDM exception). As a mandatory exception under articles 3 and 4 of the DSM Directive, it seeks to unleash the innovative potential of big data analysis and eliminate legal uncertainty surrounding the application of IP rights to automated computational analysis.[64] The data-driven crisis management implies an informed decision-making process. As heterogeneous data sources lay its foundation, a working and efficient mechanism for data mining has been long overdue. The actual scope of the TDM exception, however, raises serious concerns as to its ability to deliver the promise, not least due to the chosen particular group of beneficiaries,[65] and the requirement of "lawful access" as a precondition for its application.[66] Again, it remains to be seen how the issue will be approached in the national implementation of Member States.[67]

Databases

Important limitations to access to health data and information as such may follow from the EU-database Directive (DBdir).[68] The DBdir defines "databases" as "collections of independent works, data or other materials arranged in a systematic or methodical way and individually accessible by electronic or other means". The definition is by design broad and "technology-neutral",[69] and, therefore,

---

64 DSM Directive, rec 8.
65 Such as research organisations and cultural heritage institutions in article 3 but also a significantly narrow scope afforded to other beneficiaries in article 4.
66 See more on TDM in Christophe Geiger, Giancarlo Frosio and Oleksandr Bulayenko 'The Exception for Text and Data Mining (TDM) in the Proposed Directive on Copyright in the Digital Single Market-Legal Aspects' (*Centre for International Intellectual Property Studies (CEIPI) Research Paper* 2018) <www.europarl.europa.eu/RegData/etudes/IDAN/2018/604941/IPOL_IDA(2018)604941_EN.pdf> accessed 30 March 2021; and Maria Canellopoulou-Bottis and others, 'Text and Data Mining in Directive 2019/790/EU Enhancing Web-Harvesting and Web-Archiving in Libraries and Archives' (2019)9 *Open Journal of Philosophy* 369 <https://doi.org/10.4236/ojpp.2019.93024> accessed 30 March 2021.
67 In the meantime, one can point to a rather concerning report on technical blocking that is certainly undermining the potential for researchers to rely on the exception in times of crisis, see Association of European Research Libraries, 'Europe's TDM Exception for Research: Will It Be Undermined by Technical Blocking From Publishers?' (*LIBER*, 10 March 2020).
68 Directive 96/9/EC of the European Parliament and of the Council of 11 March 1996 on the legal protection of databases, OJ L 77, 27.3.1996, 20–28 (DBdir).
69 ibid, recitals 13, 14 and article 1; Commission, Proposal for a Council Directive on the legal protection of databases COM (92) 24 final (13 May 1992) 21; Case C-490/14 *Freistaat Bayern v Verlag Esterbauer GmbH*), ECLI:EU:C:2015:735, para 26. See also a historical account by Mark Schneider, 'The European Union Database Directive' (1998)13 *Berkeley Technology Law Journal* 551.

potentially accommodates a wide variety of information, including data about infected persons, the efficacy of drugs or treatments or basic information about diseases.

Importantly, databases are protected not only if they are "original" in the sense described previously, for example, by way of their selection of the data or the arrangements. Even non-original databases are protected under the *sui generis*-rights, provided that there has been 'qualitatively and/or quantitatively a substantial investment in either the obtaining, verification or presentation of the contents'.[70] The threshold for the qualifying investment is, thus, quite low. However, following, the case law of the CJEU, costs incurred merely in the *creation* of new data are irrelevant.[71] Therefore, efforts must have been employed to seek out existing independent materials and collect them in the database. Such qualifying efforts can be undertaken by the same entity that has "created" the data and may qualify even if the data has not been made public. In this way, a "protective environment" can be created by and within the same undertaking. It is for this reason, that the authors have argued elsewhere that the DBdir casts the net very wide.[72]

It is to be expected that health information is regularly covered by the protection offered by the Directive. For such data, third parties may not: without the consent of the holder of the *sui generis* rights; extract and/or re-utilize the whole or a substantial part of the database contents; or engage in acts of repeated and systematic extraction even of an insubstantial part of thereof.[73] Following the case law of the CJEU, article 7 offers substantial leeway for finding infringement in Big Data contexts.[74] Moreover, access could be denied to non-substantial parts of the database where it is of a 'repeated and systematic' nature.[75] Also, since the publication of the contents of a database does not terminate protection, downstream uses of the contents of databases (including, sometimes, even the data),

---

70   DBdir, art 7(1).
71   Case C-203/02 *BHB v Hill,* ECLI:EU:C:2004:695, as well as a series of rulings on Fixtures Marketing, see Case C-444/02 *Fixtures Marketing v Organismos prognostikon,* ECLI:EU:C:2004:697; Case C-46/02 *Fixtures Marketing v Oy Veikkaus AB* ECLI:EU:C:2004:694; and Case C-338/02 *Fixtures Marketing v Svenska Spel AB,* ECLI:EU:C:2004:696.
72   Jens Schovsbo and Olga Kokoulina, 'Cutting into Diamonds: Competition Law, IPR, Trade Secrets and the Case of "Big Data"' *Liber Discipulorum for Hanns Ullrich* (Springer 2021 forthcoming), University of Copenhagen Faculty of Law Research Paper No 2020-94 <https://papers.ssrn.com/sol3/papers.cfm?abstract_id=3604063> accessed 30 March 2021.
73   DBdir, art 7.
74   Schovsbo and Kokoulina (n 72), with references to Case C-304/07 *Directmedia Publishing Gmbh v Albert-Ludwigs Universität Freiburg,* ECLI:EU:C:2008:552; Case C-545/07 *Apis – Hristovich EOOD v Lakorda AD,* ECLI:EU:C:2009:132; and Case C-202/12 *Innoweb BV v. Wegener ICT Media BV and Wegener Mediaventions BV,* ECLI:EU:C:2013:850 (Case C-202/12 Innoweb BV).
75   DBDir, art 7(5).

also constitutes an infringement if the data has been made available to the public by the right holder and is used as a part of something bigger.[76]

Thus, the DBdir combines a very broad scope with far-reaching exclusivity. The protection is exacerbated by the rules on protection that allow for perpetual prolongation based on periods of 15-years. Finally, the Directive relies on the system of limitations and exceptions found in copyright law in general. This includes a limitation of the *sui generis* right for extraction and/ or re-utilisation for the purposes of public security or an administrative or judicial procedure (article 9 litra c), which should be interpreted along the lines described earlier.

Patent law

Patent law grants exclusive rights to inventors for a limited period of time. Patent protection is open within "all fields of technology" provided the basic criteria are met: novelty, inventive step and industrial applicability.[77] Pharmaceuticals and medical devises are patentable under normal conditions and many of the drugs and vaccines related to COVID-19 are patent protected.[78]

The international base line for patent law is the Agreement on Trade-Related Aspects of Intellectual Property Rights (TRIPS Agreement). The TRIPS not only obliges Member States to grant patent rights on the conditions outlined previously, but also contains safeguards that allow Members to provide for limitations or exceptions in their national legislation. By this token, Members may limit protection to protect human health for reasons of *ordre public* or morality, or through the exclusion of diagnostic, therapeutic and surgical methods for the treatment of humans. These are narrow

---

76 Case C-202/12 Innoweb BV.

77 Agreement on Trade-Related Aspects of Intellectual Property Rights (TRIPS), art 27; For Europe, see European Patent Convention (EPC), art 52. The obligations under TRIPS may be waived. Also according to article 73 states may take 'any action which it considers necessary for the protection of its essential security interests'. Both of these avenues have been explored in the context of the COVID-19 crisis, see e.g. *The TRIPS Waiver Request* submitted by India and South Africa, available at World Trade Organization, 'Members Discuss TRIPS Waiver Request, Exchange Views on IP Role Amid a Pandemic' (*WTO*, 23 February 2021) <www.wto.org/english/news_e/news21_e/trip_23feb21_e.htm> accessed 30 March 2021; Emmanuel Kolawole Oke, 'Is the National Security Exception in the TRIPS Agreement a Realistic Option in Confronting COVID-19?' (*EJIL: TALK*, 6 August 2020) <www.ejiltalk.org/is-the-national-security-exception-in-the-trips-agreement-a-realistic-option-in-confronting-covid-19/> accessed 30 March 2021. We will not address these options further in the following. Instead, we focus on compulsory licenses as these are emblematic to the traditional patent law responses to third parties' claim for access to work inventions.

78 José Adão Carvalho Nascimento Junior and others, 'SARS, MERS and SARS-CoV-2 (COVID-19) Treatment: A Patent Review' (2020)30(8) *Expert Opinion on Therapeutic Patents* 567.

limitations and do not allow states to, for example, refuse to grant patents for pharmaceuticals outright.[79]

Apart from the "internal" and predefined limitations and exceptions (which in some countries include exemptions for research), patent law has long-acknowledged the use of compulsory licenses; in other words, licenses issued by competent authorities to third parties or governments to manufacture patented technology without the consent of the patent holder.[80] As an "emergency brake", compulsory licensing is allowed only to 'prevent the abuses which might result from the exercise of the exclusive rights conferred by the patent, for example, failure to work'.[81] For this to be triggered, a firm basis in law must be established.

Nowadays, to find the international base line for compulsory licenses we once more turn to the TRIPS.[82] Article 31 establishes a number of conditions. First, a compulsory license is a matter for the national legal system, so the remedy has to be provided for in national law. Moreover, those laws may only provide for compulsory licenses if the conditions specified in article 31 have been met. These include a case-by-case determination of compulsory license applications (either by a court or by another public authority), the need to demonstrate prior (unsuccessful) negotiations with the patent owner for a voluntary license, and the payment of adequate remuneration to the patent holder. Where compulsory licenses are granted to address a national emergency or other circumstances of extreme

---

79   Article 53(c) of the EPC on the exclusion regarding methods for treatment etc. does not apply to products, in particular substances or compositions, for use in any of these methods.

80   In some countries granting compulsory licenses are a matter for courts (such as Denmark) whereas other countries have also authorised the national Intellectual Property Office (such as the UK) or competition authorities (such as Norway).

81   Paris Convention for the Protection of Industrial Property, art 5A(1). "Abuses" cover a wide variety of issues including: refusal to deal; nonworking or inadequate supply of the market; public interest; abusive and/or anticompetitive practices; government use; dependent or "blocking" patents (on improvements to prior inventions); special product regimes, such as pharmaceuticals and food; licenses of right, see Jerome H Reichman and Cathy Hasenzahl, 'Non-Voluntary Licensing of Patented Inventions Historical Perspective, Legal Framework under TRIPS, and an Overview of the Practice in Canada and the USA' (2003)5 *UNCTAD – ICTSD* 10. The US patent law has no general statutory provisions for compulsory licensing of unexploited patents but contains very narrowly and never used compulsory options for government-funded technology (introduced by the Bay-Dole act). The Chinese patent law contains rules on compulsory licensing but so far none have been issued, see Enrico Bonadio and Andrea Baldini, 'COVID-19, Patents and the Never-Ending Tension Between Proprietary Rights and the Protection of Public Health' (2020)11(2) *European Journal of Risk Regulation* 390. For EU countries, the Directive 98/44/EC of the European Parliament and of the Council of 6 July 1998 on the legal protection of biotechnological inventions OJ L 213, 30.7.1998, art 13–21, article 12 provides for rules on compulsory cross-licensing where the exploitation of a patent issued for a biotechnological invention would infringe a prior plant patent, and vice versa.

82   Some countries may be limited by Bilateral Trade Agreements to use compulsory licensing, but this is disregarded here. Even prior to TRIPs, compulsory licensing was a widely accepted tool in patent law. About one hundred countries recognised some form of non-voluntary licensing in their patent laws by the early 1990s. See Reichman and Hasenzahl (n 81).

urgency, the requirement to obtain authorisation prior to the use is waived, which can be found at article 31(a) of the TRIPS.

The role and function of compulsory licenses was further clarified by the Doha Declaration.[83]According to the Declaration, the reference in article 31 to national emergency or other circumstances of extreme urgency covers public health crises, including those relating to HIV/AIDS, tuberculosis, malaria and other epidemics. This was not surprising, because around the time of the adoption of the Doha Declaration in 2001 a number of countries issued compulsory licenses for one or more (Brazil, Indonesia and Thailand) or all (Ghana and Zambia) of the antiretroviral drugs used to treat HIV/AIDS; this was to keep the price at an affordable level (or to provide for free treatment).[84]

In the light of the foregoing, which has established compulsory licensing as a tool to be used by countries in response to, *inter alia*, public health crises and national emergencies, it is hardly surprising that the ongoing COVID-19 pandemic has spurred a renewed interest in compulsory licensing. This time around, interest is also coming from developed countries. In mid-March 2020, Israel issued a compulsory license to import generic versions of lopinavir/ronavir, but has yet to rely on the option.[85] In addition, legislators in Chile and Ecuador have prepared their legislation for a faster assessment of claims for compulsory licenses.[86] In the same vein, the Canadian Patent Act was amended in March 2020, and now makes it possible for the federal government – or anyone it designates – to make, use of and sell patented inventions 'to the extent necessary to respond to a public health emergency'.[87] In addition, the German patent provisions have been streamlined and now empower the Federal Health Minister to issue an administrative order with regard to, for example, pharmaceuticals and medical devices that enable the government or any designee to use the patent for reasons of public welfare.[88]

Thus, compulsory licensing is a time-honoured tool in many national patents systems and has long been acknowledged in the international patent law framework. TRIPS made it clear beyond doubt that licenses may be issued in accordance with the stringent criteria set out in article 31 for reasons of public

---

83 Declaration on the TRIPS Agreement and Public Health, Doha, WT/MIN(01)/DEC/W/2 (9–14 November 2001) <www.who.int/medicines/areas/policy/tripshealth.pdf?ua=1> accessed 17 May 2021.

84 Hilary Wong, 'The Case for Compulsory Licensing During COVID-19' (2020)10(1) *Journal of Global Health* 2. The role and function of compulsory licensing position was further clarified with the adoption of article 31bis of the TRIPS which amended TRIPS with effect from 2017 (a waiver was adopted in 2003).

85 See an unofficial translation of the Israel's Permit to the State to Exploit an Invention Pursuant to Chapter Six, Article Three of the Patents Law 5727–1967 <www.keionline.org/32503> accessed 30 March 2021.

86 Wong (n 84).

87 An Act respecting certain measures in response to COVID-19 <https://laws-lois.justice.gc.ca/PDF/2020_5.pdf> accessed 17 May 2021.

88 German Patent Act § 13 as amended by the Protection Against Infection Act.

health, and that in case of emergencies the criteria are relaxed. However, as a mechanism compulsory licensing is always based on an ex-post perspective and is reactive and not proactive. Even the Israeli patent license needs to be triggered by a specific market failure. In this way compulsory licensing may gloss over more general critique of the patent system as such, the pharmaceutical patent in particular, and of granting practices such as disclosure and enablement.[89]

Finally, there have been repeated calls to open access to both patented and non-patented information needed to prevent the spreading of the COVID-19 or for the treatment of patients. The crisis has spurred several initiatives to this end, including the establishment of so-called Regional Pharmaceutical Supply Centers for the collective procurement of such products,[90] and arrangements aimed at furthering knowledge-sharing.[91] In the same vein, voluntary, unilateral or coordinated pledges to make Intellectual Property Rights (IPR) available to address public health crises have been made by several patent holders.[92]

Conclusion: looking across the rights

Information law has traditionally aspired to find the right type of fencing that would mark its boundaries. Ideally, it should be flexible and robust enough to quarter ubiquitous and intangible assets. At the same time, its thresholds should be flexible enough to protect a particular valuable category of information, whilst enabling a general flow of information within its confines. Finally, it should be attractive enough to incentivise the growth and accumulation of data, and secure enough to prevent any type of its abuse.

In some ways, the public health crisis, tests all these qualities of outer limits, whilst also challenging the inner partitions and structures of the information law domain. The regulatory landscape is presented with various patterns of rights protection that intersect, overlap, and run in parallel. For example, rules on copyright and database protection apply without prejudice to data

---

89 Bonadio and Baldini (n 81) of the attempt by researchers at the Wuhan Institute of Virology to file a patent for the use of the drug Remdesevir which was produced and patented by Gilead Sciences.

90 Frederick M Abbott and Jerome H Reichman, 'Facilitating Access to Cross-Border Supplies of Patented Pharmaceuticals: The Case of the COVID-19 Pandemic' (2020)23(3) *Journal of International Economic* Law 535 <https://doi.org/10.1093/jiel/jgaa022> accessed 30 March 2021.

91 W Nicholson Price, Arti K Rai and Timo Minssen, 'Knowledge Transfer for Large-Scale Vaccine Manufacturing' (2020)369(6506) *Science* 912 <https://science.sciencemag.org/content/369/6506/912> accessed 14 April 2021.

92 Jorge L Contreras, 'Pledging Intellectual Property for COVID-19' (2020)38 *Nature Biotechnology* 1146 <https://doi.org/10.1038/s41587–020–0682–1> accessed 30 March 2021.

protection legislation.[93] In other words, conceptually, the IPR layer of protection does not affect the rights accorded under the PD layer. By the same token, the fact that information contains personal information does not impact on its eligibility for protection under copyright or patent law. However, depending on the perspective, protection layers under different labels of PD or IPR might overlap, demanding careful and in-depth analysis. In the context of a health crisis, an all-embracing figure of "research" is just that case in point. Automated analytical techniques are being increasingly applied across a wide range of knowledge domains. This quest for patterns, trends and correlation requires large datasets that might consist of various types of data. The ensuing processes of accessing, extracting/copying, presenting and re-using this data is often complicated by difficulties of identifying and clearing boundaries of, for instance, personal data, database and copyright protection.

By default, the boundaries of distinct rights protection regimes are defined differently. For example, some information protection regimes, such as database and PD, are initially posited, or further interpreted to rely on, rather generic and open-ended concepts defining their material scope. The approach naturally entails a trade-off: a potential flexibility to accommodate future technological developments comes with the challenge of a meaningful enforcement of associated rights. In other cases, the boundaries of the protection regime are much more discernible and stable, for example, through patent claims of patent application. That is not to say that theoretical foundations of protection are easy to apply as qualifiers for future scientific and technological advancements; for example, the distinction between idea and embodiment in patent law, idea/expression dichotomy in copyright.

As for "flexible" legal mechanisms for enabling access to protected information, these could be traced on different levels. Thus, the means allowing for revisiting and reconfiguring the balance of rights and interests could be seen in the very logic of the protection regime, such as defining the rules of lawful processing and demanding appropriate safeguards in data protection law and establishing exceptions to distinct rights in copyright. These could be triggered under various tags of "public interest", "epidemics" and "situations of humanitarian emergencies". As mechanisms, they could be actively evoked or merely used as a threat to promote desirable behavioural response, a compulsory license for example. At a more nuanced level, the flexible mechanisms could be internalised in individual provisions of law, allowing for a special arrangement or affording a privileged regime for certain types or certain areas of activity, such as pseudonymised data, research and text and data mining. Finally, there is an array of external mechanisms for facilitating access to protected information. They vary in their scope, reach and conditions of application. For example, access to information might be

---

93   DBdir points 35 and 48. See also and in the same vein Infosoc Directive point 57.

a primary ambition or a collateral effect of different user-generated solutions,[94] the scrutiny of competition law,[95] or various policy initiatives.[96]

In a broad sense, there is no dearth of distinct mechanisms that could advance a data-driven and informed decision-making in time of a health crisis. But, as the pandemic knows no borders traversing the globe, the only efficient response strategy should be based on consistent and concerted efforts of various stakeholders. Only greater coordination could unleash a full potential of data access and sharing: in order to succeed, we need to build the bridges, instead of fortifying walls and blocking the gates of distinct information law domains.

Bibliography

Abbott F and Reichman J, 'Facilitating Access to Cross-Border Supplies of Patented Pharmaceuticals: The Case of the COVID-19 Pandemic' (2020)23(3) *Journal of International Economic Law* 535 <https://doi.org/10.1093/jiel/jgaa022> accessed 30 March 2021.

Black N, 'Why We Need Observational Studies to Evaluate the Effectiveness of Health Care' (1996)312(7040) *BMJ: British Medical Journal* 1215.

Bohannon J, 'Genealogy Databases Enable Naming of Anonymous DNA Donors' (2013)339(6117) *Science* 262.

Boisot M and Agustí C, 'Data, Information and Knowledge: Have We Got It Right?' (2004)14(1) *Journal of Evolutionary Economics* 43.

Bonadio E and Baldini A, 'COVID-19, Patents and the Never-Ending Tension Between Proprietary Rights and the Protection of Public Health' (2020)11(2) *European Journal of Risk Regulation* 390.

Burgin M, *Theory of Information: Fundamentality, Diversity and Unification* (Los Angeles, World Scientific Publishing 2010).

Bygrave L, 'Information Concepts in Law: Generic Dreams and Definitional Daylight' (2015)35(1) *Oxford Journal of Legal Studies* 91.

Canellopoulou-Bottis M and others, 'Text and Data Mining in Directive 2019/790/EU Enhancing Web-Harvesting and Web-Archiving in Libraries and Archives' (2019)9 *Open Journal of Philosophy* 369 <https://doi.org/10.4236/ojpp.2019.93024> accessed 30 March 2021.

Choi H and Varian H, 'Predicting the Present with Google Trends' (2012)88(1) *Economic Record* 2.

Contreras J, 'Pledging Intellectual Property for COVID-19' (2020)38 *Nature Biotechnology* 1146 <https://doi.org/10.1038/s41587-020-0682-1> accessed 30 March 2021.

---

94 Thomas Riis (ed), *User Generated Law: Re-Constructing Intellectual Property Law in a Knowledge Society* (Cheltenham, Edward Elgar Publishing 2016); Geertrui van Overwalle (ed), *Gene Patents and Collaborative Licensing Models: Patent Pools, Clearinghouses, Open Source Models and Liability Regimes* (Cambridge, Cambridge UP 2009).

95 Schovsbo and Kokoulina (n 72).

96 See examples: Directive (EU) 2019/1024 of the European Parliament and of the Council of 20 June 2019 on open data and the re-use of public sector information OJ L 172, 26.6.2019, 56–83; and also various EU initiatives under 2020 European Strategy for Data.

Copydan Tekst & Node, *Godkendelse af Copydan Tekst & Node i henhold til ophavs-retsloven § 50, stk. 4, jf. § 50, stk. 2 – tillæg til aftale om tilgængeliggørelse af ophavs-retligt beskyttet avismateriale mellem Det Kgl. Bibliotek og Copydan Tekst og Node og VISDA* (Approval of Copydan Text & Node by Way of the Copyright Act § 50(4), cf. § 50(2) – Addendum to Agreement on the Making Available of Copyright Pro-tected Newspaper-Material Between the Royal Library and Copydan Tekst & Node and VISDA) (23 December 2020) <https://kum.dk/fileadmin/user_upload/ Godkendelse_-_Covid-tillaeg_til_aftale_om_avisdigitalisering__december_2020. pdf> accessed 17 May 2021.

Docksey C, 'Four Fundamental Rights: Finding the Balance' (2016)6(3) *International Data Privacy Law* 195.

Floridi L, 'Philosophical Conceptions of Information' in Sommaruga G (ed), *Formal Theories of Information: From Shannon to Semantic Information Theory and General Concepts of Information* (Berlin, Springer 2009).

Foucault M, *Discipline and Punish: The Birth of the Prison* (Paris, Gallimard 1975).

Foucault M, *Security, Territory, Population: Lectures at the Collège de France* (London, Palgrave Macmillan 2009).

Geiger C, Frosio G and Bulayenko O 'The Exception for Text and Data Mining (TDM) in the Proposed Directive on Copyright in the Digital Single Market-Legal Aspects' (*Centre for International Intellectual Property Studies (CEIPI) Research Paper* 2018) <www.europarl.europa.eu/RegData/etudes/IDAN/2018/604941/ IPOL_IDA(2018)604941_EN.pdf> accessed 30 March 2021.

Gostin L and Wiley L, *Public Health Law: Power, Duty, Restraint* (3rd edn, Oakland, CA, California UP 2016).

Hildebrandt M, 'Law As Computation in the Era of Artificial Legal Intelligence: Speaking Law to the Power of Statistics' (2018)68(supplement 1) *University of Toronto Law Journal* 12.

Hoeyer K, 'Denmark at a Crossroad? Intensified Data Sourcing in a Research Radical Country' in Mittelstadt BD and Floridi L (eds), *The Ethics of Biomedical Big Data* (Cham, Switzerland, Springer 2016).

Mallappallil M and others, 'A Review of Big Data and Medical Research' (2020)8 *Sage Open Medicine* 1.

Mestan K and others, 'Genomic Sequencing in Clinical Trials' (2011)9(1) *Journal of Translational Medicine* 1.

Moses L, 'Adapting the Law to Technological Change: A Comparison of Common Law and Legislation' (2003)26 *U New South Wales LJ* 394.

Olson D and others, 'Reassessing Google Flu Trends Data for Detection of Seasonal and Pandemic Influenza: A Comparative Epidemiological Study at Three Geo-graphic Scales' (2013)9(10) *PLoS Computational Biology* e1003256.

Price N, Rai A and Minssen T, 'Knowledge Transfer for Large-Scale Vaccine Manu-facturing' (2020)369(6506) *Science* 912 <https://science.sciencemag.org/con-tent/369/6506/912> accessed 30 March 2021.

Purtova N, 'The Law of Everything: Broad Concept of Personal Data and Future of EU Data Protection Law' (2018)10(1) *Law, Innovation and Technology* 40.

Reichman J and Hasenzahl C, 'Non-Voluntary Licensing of Patented Inventions His-torical Perspective, Legal Framework Under TRIPS, and an Overview of the Prac-tice in Canada and the USA' (2003)5 *UNCTAD – ICTSD.*

Richesson R, Horvath M and Rusincovitch S, 'Clinical Research Informatics and Electronic Health Record Data' (2014)9(1) *Yearbook of Medical Informatics* 215.

Riis T (ed), *User Generated Law: Re-Constructing Intellectual Property Law in a Knowledge Society* (Cheltenham, Edward Elgar Publishing 2016).

Rosati E, *Copyright and the Court of Justice of the European Union* (Oxford, OUP 2019).

Rose G, 'Sick Individuals and Sick Populations' (2001)30(3) *International Journal of Epidemiology* 427.

Schneider M, 'The European Union Database Directive' (1998)13 *Berkeley Technology Law Journal* 551.

Schovsbo J and Kokoulina O, 'Cutting into Diamonds: Competition Law, IPR, Trade Secrets and the Case of "Big Data"' in *Liber Discipulorum for Hanns Ullrich* (Springer 2021 forthcoming), University of Copenhagen Faculty of Law Research Paper No 2020–94 <https://papers.ssrn.com/sol3/papers.cfm?abstract_id=3604063> accessed 30 March 2021.

Shapiro C and Varian H, *Information Rules: A Strategic Guide to the Network Economy* (Boston, Harvard Business Press 1998).

Sweeney L, 'Simple Demographics Often Identify People Uniquely' (2000)671(2000) *Health (San Francisco)* 1.

Taglang G and Jackson D, 'Use of "Big Data" in Drug Discovery and Clinical Trials' (2016)14(1) *Gynecologic Oncology* 17.

Tenforde M, Fisher K, and Patel M, 'Identifying COVID-19 Risk Through Observational Studies to Inform Control Measures' (2021)325(14) *The Journal of the American Medical Association* 1464.

Thadhani R, 'Formal Trials Versus Observational Studies' in Mehta A and others (eds), *FABRY Disease: Perspectives from 5 Years of FOS* (Oxford, PharmaGenesis 2006)

Van Overwalle G (ed), *Gene Patents and Collaborative Licensing Models: Patent Pools, Clearinghouses, Open Source Models and Liability Regimes* (Cambridge, Cambridge UP 2009).

Weng C and Kahn M, 'Clinical Research Informatics for Big Data and Precision Medicine' (2016)1 *Yearbook of Medical Informatics* 211.

Wong H, 'The Case for Compulsory Licensing During COVID-19' (2020)10(1) *Journal of Global Health* 2.

3 Fashion after COVID-19

Virtually the same, but different

Johanna Gibson

Introduction

The effect of COVID-19 has been far-reaching and indiscriminate, not only for the maintenance of the practical and commercial infrastructure of the fashion industry, but also for the very identity of fashion itself: 'We turned out to be so small. A miracle of nothing'.[1] The pandemic has presented specific challenges to the fashion industry, some well beyond the immediate retail relationship or shop-front. The impact of the virus on production, including the closure of factories, has magnified already existing attention on outsourcing and the uncertain welfare of workers in poorer economies manufacturing the bulk of fast fashion,[2] as well as the sustainability and impact of existing supply models. Not only individual brands and the intellectual property strategies behind them, but also, to a large extent, the industry itself, have been forced to re-position in order to secure identity and resilience. While for quite obvious reasons, some retail industries flourished, such as groceries and hygiene products, the impact on the fashion industry was sudden and somewhat catastrophic. Doors closed, fashion weeks were cancelled, shows went online[3] and people stayed home. It was all, quite suddenly, just window-shopping. However, just as suddenly, parts of the industry reframed the community of fashion through engaging in the business of the pandemic itself, as it were. In the first instance there was the very direct response of

1   Alessandro Michele, 'Notes from the Silence' (*Instagram Post*, 24 May 2020, Original note dated 29 March 2020), 'We turned out to be so small'). All weblinks accessed and accurate on 1 June 2021.
2   Tansy Hoskins, 'Can Workers Reset the System?' (*New Internationalist*, 6 October 2020) <https://newint.org/features/2020/08/11/can-workers-reset-system>; Isabella Fish, 'The Search for Fashion Supply Chain Transparency' (*Drapers*, 8 February 2020) <www.drapersonline.com/topics/sustainable-fashion/the-search-for-fashion-supply-chain-transparency>; see further on Boohoo workers' conditions in Howard Mustoe, 'Boohoo Tells Suppliers Not to Subcontract, Raising Job Fears' (*BBC News*, 8 February 2020) <www.bbc.co.uk/news/business-55974075>.
3   Georgia Wright, 'What Will Fashion Weeks Look Like Post-Coronavirus?' (*Retail Gazette*, 16 February 2020) <www.retailgazette.co.uk/blog/2021/02/what-will-fashion-weeks-look-like-post-coronavirus/>.

DOI: 10.4324/9781003176848-5

turning factories over to the production of personal protective equipment[4] and the positioning of the face mask as a fashion item.[5] But beyond this immediate response the disruption and transformation of the industry is likely to be felt for some time to come. COVID-19 has challenged not only the adaptability and production of fashion,[6] but also the very community of the industry itself.[7] This includes the community of consumers, with which this chapter is concerned. After COVID-19, what will the new consumer look like, desire, experience and create? Has fashion finally started to enjoy the virtual power of selling nothing?

Watch the shop

The impact of COVID-19 on retail was immediate, effected by both physical constraints of lockdown as well as consumer behaviour and risk assessment. And with the first lockdowns, consumers switched swiftly to online consumption.[8] In the apparel, fashion and luxury sector (AF&L), McKinsey & Company reported 'a marked shift . . . toward online or omnichannel sales, with a projected post-pandemic increase in e-commerce penetration of 10 to 15 per cent.'[9] At the

4   Leah Harper, 'UK Fashion Designers Join Hands to Make Scrubs for Key Workers' (*The Guardian*, 17 April 2020) <>www.theguardian.com/fashion/2020/apr/17/uk-fashion-designers-join-hands-to-make-scrubs-for-key-workers>.

5   Roggeveen and Sethuraman, writing at the beginning of the pandemic: 'Some manufacturers and retailers are even pivoting and changing their product mix to suit the demand arising from the COVID-19 crisis (e.g., shoe manufacturers creating facemasks, spirit manufacturers using the same alcohol ingredient for producing and selling hand sanitizers during the present crisis)'. See Anne Roggeveen and Raj Sethuraman, 'How the COVID-19 Pandemic May Change the World of Retailing' (2020)96(2) *Journal of Retailing* 169–71; see further May McMaster and others, 'Risk Management: Rethinking Fashion Supply Chain Management for Multinational Corporations in Light of the COVID-19 Outbreak' (2020)13(173) *Journal of Risk and Financial Management* 1–16. The British Fashion Council (BFC) and the Council of Fashion Designers of America (CDFA) launched a partnership on the production of designer face masks in July 2020. See Nicky Campbell, 'CFDA and BFC Launch Great Global Designer Face Coverings' (*CFDA.com*, 12 July 2020) <https://cfda.com/news/cfda-bfc-launch-great-global-designer-face-coverings>.

6   Li Zhao and Kihyung Kim, 'Responding to the COVID-19 Pandemic: Practices and Strategies of the Global Clothing and Textile Value Chain' (2020)39(2) *Clothing and Textiles Research Journal* 157–72.

7   Taylor Brydges and Mary Hanlon argue that 'To better support garment workers impacted by crisis across GPNs [global production networks], fashion brands must expand their understanding of "community" and seek out shared-responsibility approaches which acknowledge interconnections across their global supply chains'. See Taylor Brydges and Mary Hanlon, 'Garment Worker Rights and the Fashion Industry's Response to COVID-19' (2020)10(2) *Dialogues in Human Geography* 195–98, 197.

8   Songyi Youn and others, 'Fashion Consumers' Channel Switching Behavior During the COVID-19: Protection Motivation Theory in the Extended Planned Behavior Framework' (2021)39(2) *Clothing and Textiles Research Journal* 139–56. See also McKinsey & Company, 'The Future of Shopping: Technology Everywhere' (*Report*, April 2021).

9   McKinsey & Company, 'Perspectives on Retail and Consumer Goods' (*Report*, 8 August 2020) 142. See further Emily Sutherland, 'The New Directions for Fashion

same time it was observed that 'discretionary spending in this category, however, is expected to drop 50 to 60 per cent in the next new normal' as a result of new behaviours acquired during the economic uncertainty of the pandemic.[10]

This transformation in consumer behaviour has significance not only for traditional retail strategies and shopfronts, but also for the consciousness of consumers in their spending behaviour. Recent data suggest that consumers have moved online not only to protect themselves, but also, and notably, acting altruistically in the protection of others.[11] In this context, consumer trends in sustainability are identified as continuing, alongside new consumer channels and forms of consumption.[12] That said, 'it remains to be seen whether the pandemic is going to be the sustainability reset the industry desperately needs.'[13] Further, there are concerns that the economic pressures on the industry during and post-pandemic may put additional strain on existing initiatives to address sustainability.[14]

Nevertheless, with increased movement of consumer purchasing online during the pandemic, it may be possible to harness critical shopping behaviour to address sustainability and other goals beyond the immediate health crisis: 'sustainable fashion companies should position themselves purposefully to provide an enjoyable and informative sustainable clothing experience.'[15] There is some suggestion of a long-term impact on sustainability goals in the fashion industry, with the potential for more comprehensive adoption of sustainable consumption levels across a range of consumer goods, including fashion: 'A part of this behaviour is permanent and brings in structural changes in the way we live, work and take buying decisions.'[16]

In the wider context of ethical consumption in fashion, and across a range of issues from sustainability to welfare, this shift in shopping practices has potential

Retail' (*Drapers Online*, 10 December 2020) <www.drapersonline.com/insight/analysis/the-new-directions-for-fashion-retail>.

10   ibid.

11   Lee and others (n 8) 151–52.

12   BCG-Vestiaire, 'The Consumers Behind Fashion's Growing Secondhand Market' (*Report*, October 2020) <>https://web-assets.bcg.com/d0/47/1fe9ce594fd8af6accb1f0ed29a0/bcg-the-consumers-behind-fashion-growing-secondhand-market-oct-2020.pdf>. The report relies on figures from the BCG x VC Resale Survey, mid-May to mid-June 2020, to conclude that 'The pandemic has accelerated consumer trends in sustainability, sales channels, and fashion consumption'.

13   Taylor Brydges and others, 'Will COVID-19 Support the Transition to a More Sustainable Fashion Industry' (2020)16(1) *Sustainability: Science, Practice and Policy* 298–308, 304.

14   ibid.

15   Julia Koch and others, 'Online Shopping Motives During the COVID-19 Pandemic: Lessons from the Crisis' (2020)12(10247) *Sustainability* 1–20, 12.

16   Seema Mehta and others, 'The New Consumer Behaviour Paradigm Amid COVID-10: Permanent or Transient?' (2020)22(2) *Journal of Health Management* 291–301, 295. The authors are optimistic that 'COVID-19 has pulled the handbrake for the humankind race to destruction and redirected attention to life and living . . . This cumulative thought will be the trigger thread for the marketing world to redefine, strategies and reshape not only their offerings but also ways of reaching out to customers' (p 299).

relevance to ethical consumer behaviour and consciousness post-pandemic. To watch the shop has taken on a whole new meaning and a particular intentionality when it comes to the investment, both economically and socially, of the post-pandemic consumer.

Slow burn

In a series of typewritten notes disseminated in an Instagram post in May 2020, Gucci's creative director, Alessandro Michele, appealed for fashion to learn from its mistakes: 'Our reckless actions have burned the house we live in. We conceived of ourselves as separated from nature.'[17] Michele confesses further in the series of diary-like entries that, 'I feel the urgent need to change a lot of things in the way I work. . . [T]his crisis has somehow amplified such transformative urgency, which can't be deferred anymore'.[18] Citing the speed, relentless cycles and "excessive performativity"[19] of fashion, Michele states, 'I will abandon the worn-out ritual of seasonalities and shows to regain a new cadence . . . I would like to leave behind the paraphernalia of leitmotifs that colonized our prior world: cruise, pre-fall, spring-summer, fall-winter. I think these are stale and underfed words, labels of an impersonal discourse that lost its meaning'.[20] As one fashion editorial responded: 'Gucci . . . is saying "*ciao*" to the traditional show schedule. *Arrivederci*, pre-collections'.[21] The industry has been forced by the pandemic to pause long enough to acknowledge "the tyranny of speed" and the "gift of inactivity".[22] But is this slowing sustainable, so to speak?

Although the immediate impact on some slow fashion movements, such as luxury rental, was their collapse, "seemingly overnight",[23] the revival of rental and resale markets seems assured. While some industry commentators speculated early on that the rental market might never recover,[24] in view of more recent reports, this may have been premature catastrophising.[25] Indeed, for the

17 Michele (n 1).
18 Alessandro Michele, 'Notes from the Silence' (*Instagram Post*, 24 May 2020, Original note dated 7 April 2020, 'About what we would not want to be the same as it was').
19 Alessandro Michele, 'Notes from the Silence' (*Instagram Post*, 24 May 2020, Original note dated 2 May 2020, 'A new creative universe').
20 Alessandro Michele, 'Notes from the Silence' (*Instagram Post*, 24 May 2020, Original note dated 3 May 2020, 'The sacred power of producing reverberations').
21 Sara McAlpine, 'Fashion's New Order: How the Coronavirus Pandemic Has Changed the Fashion Industry' (*Elle*, 29 July 2020) <www.elle.com/uk/fashion/trends/a33442347/covid-affected-fashion-industry/>.
22 Michele (n 19).
23 Taylor Brydges and others, 'Platforms and the Pandemic: A Case Study of Fashion Rental Platforms During COVID-19' (2021)187 *The Geographical Journal* 57–63, 58.
24 See further the impact of new hygiene protocols in Emily Chan, 'Will the Fashion Rental Market Ever Recover From Covid-19?' (*Vogue*, 17 May 2020) <www.vogue.co.uk/fashion/article/will-the-fashion-rental-market-recover>.
25 Cathaleen Chen, 'The Return of Rental' (*Business of Fashion*, 29 March 2021) <www.businessoffashion.com/articles/retail/the-return-of-rental>.

resale market,[26] including luxury resale, recent industry reports actually predict a boom.[27] BCG-Vestiaire points to opportunities for innovation within luxury brands, advocating participation in second-hand markets themselves.[28]

Overall, there is likely to be a shift in the way brands communicate with their audience. This includes adaptations in the actual practices of selling fashion, not only due to changing consumer behaviour in purchasing, but also because of the broader cultural and social elements of fashion retailing. Fundamentally there has been a transformative shift in fashion's identity. Ordinarily, fashion struggles with social distance and hoards trending products, but with the impact of the virus, the discourse of sustainability in fashion and the cycling of trends has become more conscientious. And fashion has, at least for now, assumed a new time, 'A time that can bring forth the promise of an epiphany, and that can linger on the dream, on the play, on the prefiguration. A time that now, more than ever, is necessary to build new and more powerful narrations.'[29] It is thus possible that the behaviours practised during isolation mean that the object of fashion's commercial model is moving even further away from that of turnover of the individual product and closer to a discourse of reuse and duration. Ultimately, and perhaps inevitably, the fashion industry has had to reconcile a retail model of selling less product rather than more.

Show stoppers

A further consequence of the pandemic was that shows too went online and the performance became an ideal digital version of itself, including in some instances the use of digital or computer-generated models. Digital models have emerged over the past few years with some novelty as well as notoriety in advertising.[30] In addition to concerns regarding what are, quite literally, unattainable standards

---

26　Resale is generally understood as a specific "curated" sub-sector of the broader second-hand market.

27　In its 2020 *Fashion Resale Market and Trend Report*, ecommerce platform thredUP predicts that resale will take over traditional thrift and donation segment by 2024. See <www.thredup.com/resale/>. See further Hyejune Park and Cosette Joyner Martinez, 'Secondhand Clothing Sales Are Booming – And May Help Solve the Sustainability Crisis in the Fashion Industry' (*The Conversation*, 16 November 2020) <>https://theconversation.com/secondhand-clothing-sales-are-booming-and-may-help-solve-the-sustainability-crisis-in-the-fashion-industry-148403>; Danielle Wightman-Stone, 'UK's Secondhand Market Skyrockets in 2020' (*Fashion United*, 2 September 2020) <https://fashionunited.uk/news/fashion/uk-s-secondhand-market-skyrocket-in-2020/2020090250676>.

28　BCG-Vestiaire (n 28).

29　Michele (n 19).

30　For example, see the Balmain campaign discussed in Rachel Hosie, 'Balmain Reveals Line-Up of Virtual Models for Latest Campaign' (*The Independent*, 3 September 2018) <>www.independent.co.uk/life-style/fashion/balmain-virtual-models-digital-campaign-fashion-shudu-a8520871.html>.

of personal appearance,[31] digital modelling agencies[32] raise questions over the employment opportunities for living models[33] as well as potential manipulation of imagery and brand legacy.[34] But in the increasing interaction between games and fashion, the "gamification" of fashion, the emergence of digital celebrities is all but inevitable, extending, as seen later in this chapter, to influencers themselves. And during the pandemic, when traditional photo shoots were impossible, 'images that are made through a combination of model and machine',[35] became 'remarkably prescient'.[36]

It may appear that fashion is becoming less "eventful," but really, the creativity and spectacle simply moved online, just not quite as before. For example, the Instagram craze of the so-called shopping bag challenge was a network of brand engagement that emerged early in lockdown. Instagram users posted images of themselves not in the products but in the shopping bags themselves, styled as "insta-worthy" outfits and accompanied by the hashtag, #shoppingbagchallenge.[37] While some bags were luxury brands, others were reusable grocery bags or simple paper bags. The styling usually involved attention to hats and footwear, or other accessories, while the clothing remained communicated, and indeed fashioned, entirely through brand – inaccessible, elsewhere and even arbitrary. The shopping bag, just like haute couture, is a kind of loss leader; that is, it is merchandising, designed to be seen and marketed, but not for sale.[38] Traditionally, the business model of luxury brands is to live for their clothing but survive on their accessories, with the majority of income derived from footwear,

---

31   On these issues in the digital manipulation of physical models' appearances, see Caitlin McBride and others, 'Digital Manipulation of Images of Models' Appearance in Advertising: Strategies for Action Through Law and Corporate Social Responsibility Incentives to Protect Public Health' (2019)45 *American Journal of Law and Medicine* 7–31; Sheila Reaves and others, 'If Looks Could Kill: Digital Manipulation of Fashion Models' (2004)19(1) *Journal of Mass Media Ethics* 56–71.

32   See The Diiigitals at <www.thediiigitals.com/models>; See further Sara Semic, 'Meet the Man Behind the World's First Digital Supermodel' (*Elle*, 15 July 2019) <www.elle.com/uk/fashion/a28394357/man-behind-worlds-first-digital-supermodel/>.

33   Lindsay Dodgson, 'Fake, Computer-Generated Instagram Influencers Are Modelling Designer Clothes, Wearing Spanx, and Attending Red Carpet Premieres' (*Insider*, 4 September 2019) <>www.insider.com/cgi-influencers-what-are-they-where-did-they-come-from-2019-8>.

34   For a discussion of CGI in acting and the use of CGI actors, please see Johanna Gibson, 'Where Have You Been? CGI Film Stars and Reanimation Horrors' (2019)10(1) *Queen Mary Journal of Intellectual Property* 1–6.

35   Maghan McDowell, 'During the Pandemic, Models Get a Digital Makeover' (*Vogue Business*, 21 April 2020) <www.voguebusiness.com/technology/during-the-pandemic-models-get-a-digital-makeover-covid-19>.

36   ibid.

37   Naomi May, 'What Is the Shopping Bag Challenge? Instagram's Latest Trend Explained' (*Evening Standard*, 28 April 2020) <www.standard.co.uk/insider/fashion/shopping-bag-instagram-lockdown-challenge-a4425861.html>.

38   With the notable exception, of course, of charges, whether as tax or charitable donation, applied in various jurisdictions to the provision of plastic shopping bags, which some high street stores still use.

handbags and other accessories.[39] In many ways, the shopping bag challenge was an incidental performance of this curious paradox in fashion. In this particular episode, fashion is translated into a discourse of brand imagery, with an emphasis on the trade mark, as distinct from conventional narratives of design. Clothing as merchandising, not product.

Further, the challenge was not only about the brand, but also the nature of shopping. The physical bag, recognisable from the bricks and mortar retail environment and the vehicle for the conspicuous display during the promenade out of the store, went digital. Indeed, carrying the shopping bag is such a strong self-branding exercise that "influencers" have been known to purchase the paper bag alone in order to maintain that display.[40] There has been for several years a somewhat established and ongoing market in luxury branded paper bags on eBay and other platforms, ironically giving rise to trade in counterfeit paper shopping bags.[41] Understanding this kind of engagement is arguably critical to the new forms of experiences and relationships with brands in the future, and 'it will be important for retailers to understand what types of experiences customers are likely to value in a store after the pandemic'.[42] The industry has been required to pivot not only on product, but also on promotion. Further, when it comes to the spectacle of intellectual property, this consumer proficiency in brand identity and engagement invites innovative perspectives on the product in other intellectual property industries, beyond the immediate performance of fashion.

How to fashion

The "event" of fashion has thus become a significant branding issue. Whether adorned in bags or in the products themselves, the display of fashion's twenty-first-century boulevardier is increasingly a mediated and virtual presence, rather than a vibrant one. The shopping bag challenge is instructive here in that the authenticity of consumer experience is itself a kind of branding

---

39   Marc Bain, 'For Luxury Brands, Selling Clothes Is Basically a Marketing Expense' (*Quartz*, 2 June 2017) <>https://qz.com/996233/big-luxury-labels-like-gucci-prada-and-louis-vuitton-arent-in-the-business-of-selling-clothes/>.

40   Chris Stokel-Walker, 'Influencers Are Buying Empty Shopping Bags to Pretend They're Rich' (*Input*, 21 October 2020) <www.inputmag.com/culture/influencers-are-pretending-theyre-rich-by-buying-empty-shopping-bags>. See further on signalling and brand prominence in Young Jee Han and others, 'Signaling Status with Luxury Goods: The Role of Brand Prominence' (2010)74(4) *Journal of Marketing* 15–30.

41   Sadie Whitelocks, 'A Chanel Bag for Less Than £5? How the Craze for Branded Paper Carriers Has Sparked Flood of Fakes' (*Daily Mail*, 3 January 2012) <>www.dailymail.co.uk/femail/article-2081642/A-Chanel-bag-5-How-craze-branded-paper-carriers-attracts-cash-strapped.html>.

42   Roggeveen and Sethuraman (n 5) 169. See further Philipp Klaus and Aikaterini Manthiou, 'Applying the EEE Customer Mindset in Luxury: Reevaluating Customer Experience Research and Practice During and After Corona' (2020)31(6) *Journal of Service Management* 1175–83.

exercise. In other words, the consumer's belief in the provenance of the fashion product (and the authenticity and assurance of labelling) becomes the object at stake and in transaction, rather than the product itself.[43] The social life of fashion thus became more difficult to recognise during COVID; but as will be seen in this chapter, with the advent of virtual fashion weeks, in-game shopping, digital clothes and more, in many ways it also became much easier to find.[44]

Thus, although COVID-19 has had a clear and tangible impact on the individual consumer's economic resources and confidence, as well as on the availability and kinds of retail opportunities, perhaps the most critical nexus between production and consumption is the desire of the new consumer themselves: 'It is very likely that some of the new behaviours adopted by retailers and consumers during the pandemic may become the new-normal. For example, retailers are likely to reconsider aspects of their supply chain, inventory, and delivery systems',[45] and 'Consumers are also likely to become accustomed to new ways of shopping.'[46]

Post-pandemic retail is to be, quite literally, a very unfamiliar exercise. The fashion industry is articulated upon the personalities of bodies, the intimacy of the product's touch and feel, the community of trends and tribes. But in a post-pandemic retail environment, the physical constraints and distance between user and product, between consumer and retailer, are likely to persist for some time. This distance extends to the experience of fashion itself. That is, consumers are not simply becoming accustomed to new ways of shopping; they are becoming accustomed to new ways of fashioning. How will a love of fashion play out, so to speak, in a post-pandemic world? What is the new playground of fashion?

---

43   Indeed, this is where non-fungible tokens or NFTs may have immediate impact for fashion's conventional business models, as discussed later in this chapter. See further the discussion of this consumption of "provenance" as distinct from product in the case of ethical veganism and fashion in Johanna Gibson, 'Brands Make Believe: Ethical Veganism and Labelling in Fashion' (2020)10(2) *Queen Mary Journal of Intellectual Property* 143–51.

44   The mainstream press has emphasised the way in which virtual shows erase the elitism of traditional fashion weeks, expanding engagement: see Jess Cartner-Morley, 'London Fashion Week Drops Elitist Traditions as Event Goes Fully Digital' (*The Guardian*, 12 June 2020) <>www.theguardian.com/fashion/2020/jun/12/london-fashion-week-drops-elitist-traditions-as-event-goes-fully-digital>; Harriet Hall, 'Digital Fashion Weeks Have Forced the Industry to Confront Some Difficult Questions' (*The Independent*, 19 February 2021) <www.independent.co.uk/voices/london-fashion-week-digital-shows-b1804599.html>. However, the industry itself still places importance on the live, in-person event: AFP, 'Pros Weigh in on Digital Fashion Week: "Runways Can't Reopen Soon Enough"' (*Fashion United*, 10 July 2020) <>https://fashionunited.uk/news/fashion/pros-weigh-in-on-digital-fashion-week-runways-can-t-reopen-soon-enough/2020071049787>.

45   Roggeveen and Sethuraman (n 5) 169.

46   ibid.

The gamification of fashion

The pandemic has transformed not only fashion retail relationships but also predominant gaming cultures.[47] Since the start of the pandemic, fashion has embraced the "new playground" of games,[48] appearing both on the characters,[49] and in shows within the games.[50] One particular phenomenon has been the translation of fashion into the fan communities of *Animal Crossing: New Horizons*,[51] the 2020 release of Nintendo's social simulation video game series, *Animal Crossing*.[52] The collaboration between the worlds of fashion and gaming became a regular press item during the series of lockdowns, but in many ways the fashioning of *Animal Crossing* and the gaming of fashion were not simply inevitable, they were also already in play.[53]

Early in the pandemic, *Animal Crossing* outsold traditionally dominant players, such as *Call of Duty*, in what could be explained as a kind of socialisation of the gaming stratosphere with a new diversity of "unlikely" gamers.[54] The popularity of the game has been attributed to timing and the desire for escapism during long periods of lockdown and self-quarantine: 'we can just consider the game world as the 'La-la land,' . . . it plays an unexpected role to provide

47   Shannon Liao, 'Why the Video Game Boom Is Here to Stay' (*CNN*, 13 December 2020) <https://edition.cnn.com/2020/12/13/tech/gaming-recession-proof/index.html>; Catherine Salfino, 'In New Retail Landscape, Brands Can Connect Through Gaming' (*Sourcing Journal*, 16 April 2020) <>https://sourcingjournal.com/topics/lifestyle-monitor/cotton-incorporated-coronavirus-gaming-mobile-advertising-fortnite-205869/>.

48   Annachiara Biondi, 'Fashion's New Playground: Esports and Gaming' (*Vogue Business*, 28 August 2020) <www.voguebusiness.com/technology/fashion-esports-gaming-monetisation>.

49   Cristina Criddle, 'Burberry Designs Skins for Honor of Kings Characters' (*BBC News*, 24 March 2021) <www.bbc.co.uk/news/technology-56511343>.

50   Khanh Tran, 'Video Games Are the New Runway' (*Los Angeles Times*, 4 December 2020) <>www.latimes.com/lifestyle/story/2020–12–04/covid-19-fashion-brands-experiment-video-games>.

51   Worldwide release, 20 March 2020.

52   The premise of *Animal Crossing: New Horizons* is to start a new life on an island, where your character performs daily activities in real time, including collecting various items, basic agriculture, shopping, trading, socialising, as well as participating in in-game events. The game is open-ended and without specific objectives, apart from maintaining the general activities associated with developing your island.

53   For a more detailed discussion of gaming in fashion, including through the example of *Animal Crossing*, see Johanna Gibson, 'When Games Are the Only Fashion in Town: COVID-19, *Animal Crossing* and the Future of Fashion' (2021)11(2) *Queen Mary Journal of Intellectual Property* 116–23.

54   Mark Sweney, 'Family-Friendly Animal Crossing Takes Video Game Top Spot Amid Lockdown' (*The Guardian*, 23 April 2020) <>www.theguardian.com/games/2020/apr/23/family-friendly-animal-crossing-takes-video-game-top-spot-amid-lockdown>.   Sweney notes the 'wider multigenerational family fanbase than most bestselling titles', with 'Animal Crossing is now the biggest single game launched on Nintendo Switch . . . proving to be an escapist antidote to the coronavirus pandemic'.

comfort and social connection in a time of isolation and struggle'.[55] With its tag-line of "Your island, your life!"[56] *Animal Crossing* promised players the tonic of a kind of control and social life that might otherwise be missing in the uncertainty of pandemic existence. As such, *Animal Crossing* became a new kind of social bazaar, where participation in the game developed into a twenty-first-century virtual promenade, showcasing fashion, taste, and mobility, as it were, in a para-doxically secluded consumer society.[57]

Play in the course of trade

The fashion credentials of *Animal Crossing* are extensive. In May 2020, Refer-ence Festival, a 24 hour fashion festival launched in 2019, produced a virtual fashion show in collaboration with Animal Crossing Fashion Archive and Marc Goehring, fashion director of 032C Magazine.[58] The show consisted of *Ani-mal Crossing* avatars dressed in current collections by Prada, Loewe and GmbH, reimagined for the virtual environment.[59] The game itself includes a tailor shop, run by the Able Sisters – Mabel, Sable and Label.[60] But fans themselves have also developed collections,[61] as well as fashion inspired by a range of luxury brands,[62] and even character costumes for digital cosplay,[63] raising some interesting ques-tions regarding intellectual property. Of particular interest in this context is the

55   Lin Zhu, 'The Psychology Behind Video Games During COVID-19 Pandemic: A Case Study of *Animal Crossing: New Horizons*' (2021)3 *Human Behavior and Emerging Tech-nologies* 157–59, 158.

56   See the YouTube promotional video at <https://youtu.be/5LAKjL3p6Gw>. One of the key characters throughout the whole *Animal Crossing* series is Tom Nook (also the game's real estate broker). With the release of *New Horizons*, Nook promised, 'With our Deserted Island Getaway Package, a carefree new life awaits you on a peaceful paradise of your own making, yes, yes!' See further the launch announcement at <www.nintendo.co.uk/Games/Nintendo-Switch/Animal-Crossing-New-Horizons-1438623.html>.

57   Keza MacDonald, video games editor for *The Guardian*, says, 'it's a game about self-expression.' See Ellie Bramley, ' "It's a Way to Live Out Fantasies": How Animal Cross-ing Became Fashion's New Catwalk' (*The Guardian*, 21 May 2000) <>www.theguardian.com/fashion/2020/may/21/its-a-way-to-live-out-fantasies-how-animal-crossing-became-fashions-new-catwalk>.

58   See <https://032c.com>.

59   Steff Yotka, 'The World's First Animal Crossing Fashion Show Is Here' (*Vogue*, 25 May 2020) <www.vogue.co.uk/news/article/animal-crossing-fashion-show>.

60   See the explanation of Label's fashion challenge at *Eurogamer* <www.eurogamer.net/articles/animal-crossing-label-fashion-challenge-rewards-new-horizons-7018>.

61   For example, see the discussion of the development of an artistic community of fashion designers in Cass Marshall, 'Animal Crossing Keeps Growing a Vibrant Fashion Com-munity' (*Polygon*, 11 September 2020) <>www.polygon.com/2020/9/11/21432219/animal-crossing-fashion-influencers-designers-dress-sharing-community>.

62   See the Creative Bloq feature on fashion designs at <www.creativebloq.com/features/animal-crossing-fashion/3>.

63   See the Creative Bloq feature on cosplay at <www.creativebloq.com/features/animal-crossing-fashion>.

use of trade marks, including examples of logomania and character merchandising within the game.

The application of trade marks within the game challenges definitions of use and trade in trade mark law. The economy of Bells is thriving within *Animal Crossing*, but does this use of trade marks constitute use in the course of trade? And, if so, is there some critical insight here for how the understanding of "trade" must develop in order to account for brand development in social media? As influencers present more and more complications for advertising and authenticity, the co-option of trade marks in their own self-branding has become an uncertain and contentious area. In this context, the phenomenon of fashion in *Animal Crossing* is especially interesting for compelling critical attention on a more innovative approach to the question of "trade" in a hybrid physical/digital retail environment.

While "bootleg" collections have proliferated within the game,[64] other brands have created official *Animal Crossing* collections. Both Valentino[65] and Marc Jacobs[66] were early in populating the game with official collections or re-worked designs which users could download, thereby directing engagement with the brands' official Instagram accounts.[67] *Hypebae*, the fashion editorial division of *Hypebeast*, hosted their own live fashion show within the game in May 2020, in which players were invited to model their creations on an island customised with its own outdoor runway.[68] Nook Street Market opened the show in a reimagined Jean Paul Gaultier Fall/Winter 1995.[69] And a few months later, Carolina Sarria presented her latest fashion show[70] within the game, with an in-game collection valued in an outside-game economy, each item bearing the modest price of $5.00

---

64 Bramley (n 57). To date there is little evidence of producers pursuing bootleg versions, and it may be speculated that in the present circumstances this kind of engagement is unlikely to be damaging or sustained, and more likely to be instrumental in maintaining brand connections with consumers.

65 For example, see <>www.instagram.com/p/B_r6dOLpHca/?hl=en>.

66 For example, see <>www.instagram.com/p/B_szSLRDdW3/?hl=en>.

67 See further the discussion in J Fingas, 'Top Fashion Houses Are Showing Their Latest Styles in "Animal Crossing"' (*Engadget*, 10 May 2020) <>www.engadget.com/animal-crossing-fashion-houses-231541432.html?guccounter=1&guce_referrer=aHR0cHM6L y93d3cuZ29vZ2xlLmNvbS8&guce_referrer_sig=AQAAAD-RhwwO_1l_zImT7IxhHqy GvfwxvL0GhVtMHjOOAzo4Zvz_AtjFfx1MWnBsk0KNtF22-ANCtgOpNMYXqejMX mFiClShjOLuy8Gqe4laXWMNynXp-SWjjD504yBe-e1en7eUgRwiHlqQ_04YCs5ylm0Ni n0jOyKaMA4y2mTdStCU>.

68 A brief "behind the scenes" of the show is available at <>www.youtube.com/ watch?v=zsyj2v3PvrU&ab_channel=HYPEBAE>.

69 See the full story at Lily Chen, 'Watch Hypebae's Animal Crossing Fashion Show' (*Hypebae*, 28 May 2020) <>https://hypebae.com/2020/5/hypebae-animal-crossing-new-horizons-fashion-show-runway-online-virtual-event-nintendo-switch-stream>.

70 See the show at <>www.youtube.com/watch?v=ayHvG23Tk9w&feature=emb_logo>. See further Steff Yotka, 'Carolina Sarria Brings the Community of Fashion Week to an Animal Crossing Show' (*Vogue*, 3 September 2020). <www.vogue.co.uk/fashion/article/ carolina-sarria-animal-crossing-fashion>.

for the opportunity to download to wear within the game.[71] The Instagram handle for each player model was also included in the show, emphasising the importance of growing the individual player "brand" within the economy of the game and complicating further the questions of play and trade.

Whether accepted as fan-based tributes outside the course of trade or produced by the brand itself as digital products for in-game play, in this way the economy of fashion is thus reimagined outside the artefact through a familiar production with fans, and thus realising value outside the physical object itself. At the same time, quite importantly, this raises questions about the commercial context for trade marks more broadly speaking. Within the *Animal Crossing* universe, the use of fashion trade marks is arguably transformed, yet still within a wholly commercial relationship.

Play to sell

This gamification of fashion imports the logic of the game into fashion itself. Balenciaga launched its autumn/winter 2021 collection in an original video game,[72] exploiting the similarly interactive fashion environment identified in *Animal Crossing*. Through the immersive, narrative aspects of the video game, consumers were offered a kind of intimacy with the product at a time when traditional forms of fashion interaction were either challenging or impossible. This use of so-called "advergames," a form advertising in which a game is developed for the purpose of advertising a particular product,[73] has actually been around in fashion for some time. In fact, the first known example of what would become known as an advergame was in fashion, when in 1978 Polo developed, but ultimately cancelled before release, a game for Atari 2600 to launch a cologne.[74]

With the current attention on sustainability and post-COVID restraint, and the increasing interest in gamification in marketing more generally,[75] the relationship between games and fashion has entered the mainstream. The appropriation by "unlikely" gamers is translating fashion consumer culture into an economy of

---

71 See <www.carolinasarria.com/animal-crossing-collection>.

72 BBC Editorial, 'Balenciaga to Unveil New Collection in Video Game' (*BBC News*, 27 November 2020) <www.bbc.co.uk/news/technology-55103957>.

73 One of the first examples of the use of the term "advergame" is in *Wired*'s "Jargon Watch" where it is defined as 'A downloadable or Web-based game created solely to enable product placements' at <www.wired.com/2001/10/jargon-watch-75/>. See further the extensive treatment of advergames (including their use in the Jean Paul Gaultier and Björn Borg examples discussed next) in Teresa dela Hera, *Digital Gaming and the Advertising Landscape* (Amsterdam, Amsterdam UP 2019) Chapter 6.

74 See at <www.atariprotos.com/2600/software/polo/polo.htm>.

75 S Hamada and Y Wakabayashi, 'Gamification in Marketing: An Empirical Study of Differences in User Psychology Among Services Using Gamification' (2014)83(1–2) *The Kyoto Economic Review* 27–57, 51; Ralf Terlutter and Michael Capella, 'The Gamification of Advertising: Analysis and Research Directions of In-Game Advertising, Advergames, and Advertising in Social Network Games' (2013)42(2–3) *Journal of Advertising* 95–112.

cultural as distinct from financial capital: 'It's a way to live out fashion fantasies without having to pay the steep price.'[76] In this way, it is possible that games such as *Animal Crossing* are repositioning both consumers and producers, ultimately teaching fashion how to sell more by making less.

Give me land

Giving new meaning to the "bricks and mortar" business model of retail, a major aspect of *Animal Crossing* is real estate and stock trading through the local currency of Bells and trading on the Stalk Market. The interaction between this virtual economy and "real world" systems and traditions of property is instructive. In developing one's island and real estate, players rely primarily on a system of manners and rules of etiquette, rather than conventional approaches to property. That is, in contrast to property norms and legal conventions, including those in intellectual property, where property 'does not depend on another's courtesy',[77] in "La-la land", player courtesy prevails. Indeed, this is an economy of abundance rather than rivalry. There is competition, but it is not a rivalry of products: 'The *Animal Crossing* fashion community can be intense. There's a lot of competition – not personal, or with each other, it's just getting eyes on your stuff. There's a lot of signal to noise.'[78] If there is any competition it is only with attention, with the performance of the brand. Indeed, what can be more abundant than the performative excess of play? In this context, as long as there is room for attention, there is no limit to the fashion or the market.

Animal Crossing thus performs the kind of mobile, sociable territories of the digital that frequently confound received conventions of intellectual property.[79] The kind of normative approach to "regulating" the interactive environment within play provides insight for the "interactivity" seen in other cultural forms, including fashion, and the interplay with dominant configurations within intellectual property environments. When it comes to intellectual property in fashion and the communication with fan communities and dynamic and "interactive" self-identity, the game thus becomes particularly compelling as a critical approach to the nature of property, including fashion. Gaming in fashion is thus not only an escape, but also an intervention in the nature of fashion, property and brands.[80] Through games consumers may be answering fashion's "expressive call"

76 Michele Yue of Nook Street Market quoted in Bramley (n 57).
77 Daniel Greenberg (ed), *Jowitt's Dictionary of English Law* (5th edn, London, Sweet & Maxwell 2019) "Property". I have examined property conventions and the nature of manners and courtesy towards a more sociable model of property in Johanna Gibson, *Owned, an Ethological Jurisprudence of Property* (London, Routledge 2020) 2–4 *passim*.
78 Riley (*Animal Crossing* designer) quoted in Marshall (n 61).
79 On mobility in territory and sociable properties in intellectual property, see further Gibson (n 77), particularly Chapter 12, *Res famliaris*.
80 The quality of gaming has been utilised as a pedagogical tool in a number of contexts: Sara de Freitas, 'Are Games Effective Learning Tools? A Review of Educational Games'

and facilitating the industry's transformation and reconnection post-COVID.[81] And they are doing so through play.

Thus, other virtual worlds may provide significant attention from the new consumers of post-pandemic fashion. For example, Phil Klaus and Aikaterini Manthiou maintain that 'An excellent example of how luxury companies can use insights about the new consumer mindset is the newly created virtual world of Decentraland . . . The current crisis with consumers seeking protection while still thriving for social contact and experiences will most certainly boost the already existing appeal of virtual social interaction platforms such as Decentraland.'[82] Decentraland is a shared virtual world or metaverse which 'began as a proof of concept for allocating ownership of digital real estate to users on a blockchain'.[83] Users trade in property as non-fungible digital assets and, although this structure creates scarcity within the economy through singularities, the value of property is premised upon attention towards the channelling of revenue to content creators.[84] Social networking thus becomes both disruptor and opportunity.[85] In a post-pandemic retail environment, 'Luxury brands can take advantage of this opportunity and build their virtual stores in Decentraland's most popular communities.'[86] Returning to the community of the industry itself, the interactivity of virtual worlds is becoming more relevant not only in terms of product launches and shows, but also in terms of the "look and feel" of brand loyalty and co-creative fashion experiences.[87] To play in fashion is to provide the "bricks and mortar" experience in the sense of a fundamental engagement with brand, where one's money is good for nothing. If the fashion world after COVID-19 looks

---

(2018)21(2) *Educational Technology & Society* 74–84. For example, for the application of gaming in farmed animal welfare education, see Roxanne Hawkins and others, 'The Development and Evaluation of "Farm Animal Welfare": An Educational Computer Game for Children' (2019)9 *Animals* 91. For application in the environmental humanities see Megan Condis, 'Live in Your World, Play in Ours': Video Games, Critical Play, and the Environmental Humanities' (2015)2(3) *Resilience: A Journal of the Environmental Humanities* 87–104. For use in the classical antiquities see Paul Christesen and Dominic Machado, 'Video Games and Classical Antiquity' (2010)104(1) *The Classical World* 107–10.

81   Michele (n 20).
82   Klaus and Manthiou (n 42) 1179.
83   Esteban Ordano and others, 'Decentraland: A Blockchain-Based Virtual World. White Paper' (2018) 5 <https://decentraland.org/whitepaper.pdf>. See further the discussion in Catalina Goanta, 'Selling LAND in Decentraland: The Regime of Non-fungible Tokens on the Ethereum Blockchain Under the Digital Content Directive' in Amon L and Ronit LS (eds), *Disruptive Technology, Legal Innovation, and the Future of Real Estate* (Amsterdam, Springer 2020) 139–54.
84   Ordano and others (n 83).
85   Templeton GF and others, 'Information Technology Firms: Creating Value through Digital Disruption' (2019)44(35) *Communications of the Association for Information Systems* 748–63, 753.
86   Klaus and Manthiou (n 42) 1179.
87   ibid.

like the hedonism of the last post-pandemic period of the "Roaring Twenties,"[88] it may be that rather than making and spending more, that abundance will be enjoyed through slowing down and playing up, in a manner of speaking. To recall Alessandro Michele, it will be to 'linger on the dream, on the play'.[89]

Money buys nothing

It is surely no coincidence that the economy of *Animal Crossing* runs on the local currency of Bells and the precious yet abundant commodity of attention. The first recorded use of the phrase, "Bells and Whistles", is in relation to efforts to attract attention, often quite literally through the noise of bells; but the later and contemporary use of the phrase is to convey additional features and the latest technological developments.[90] As a result of the lessons learned during the pandemic, it is predicted that a range of industries, not only fashion, will continue to embrace technology and the reach of virtual enterprise and experience.[91] The future of fashion is, in every sense, bells and whistles.

The intensification during the pandemic of fashion's practice with the digital has perhaps also driven industry interest in non-fungible tokens (NFTs). Unlike money and Bitcoin, which are fungible forms of currency, NFTs are unique, irreplaceable and non-fungible. In the abundance of the virtual world, NFTs are a way of creating an artificial scarcity. However, and perhaps most importantly, that scarcity is not in the product, but in the owner; that is, in the consumer identity.[92] In this way, the NFT provides a kind of mechanism of authenticity for the user and brand relationship in a digital marketplace; they provide their "owner" with a digital singularity second to none. In their application in fashion, NFTs are attracting attention not only for marketing and celebrity,[93] but also as tools for

88 The industry and mainstream press have been crowded with optimistic reference to the period of the Roaring Twenties following the Spanish flu pandemic of 1918–20, where there was experienced a period of not only economic boom but also creative freedom and hedonism. For example, see Priya Elan, 'Roaring 20s: Fashion World Predicts Post-Covid Boom' (*The Guardian*, 31 January 2021) <www.theguardian.com/fashion/2021/jan/31/economists-predict-post-covid-fashion-boom>. See also Tom Ryan, 'Will the Post-pandemic Era be America's Next Roaring 20s?' (*RetailWire*, 1 March 2021) <www.retail wire.com/discussion/will-the-post-pandemic-era-be-americas-next-roaring-20s/>.

89 Michele (n 20).

90 *Oxford English Dictionary* and E Brewer and Susie Dent, *Brewer's Phrase and Fable* (20th edn, London, Chambers 2018).

91 Janna Anderson and others, 'Experts Say the "New Normal" in 2025 Will Be Far More Tech-Driven, Presenting More Big Challenges, Report' (*Pew Research Center*, 18 February 2021) <>www.pewresearch.org/internet/2021/02/18/experts-say-the-new-normal-in-2025-will-be-far-more-tech-driven-presenting-more-big-challenges/>.

92 See further the discussion of NFTs in relation to ownership in Johanna Gibson, 'The Thousand-and-Second Tale of NFTs, as Foretold by Edgar Allan Poe' (2021)11(3) *Queen Mary Journal of Intellectual Property* 249–69.

93 For example, see Shelby Hyde, 'Kate Moss Ventures into the NFT Art Market by Sharing Some of Her Most Intimate Moments' (*Harper's Bazaar*, 13 April 2021) <www.

securing provenance for the singularity of the brand as applied to the multiplicity of the mass-produced product. More specifically, it does so in the creation of social media images using digital clothing,[94] as well as in collaboration with virtual worlds and marketing of outfits within games.[95]

The emperor's new clothes

Customer proficiency as well as desire in the technology of a mainstreamed virtual marketplace is assisted further by an environment that already has an appetite for virtual fashion. In 2019, a digital dress, existing solely virtually, was sold for $9,500 at auction on blockchain.[96] And a few months later, Scandinavian retailer, Carlings, offered an entirely digital collection.[97] The

harpersbazaar.com/celebrity/latest/a36099278/kate-moss-enters-nft-art-market/>, as well as the much-publicised interaction between Richard Prince and Emily Ratajkowski in Caroline Goldstein, 'Model Emily Ratajkowski Blasted Richard Prince for Stealing Her Image. Now, She's Taking It Back – and Selling It as an NFT' (*Artnet*, 23 April 2021) <https://news.artnet.com/market/emily-ratajkowski-nft-christies-1961581>.

94 Anna Tong, 'Luxury Fashion Brands Poised to Join the NFT Party' (*Vogue Business*, 5 April 2021) <www.voguebusiness.com/technology/luxury-fashion-brands-poised-to-join-the-nft-party>; Danny Parisi, 'Beyond the Hype: How NFTs Stand to Benefit Fashion Brands' (*Glossy*, 24 March 2021) <www.glossy.co/fashion/beyond-the-hype-nfts-stand-to-benefit-fashion-brands-in-the-future/>.

95 M Nanda, 'What the NFT Gold Rush Means for Fashion' (*Business of Fashion*, 24 March 2021) <www.businessoffashion.com/articles/technology/what-the-nft-gold-rush-means-for-fashion> (reporting on the example of the collaboration between RTKFT and digital artist, FEWOCiOUS, to produce 621 pairs of shoes issued as NFTs, selling for approximately $3.1M total). See also Greta Jelen, 'Why NFTs Could Mean Windfall Profits for Fashion' (*L'Officiel*, 25 March 2021) <www.lofficielusa.com/fashion/nfts-impact-fashion-industry-crypto-currency>; Zak Maoui, 'The Fashion Industry Is Getting in on the NFT Game' (*GQ*, 14 April 2021) <www.gq-magazine.co.uk/fashion/article/angelo-galasso-nft>; Leigh Cuen, 'NFTs Could Bridge Video Games and the Fashion Industry' (*TechCrunch*, 22 March 2021) <>https://techcrunch.com/2021/03/22/nfts-could-bridge-video-games-and-the-fashion-industry/?guccounter=1&guce_referrer=aHR0cHM6Ly93d3cuZ29vZ2xlLmNvbV88&guce_referrer_sig=AQAAAHcBysl9Br7gjO2GgGqrIakNa8YcVAvOoz1tN7vj_cItSuXm-OEZ04skk-6tpYvoBPNA2etY8XShl5n3pKGr6nc1GLa_RQTniMTVN-t1nRkugwOk7Whhw8gm_JLJ4Cv44R0sD4v2ynnlqYMh4beUmwX9uxO2A6QK3E8zJTgs_gf0>.

96 See <>www.instagram.com/p/BxVzibUopFM/?hl=en>; see further the discussion in J Fingas, 'A Digital "Dress" Sold for $9500' (*Engadget*, 27 May 2019) <>www.engadget.com/2019–05–27-fabricant-blockchain-digital-dress.html>; Cody Godwin, 'The £7,500 Dress That Does Not Exist' (*BBC News*, 15 November 2019) <www.bbc.co.uk/news/business-49794403>; Annabelle Williams, 'What Is Digital Fashion?' (*Yahoo!News*, 21 April 2021) <https://news.yahoo.com/digital-fashion-spoke-fashion-house-145718109.html>.

97 See <www.jantrendman.com/en/trends/carlings-digital-collection>. See further the report in Naomi May, 'These Clothes Aren't Real, They're All Digital: Is This the Future of Fashion?' (*Evening Standard*, 14 November 2019) <www.standard.co.uk/insider/fashion/digital-fashion-the-fabricant-carlings-a4286496.html>.

rationale for such a collection is that the nature of fashion consumption is increasingly through brand and image, as distinct from product: 'Online influencers wear "real" clothes. But why? Their followers only see the digital image of the clothes. Swipe, like and move on to the next image. Three seconds of exposure and the look is old news. The solution: digital clothes. One algorithm fits all.'[98]

A digital collection thus responds to desired experiences and at the same time achieves momentum towards selling more by making less. What could be less than nothing? Abi Buller, The Future Laboratory, says,

> We could see brands launching a digital twin of physical products. We know that consumers shop to buy new outfits that they can share on social media, but they don't necessarily have to buy a physical garment to do that. They could buy digital versions of clothing products that could be added into photos and get the same experience.[99]

This not only captures the behaviour of Instagram, but also the abundance of play. *Animal Crossing*, in ways very similar to Instagram's #OOTD (outfit of the day), plays, as it were, into this very social environment of attention and an economy of nothing.

Paper tigers and hollow people

As well as the digital performers through games, virtual models and so on, the nature of influence in fashion is also changing. Possibly even more intriguing, as well as presenting further challenges in terms of consumer welfare and representation,[100] is the development of virtual influencers, where artificial intelligence characters are created and crafted as influencers and brands in their own capacity.[101] Marketers recognise that 'live platforms are limited by the fact that the influencers, being human, need to sleep and do other activities offline. Virtual influencers . . . have no such limitations',[102] leading to predictions that such virtual influencers 'will become more prominent on social media, being

---

98 See <www.jantrendman.com/en/trends/carlings-digital-collection>.
99 Quoted in Sutherland (n 9). Buller goes on to note the influence of *Animal Crossing*: 'Virtual fashion is already a growing trend – many brands have launched digital versions of products for avatars in Animal Crossing.'
100 Alice Newbold, 'The Numerous Questions Around the Rise of CGI Models and Influencers' (*Vogue*, 18 August 2018) <www.vogue.co.uk/article/cgi-virtual-reality-model-debate>. (on the creation of Shudu, a black female model, by Cameron-James Wilson, a white male).
101 Georgia Graham, '2018 Was the Year AI Influencers and Digital Models Took Over Fashion' (*Dazed*, 10 December 2018) <>www.dazeddigital.com/fashion/article/42484/1/cgi-models-ai-influencers-lil-miquela-digital-models-trend-shudu-noonoouri>.
102 G Appel and others, 'The Future of Social Media in Marketing' (2020)48 *Journal of the Academy of Marketing Science* 79–95, 83.

able to invariably represent and act on brand values and engage with followers anytime'.[103]

Further, artificial intelligence is perhaps, somewhat paradoxically, more effective at communicating with individual fans than its human counterparts, thus providing a kind of intimacy and familiarity in the post-pandemic branding environment through a curiously "authentic" community with followers: 'an AI influencer can become attuned to followers' personalities and subsequently use this information to better inform the ways in which to interact with these followers'.[104] The "vulnerability" of influencer brands became especially apparent during the pandemic, with influencers seemingly flouting travel rules, drawing heavy criticism from their followers who remained in lockdown.[105] During the height of a pandemic, virtual influencers can travel anywhere, anytime, without compromising their brand value. In many respects, unlike their living counterparts, virtual influencers can provide the kind of escapism desired with all of the attention and none of the competition. And what could be more playful and hedonistic than the influence of nothing? In taking influence virtual, fashion is not only grappling with the narrative of intentionality and brand authenticity, but also introducing a fresh debate into "authorship" in the digital environment.

Conclusion: amounting to nothing

As fashion moved entirely online, both in its production and in its performance and consumption, the industry was compelled to examine the time and place of fashion. From the time of the incessant "ritual of seasonality" to the slow burn of fashion's environmental accountability, from the earthly promenade to the digital bazaar of games and virtual influencers, the only constant for fashion has been the brand. The transformation of the brand through COVID was not merely an intense shift in marketing and merchandising. The pandemic has been a merciless apprenticeship in the plasticity in the use and meaning of trade marks. In particular, the conservative approach to the concept of "trade" in the use of trade marks is almost in vain, so to speak, in the uncertain environment of social media. Above all, the message to fashion is unforgiving of the emphasis on product. Post-pandemic fashion is very *on brand*.

It would seem, but appearances can be deceptive, that in predicting the future of fashion after COVID-19 there is everything to play for and nothing to lose. Nothing at all.

---

103 ibid.
104 Veronica Thomas and Kendra Fowler, 'Close Encounters of the AI Kind: Use of AI Influencers as Brand Endorsers' (2021)50(1) *Journal of Advertising* 11–25, 13.
105 Lauren Cochrane, 'Perfect Storm: Have the Influencers Selling a Dream Lost Their Allure?' (*The Guardian*, 6 February 2021) <>www.theguardian.com/media/2021/feb/06/perfect-storm-have-the-influencers-selling-a-dream-lost-their-allure>.

Bibliography

AFP, 'Pros Weigh in on Digital Fashion Week: "Runways Can't Reopen Soon Enough"' (*Fashion United*, 10 July 2020) <https://fashionunited.uk/news/fashion/pros-weigh-in-on-digital-fashion-week-runways-can-t-reopen-soon-enough/2020071049787>.

Appel G and others, 'The Future of Social Media in Marketing' (2020)48 *Journal of the Academy of Marketing Science* 79–95.

Bain M, 'For Luxury Brands, Selling Clothes Is Basically a Marketing Expense' (*Quartz*, 2 June 2017) <https://qz.com/996233/big-luxury-labels-like-gucci-prada-and-louis-vuitton-arent-in-the-business-of-selling-clothes/>.

BBC Editorial, 'Balenciaga to Unveil New Collection in Video Game' (*BBC News*, 27 November 2020) <www.bbc.co.uk/news/technology-55103957>.

BCG-Vestiaire, 'The Consumers Behind Fashion's Growing Secondhand Market' (*Report*, October 2020) <https://web-assets.bcg.com/d0/47/1fe9ce594fd8af6accb1f0ed29a0/bcg-the-consumers-behind-fashion-growing-secondhand-market-oct-2020.pdf>.

Biondi A, 'Fashion's New Playground: Esports and Gaming' (*Vogue Business*, 28 August 2020) <www.voguebusiness.com/technology/fashion-esports-gaming-monetisation>.

Bramley E, ' "It's a Way to Live Out Fantasies": How Animal Crossing Became Fashion's New Catwalk' (*The Guardian*, 21 May 2000) <www.theguardian.com/fashion/2020/may/21/its-a-way-to-live-out-fantasies-how-animal-crossing-became-fashions-new-catwalk>.

Brydges, T and Hanlon M, 'Garment Worker Rights and the Fashion Industry's Response to COVID-19' (2020)10(2) *Dialogues in Human Geography* 195–98.

Brydges T and others, 'Will COVID-19 Support the Transition to a More Sustainable Fashion Industry' (2020)16(1) *Sustainability: Science, Practice and Policy* 298–308.

Brydges T and others, 'Platforms and the Pandemic: A Case Study of Fashion Rental Platforms During COVID-19' (2021)187 *The Geographical Journal* 57–63.

Campbell N, 'CFDA and BFC Launch Great Global Designer Face Coverings' (*CFDA.com*, 12 July 2020) <https://cfda.com/news/cfda-bfc-launch-great-global-designer-face-coverings>.

Cartner-Morley J, 'London Fashion Week Drops Elitist Traditions as Event Goes Fully Digital' (*The Guardian*, 12 June 2020) <www.theguardian.com/fashion/2020/jun/12/london-fashion-week-drops-elitist-traditions-as-event-goes-fully-digital>.

Chan E, 'Will the Fashion Rental Market Ever Recover From Covid-19?' (*Vogue*, 17 May 2020) <www.vogue.co.uk/fashion/article/will-the-fashion-rental-market-recover>.

Chen C, 'The Return of Rental' (*Business of Fashion*, 29 March 2021) <www.businessoffashion.com/articles/retail/the-return-of-rental>.

Christesen P and Machado D, 'Video Games and Classical Antiquity' (2010)104(1) *The Classical World* 107–10.

Cochrane L, 'Perfect Storm: Have the Influencers Selling a Dream Lost Their Allure?' (*The Guardian*, 6 February 2021) <www.theguardian.com/media/2021/feb/06/perfect-storm-have-the-influencers-selling-a-dream-lost-their-allure>.

Condis A, 'Live in Your World, Play in Ours': Video Games, Critical Play, and the Environmental Humanities' (2015)2(3) *Resilience: A Journal of the Environmental Humanities* 87–104.

Criddle C, 'Burberry Designs Skins for Honor of Kings Characters' (*BBC News*, 24 March 2021) <www.bbc.co.uk/news/technology-56511343>.

Cuen L, 'NFTs Could Bridge Video Games and the Fashion Industry' (*TechCrunch*, 22 March 2021) <https://techcrunch.com/2021/03/22/nfts-could-bridge-video-games-and-the-fashion-industry/?guccounter=1&guce_referrer=aHR0cH M6Ly93d3cuZ29vZ2xlLmNvbS8&guce_referrer_sig=AQAAAHcBysl9Br7gjO 2GgGqrIakNa8YcVAvOoz1tN7vj_cItSuXm-OEZ04skk-6tpYvoBPNA2etY8XS hl5n3pKGr6nc1GLa_RQTniMTVN-t1nRkugwOk7Whhw8gm_JLJ4Cv44R0s D4v2ynnlqYMh4beUmwX9uxO2A6QK3E8zJTgs_gf0>.

de Freitas S, 'Are Games Effective Learning Tools? A Review of Educational Games' (2018)21(2) *Educational Technology & Society* 74–84.

Dodgson L, 'Fake, Computer-Generated Instagram Influencers Are Modelling Designer Clothes, Wearing Spanx, and Attending Red Carpet Premieres' (*Insider*, 4 September 2019) <www.insider.com/cgi-influencers-what-are-they-where-did-they-come-from-2019-8>.

Elan P, 'Roaring 20s: Fashion World Predicts Post-Covid Boom' (*The Guardian*, 31 January 2021) <www.theguardian.com/fashion/2021/jan/31/economists-predict-post-covid-fashion-boom>.

Fingas J, 'A Digital "Dress" Sold for $9500' (*Engadget*, 27 May 2019) <www.engadget.com/2019-05-27-fabricant-blockchain-digital-dress.html>.

Fingas J, 'Top Fashion Houses Are Showing Their Latest Styles In "Animal Crossing"' (*Engadget*, 10 May 2020) <www.engadget.com/animal-crossing-fashion-houses-231541432.html?guccounter=1&guce_referrer=aHR0cHM6Ly93d3cu Z29vZ2xlLmNvbS8&guce_referrer_sig=AQAAAD-RhwwO_1l_zImT7IxhHqy GvfwxvL0GhVtMHjOOAzo4Zvz_AtjFfx1MWnBsk0KNtF22-ANCtgOpNMYX qejMXmFiClShjOLuy8Gqe4laXWMNynXp-SWjjD504yBe-e1en7eUg RwiHlqQ_04YCs5ylm0Nin0jOyKaMA4y2mTdStCU>.

Fish I, 'The Search for Fashion Supply Chain Transparency' (*Drapers*, 8 February 2020) <www.drapersonline.com/topics/sustainable-fashion/the-search-for-fashion-supply-chain-transparency>.

Gibson J, 'Where Have You Been? CGI Film Stars and Reanimation Horrors' (2019)10(1) *Queen Mary Journal of Intellectual Property* 1–6.

Gibson J, 'Brands Make Believe: Ethical Veganism and Labelling in Fashion' (2020)10(2) *Queen Mary Journal of Intellectual Property* 143–51.

Gibson J, *Owned, an Ethological Jurisprudence of Property* (London, Routledge 2020).

Gibson J, 'The Thousand-and-Second Tale of NFTs, as Foretold by Edgar Allan Poe' (2021)11(3) *Queen Mary Journal of Intellectual Property* 249–69.

Gibson J, 'When Games Are the Only Fashion in Town: COVID-19, *Animal Crossing* and the Future of Fashion' (2021)11(2) *Queen Mary Journal of Intellectual Property* 116–23.

Goanta C, 'Selling LAND in Decentraland: The Regime of Non-Fungible Tokens on the Ethereum Blockchain Under the Digital Content Directive' in Amon L and Ronit LS (eds), *Disruptive Technology, Legal Innovation, and the Future of Real Estate* (Amsterdam, Springer 2020) 139–54.

Godwin C, 'The £7,500 Dress That Does Not Exist' (*BBC News*, 15 November 2019) <www.bbc.co.uk/news/business-49794403>.

Goldstein C, 'Model Emily Ratajkowski Blasted Richard Prince for Stealing Her Image. Now, She's Taking It Back – and Selling It as an NFT' (*Artnet*, 23 April 2021) <https://news.artnet.com/market/emily-ratajkowski-nft-christies-1961581>.

Graham G, '2018 Was the Year AI Influencers and Digital Models Took Over Fashion' (*Dazed*, 10 December 2018) <www.dazeddigital.com/fashion/article/42484/1/cgi-models-ai-influencers-lil-miquela-digital-models-trend-shudu-noonoouri>.

Greenberg, D (ed), *Jowitt's Dictionary of English Law* (5th edn, London, Sweet & Maxwell 2019).

Hall H, 'Digital Fashion Weeks Have Forced the Industry to Confront Some Difficult Questions' (*The Independent*, 19 February 2021) <www.independent.co.uk/voices/london-fashion-week-digital-shows-b1804599.html>.

Hamada S and Wakabayashi Y, 'Gamification in Marketing: An Empirical Study of Differences in User Psychology Among Services Using Gamification' (2014)83(1–2) *The Kyoto Economic Review* 27–57.

Han Y-J and others, 'Signaling Status with Luxury Goods: The Role of Brand Prominence' (2010)74(4) *Journal of Marketing* 15–30.

Harper L, 'UK Fashion Designers Join Hands to Make Scrubs for Key Workers' (*The Guardian*, 17 April 2020) <www.theguardian.com/fashion/2020/apr/17/uk-fashion-designers-join-hands-to-make-scrubs-for-key-workers>.

Hawkins R and others, 'The Development and Evaluation of "Farm Animal Welfare": An Educational Computer Game for Children' (2019)9 *Animals* 91.

Hera T de la, *Digital Gaming and the Advertising Landscape* (Amsterdam, Amsterdam UP 2019).

Hosie R, 'Balmain Reveals Line-Up of Virtual Models for Latest Campaign' (*The Independent*, 3 September 2018) <www.independent.co.uk/life-style/fashion/balmain-virtual-models-digital-campaign-fashion-shudu-a8520871.html>.

Hoskins T, 'Can Workers Reset the System?' (*New Internationalist*, 6 October 2020) <https://newint.org/features/2020/08/11/can-workers-reset-system>.

Hyde S, 'Kate Moss Ventures into the NFT Art Market by Sharing Some of Her Most Intimate Moments' (*Harper's Bazaar*, 13 April 2021) <www.harpersbazaar.com/celebrity/latest/a36099278/kate-moss-enters-nft-art-market/>.

Jelen G, 'Why NFTs Could Mean Windfall Profits for Fashion' (*L'Officiel*, 25 March 2021) <www.lofficielusa.com/fashion/nfts-impact-fashion-industry-crypto-currency>.

Klaus P and Manthiou A, 'Applying the EEE Customer Mindset in Luxury: Reevaluating Customer Experience Research and Practice During and After Corona' (2020)31(6) *Journal of Service Management* 1175–83.

Koch J and others, 'Online Shopping Motives During the COVID-19 Pandemic: Lessons from the Crisis' (2020)12(10247) *Sustainability* 1–20.

Liao S, 'Why the Video Game Boom Is Here to Stay' (*CNN*, 13 December 2020) <https://edition.cnn.com/2020/12/13/tech/gaming-recession-proof/index.html>.

Maoui Z, 'The Fashion Industry Is Getting in on the NFT Game' (*GQ*, 14 April 2021) <www.gq-magazine.co.uk/fashion/article/angelo-galasso-nft>.

Marshall C, 'Animal Crossing Keeps Growing a Vibrant Fashion Community' (*Polygon*, 11 September 2020) <www.polygon.com/2020/9/11/21432219/animal-crossing-fashion-influencers-designers-dress-sharing-community>.

May N, 'These Clothes Aren't Real, They're All Digital: Is This the Future of Fashion?' (*Evening Standard*, 14 November 2019) <www.standard.co.uk/insider/fashion/digital-fashion-the-fabricant-carlings-a4286496.html>.

May N, 'What Is the Shopping Bag Challenge? Instagram's Latest Trend Explained' (*Evening Standard*, 28 April 2020) <www.standard.co.uk/insider/fashion/shopping-bag-instagram-lockdown-challenge-a4425861.html>.

McAlpine S, 'Fashion's New Order: How the Coronavirus Pandemic Has Changed the Fashion Industry' (*Elle*, 29 July 2020) <www.elle.com/uk/fashion/trends/a33442347/covid-affected-fashion-industry/>.

McBride C and others, 'Digital Manipulation of Images of Models' Appearance in Advertising: Strategies for Action Through Law and Corporate Social Responsibility Incentives to Protect Public Health' (2019)45 *American Journal of Law and Medicine* 7–31.

McDowell M, 'During the Pandemic, Models Get a Digital Makeover' (*Vogue Business*, 21 April 2020) <www.voguebusiness.com/technology/during-the-pandemic-models-get-a-digital-makeover-covid-19>.

McKinsey & Company, 'Perspectives on Retail and Consumer Goods' (*Report*, 8 August 2020).

McKinsey & Company, 'The Future of Shopping: Technology Everywhere' (*Report*, April 2021).

McMaster M and others, 'Risk Management: Rethinking Fashion Supply Chain Management for Multinational Corporations in Light of the COVID-19 Outbreak' (2020)13(173) *Journal of Risk and Financial Management* 1–16.

Mehta S and others, 'The New Consumer Behaviour Paradigm Amid COVID-10: Permanent or Transient?' (2020)22(2) *Journal of Health Management* 291–301.

Michele, A, 'Notes from the Silence' (*Instagram Post*, 24 May 2020) <www.instagram.com/p/CAkszCYpBJV/>.

Mustoe H, 'Boohoo Tells Suppliers Not to Subcontract, Raising Job Fears' (*BBC News*, 8 February 2020) <www.bbc.co.uk/news/business-55974075>.

Nanda M, 'What the NFT Gold Rush Means for Fashion' (*Business of Fashion*, 24 March 2021) <www.businessoffashion.com/articles/technology/what-the-nft-gold-rush-means-for-fashion>.

Newbold A, 'The Numerous Questions Around the Rise of CGI Models and Influencers' (*Vogue*, 18 August 2018) <www.vogue.co.uk/article/cgi-virtual-reality-model-debate>.

Ordano E and others, 'Decentraland: A Blockchain-Based Virtual World. White Paper' (2018) 5 <https://decentraland.org/whitepaper.pdf>.

Parisi D, 'Beyond the Hype: How NFTs Stand to Benefit Fashion Brands' (*Glossy*, 24 March 2021) <www.glossy.co/fashion/beyond-the-hype-nfts-stand-to-benefit-fashion-brands-in-the-future/>.

Park H and Joyner Martinez C, 'Secondhand Clothing Sales Are Booming – And May Help Solve the Sustainability Crisis in the Fashion Industry' (*The Conversation*, 16 November 2020) <https://theconversation.com/secondhand-clothing-sales-are-booming-and-may-help-solve-the-sustainability-crisis-in-the-fashion-industry-148403>.

Pew Research Center, 'Experts Say the "New Normal" in 2025 Will Be Far More Tech-Driven, Presenting More Big Challenges, Report' (*Pew Research Center*, 18 February 2021) <www.pewresearch.org/internet/2021/02/18/experts-say-the-new-normal-in-2025-will-be-far-more-tech-driven-presenting-more-big-challenges/>.

Reaves S and others, 'If Looks Could Kill: Digital Manipulation of Fashion Models' (2004)19(1) *Journal of Mass Media Ethics* 56–71.

Roggeveen A and Sethuraman R, 'How the COVID-19 Pandemic May Change the World of Retailing' (2020)96(2) *Journal of Retailing* 169–171.

Ryan T, 'Will the Post-Pandemic Era be America's Next Roaring 20s?' (*Retail-Wire*, 1 March 2021) <www.retailwire.com/discussion/will-the-post-pandemic-era-be-americas-next-roaring-20s/>.

Salfino C, 'In New Retail Landscape, Brands Can Connect Through Gaming' (*Sourcing Journal*, 16 April 2020) <https://sourcingjournal.com/topics/lifestyle-monitor/cotton-incorporated-coronavirus-gaming-mobile-advertising-fortnite-205869/>.

Semic S, 'Meet the Man Behind the World's First Digital Supermodel' (*Elle*, 15 July 2019) <www.elle.com/uk/fashion/a28394357/man-behind-worlds-first-digital-supermodel/>.

Stokel-Walker C, 'Influencers Are Buying Empty Shopping Bags to Pretend They're Rich' (*Input*, 21 October 2020) <www.inputmag.com/culture/influencers-are-pretending-theyre-rich-by-buying-empty-shopping-bags>.

Sutherland E, 'The New Directions for Fashion Retail' (*Drapers Online*, 10 December 2020) <www.drapersonline.com/insight/analysis/the-new-directions-for-fashion-retail>.

Templeton GF and others, 'Information Technology Firms: Creating Value through Digital Disruption' (2019)44(35) *Communications of the Association for Information Systems* 748–63.

Terlutter R and Capella M, 'The Gamification of Advertising: Analysis and Research Directions of In-Game Advertising, Advergames, and Advertising in Social Network Games' (2013)42(2–3) *Journal of Advertising* 95–112.

Thomas V and Fowler K, 'Close Encounters of the AI Kind: Use of AI Influencers as Brand Endorsers' (2021)50(1) *Journal of Advertising* 11–25.

Tong A, 'Luxury Fashion Brands Poised to Join the NFT Party' (*Vogue Business*, 5 April 2021) <www.voguebusiness.com/technology/luxury-fashion-brands-poised-to-join-the-nft-party>.

Tran KTL, 'Video Games Are the New Runway' (*Los Angeles Times*, 4 December 2020) <www.latimes.com/lifestyle/story/2020-12-04/covid-19-fashion-brands-experiment-video-games>.

Whitelocks S, 'A Chanel Bag for Less Than £5? How the Craze for Branded Paper Carriers Has Sparked Flood of Fakes' (*Daily Mail*, 3 January 2012) <www.dailymail.co.uk/femail/article-2081642/A-Chanel-bag-5-How-craze-branded-paper-carriers-attracts-cash-strapped.html>.

Wightman-Stone D, 'UK's Secondhand Market Skyrockets in 2020' (*Fashion United*, 2 September 2020) <https://fashionunited.uk/news/fashion/uk-s-secondhand-market-skyrocket-in-2020/2020090250676>.

Williams A, 'What Is Digital Fashion?' (*Yahoo!News*, 21 April 2021) <https://news.yahoo.com/digital-fashion-spoke-fashion-house-145718109.html>.

Wright G, 'What Will Fashion Weeks Look Like Post-coronavirus?' (*Retail Gazette*, 16 February 2020) <www.retailgazette.co.uk/blog/2021/02/what-will-fashion-weeks-look-like-post-coronavirus/>.

Yotka S, 'The World's First Animal Crossing Fashion Show Is Here' (*Vogue*, 25 May 2020) <www.vogue.co.uk/news/article/animal-crossing-fashion-show>.

Yotka S, 'Carolina Sarria Brings the Community of Fashion Week to an Animal Crossing Show' (*Vogue*, 3 September 2020) <www.vogue.co.uk/fashion/article/carolina-sarria-animal-crossing-fashion>.

Youn S-Y and others, 'Fashion Consumers' Channel Switching Behavior During the COVID-19: Protection Motivation Theory in the Extended Planned Behavior Framework' (2021)39(2) *Clothing and Textiles Research Journal* 139–56.

Zhao L and Kim K, 'Responding to the COVID-19 Pandemic: Practices and Strategies of the Global Clothing and Textile Value Chain' (2020)39(2) *Clothing and Textiles Research Journal* 157–72.

Zhu L, 'The Psychology Behind Video Games During COVID-19 Pandemic: A Case Study of *Animal Crossing: New Horizons*' (2021)3 *Human Behavior and Emerging Technologies* 157–59.

4 Broken copyright in the pandemic crisis – rethinking public interest in China

Luo Li

Introduction

While global business and the economy remain stagnant, with restrictions on travel and social distancing policy due to the COVID-19 pandemic, much work, study and leisure have been transformed into the home- and online-based models. Suddenly, everything related to creativity and intelligence has accelerated its digitalisation transformation, and now heavily relies on the digital platform to transmit and distribute information. Meanwhile, this radical change challenges copyright defences (exceptions and limitations) on exempting the public users from the copyright principle of permission first and use later. The education sector is one suffering copyright issues due to these changes. Traditional face-to-face classroom teaching is replaced by the online model. Therefore, there is an issue on whether those copyright defences for common situations of use (part of physical use and part of digital use) will be suitable for the pandemic situation (digital use only). Meanwhile, many educational institutions in the world provide emergency training/guidance to their staff on how to avoid potential copyright infringement during online teaching.[1] Scholars and practitioners advise how to use copyrighted works during the pandemic,[2] and many organisations either

---

1   Herbert Lee, 'Intellectual Property and Copyright in Course Materials During COVID-19 Remote Teaching: Information and Language for Instructors' (*US Santa Cruz*, 19 March 2020) <https://news.ucsc.edu/2020/03/intellectual-property-and-copyright-in-course-materials-during-covid-19-remote-teaching.html> accessed 3 March 2021; 'COVID-19: Copyright and Licensing Tips for Online Teaching' (*Imperial College London*) <www.imperial.ac.uk/admin-services/library/learning-support/copyright-guidance/copyright-for-lecturers/tips-for-online-teaching/> accessed 3 March 2021.
2   Shaoling Chen, 'Safeguarding Online Teaching from Copyright Risks During the Pandemic' (*Speedy Report (Kandian Kuaibao), Shanghai*, 11 March 2020); Samuel Trosow and Lisa Macklem, 'Fair Dealing and Emergency Remote Teaching in Canada' (*Infojustice*, 24 March 2020) <https://infojustice.org/archives/42120> accessed 3 March 2021; Anita Cade, Ted Talas and Stephen Klimis, 'Crown Use of Intellectual Property Rights in Australia' (*Ashurst*) <www.ashurst.com/en/news-and-insights/legal-updates/crown-use-of-intellectual-property-rights-in-australia/> accessed 3 March 2021.

DOI: 10.4324/9781003176848-6

interpret fair use to support education,[3] or call on publishers to make their resources temporarily publicly accessible during the pandemic.[4] This perhaps reflects an embarrassingly inadequate copyright system in considering the public interest defence compared with copyright owners' rights.

In November 2020, Chinese copyright law passed its third amendment, becoming effective on 1 June 2021.[5] Nevertheless, this amended version still focuses more on updating individuals' copyright in response to the technologies, with less consideration of public-interest-related provisions. This chapter examines the recognition of the concept of "public interest" in a Chinese copyright context after undertaking a comparative analysis at both international and national levels. The right to education is universally recognised as a basic human right[6] and it is the most justifiable copyright defence. However, during the pandemic, many countries suffer the same or similar copyright issues which could disrupt such a right to education. Thus, the chapter evaluates the flexibility of the existing Chinese copyright system in order to favour a larger interest of public education when responding to extreme situations such as COVID-19. Finally, the author calls for the introduction of a compulsory license for the public interest in extreme situations.

The concept of public interest

International context

The exclusive rights authorised in the copyright system form a monopoly scheme to guard creators' intellectual labour and creative activities. Meanwhile, the copyright system also regulates some permitted acts as limitations and exceptions. This system makes the public use of copyrighted works, either for free or payment, without infringement issues. This is 'to maintain a balance between the rights of authors and the larger public interest, particularly in education, research and access to information',[7] although protecting the rights of authors is the first goal.[8] In 1886, the Berne Convention for the Protection of Literary and Artistic

---

3   'Public Statement of Library Copyright Specialists: Fair Use & Emergency Remote Teaching & Research' (*Infojustice*, 13 March 2020) <https://infojustice.org/archives/42126> accessed 3 March 2021.
4   Canadian Association of Research Libraries (CARL) calls the publishers to waive access restrictions currently imposed on their licensed online collections because of the COVID-19. CARL, 'CARL Statement on Optimal Equitable Access to Post-Secondary Learning Resources During COVID-19' <www.carl-abrc.ca/wp-content/uploads/2020/03/CARL_statement_optimal_equitable_access_COVID19.pdf> accessed 3 March 2021.
5   Copyright Law of the People's Republic of China 2020 (Copyright Law 2020).
6   Article 26(1) of the Universal Declaration of Human Rights states everyone has the right to education.
7   WIPO Copyright Treaty 1996 (adopted 20 December 1996, entered into force 6 March 2002) WCT Preamble.
8   ibid.

Works (Berne Convention) provided permitted acts to 'meet the public's thirst for information'.[9] Subsequently, the Berne Convention (Brussels Revisions of 1948) permitted using 'copyrighted works by way of illustration for teaching'.[10] This indicates that the international interpretation of the concept of public interest could be understood as 'the public has optimal access to the rich store of knowledge products'.[11]

Nevertheless, international regulations lack detailed clarification in this aspect, making the concept of "public interest" unclear and unbalanced. The term "public interest" in an international copyright context should cover a wider scope of developing countries, least-developed countries (LDC) and developed countries. There is concern that the permitted acts of use in the Berne Convention do not address the needs of the most developing countries and LDC.[12] Developed countries, occupying massive intellectual creations in the world, are the main author-right supporter and the main policymaker in the Berne Convention, whereas the global south countries' interests rely on restricted limitations and exceptions. There are more concerns on what should be a balanced copyright system and the scope of "rights" the public should have in such a system. Alan Story argues that the Berne Convention never pursued a balance between copyright owners and the public users, despite the title of the Convention, focusing on protecting creators' exclusive rights or the proportionality of provisions between permitted acts and the use under exploitation of the work through the license scheme.[13] Jeremy Philips noted that the Berne Convention does not explicitly permit that the use of someone's copyright be treated as the public interest defence.[14] Even the three-step test in the Berne Convention is treated as a general limit on the sovereign discretion, rather than of any public interest consideration.[15] The flexibility of allowing Member States' discretion in the international copyright system, together with a non-explicit public policy from a global perspective, makes it difficult to clarify the boundary of public interest at the international level, resulting in the ineffectiveness of justifying national limitations and exceptions.

9   WIPO, 'Guide to the Berne Convention for the Protection of Literary and Artistic Works (Paris Act, 1971)' (1978) 58 <www.wipo.int/edocs/pubdocs/en/copyright/615/wipo_pub_615.pdf> accessed 2 February 2021.
10 ibid 60.
11 Ruth L Okediji, 'The International Copyright System: Limitations, Exceptions and Public Interest Considerations for Developing Countries' (2006) ix <https://unctad.org/system/files/official-document/iteipc200610_en.pdf> accessed 2 February 2021.
12 ibid.
13 Alan Story, ' "Balanced" Copyright: Not A Magic Solving Word' (2012)34(8) *European Intellectual Property Review* 493–95.
14 Jeremy Phillips, 'The Berne Convention and the Public Interest' (1986)11 *Columbia-VLA Journal of Law & the Arts* 165, 169.
15 Okediji (n 11) 4–5, 8.

The national context: China

China is a civil law country with special characters, but its copyright system is influenced by international treaties harmonizing member states' common law and civil law systems. Chinese academia often discusses public interest topics from an interest-balance perspective among individual, society and national interest.[16] Theoretically, the term "public interest" in the Chinese copyright context is reflected as promoting the public sense, and in encouraging works to be public access in enhancing democracy.[17] This achieves social development in science and culture, and enhances knowledge levels,[18] as well as links with public order, public transmission, fair competition, public security and public morality.[19] There is a view that the unbalanced nature between individual and the public interests is an incentive to update copyright law.[20] Another view supports a more restrictive control of fair dealing provisions because it believes fair dealing would damage copyright owner's rights. This view argues that public-interest fair dealing could only apply in very limited and restricted situations that would minimise the damage to copyright.[21]

At the legislative level, Chinese copyright law established a list of 12 circumstances in which users could use a copyrighted work without the copyright owner's permission and payment fee.[22] This is similar to a fair dealing list contained in the Copyright, Design and Patent Act 1988 (CDPA) in the United Kingdom (UK). Chinese copyright law also established another list of limitations referring to a statutory licence. This list permits others' use of a copyrighted work without the permission of the copyright owner but requires payment of remuneration to the copyright owner.[23] Compared with that of Chinese copyright law, the CDPA in the UK provides a wider and well-classified permitted use of defences promoting learning knowledge, culture, science and anything referring to human

16   Xiaoqing Feng, 'Research on the Theory of Balancing of Interests in Copyright Law' (2008)22 *Journal of Hunan University (Social Sciences)* 6, 113.
17   Xiaoqing Feng, '著作权法目的与利益平衡论 (The Goal of Copyright and the Theory of Rights Balance)' (2004)2 *Science Technology and Law* 86–87.
18   Yumin Zhang and Yufeng Li, 知识产权法学 (*Intellectual Property Law*) (2nd edn, Beijing, Law Press China 2011) 158.
19   Yong Yang, '著作权法中损害公共利益的认定研究 (Research on Determination of Public Interest Damage in Copyright Law)' (2016)5 *China Copyright* 13–17.
20   Chenjia Wang, '网络时代著作权相关利益再平衡研究 (Research on Re-Balanced Interest in Copyright During the Internet Age)' (2017)23 *China Publishing Journal* 44–48.
21   Bo Yuan, '细说著作权之"合理使用"不是"任性使用" (Copyright "Fair Use" Is Not "Abuse")' *China Press Publication Radio Film and Television Journal* (Beijing, 18 May 2017) 5.
22   Copyright Law of the People's Republic of China 2010 (Copyright Law 2010), art 22. In the third amendment, article 22 of the Copyright Law 2010 is renumbered as article 24 in the Copyright Law 2020. When this chapter is completed, China still implements the Copyright Law 2010. Therefore, the chapter uses articles 22 and 23 of the 2010 version instead of the amended 2020 version which would be implemented in June 2021.
23   ibid art 23, art 40, 43–44.

civilisation, thus encouraging information availability and its free movement. Besides statutory exceptions and limitations in the CDPA, in practice the courts can determine if other circumstances can constitute public interest defences. The past UK judicial experiences often concern the publication of information and, thus, link with confidentiality issues.[24] Therefore, the scope of public interest has been extended to those areas of public health, public safety, fair administration and justice, and even into the political arena,[25] being not relevant to copyright interest. From this perspective, flexible public-interest provisions in the UK provide a better scope and coverage than that of Chinese copyright law, which only provides fixed and exhaustive provisions.

United States' (US) copyright law provides a series of limitations to exclusive rights, the most important being the fair use doctrine.[26] Unlike the UK and China, the US provides a general defence of fair use in its most important and well-known defences, instead of a restricted list. American courts use a four-factor test to determine if certain use is fair (no infringement) or not (infringement).[27] 'The courts must be free to adapt the doctrine to particular situation on a case-by-case basis'.[28] The flexibility of fair use not only covers most known purposes, including the use of works for criticism, news reporting, teaching and research listed in section 107 of the American copyright law, but also provides possibilities to cover other uses being qualified as fair use. This does not mean that these uses are guaranteed in a fair-use safe zone. However, the rationale is to consider whether these public interest uses outweigh the losses or damage to the copyright owner's rights; or if the public beneficial use of certain work would be hindered by the negotiation of the copyright license.[29]

Chinese judicial practice shows an insufficient consideration of the public interest. The Beijing Frist Intermediate Court did not support Google's claim that scanning and uploading Wang's novel at Google Library constituted fair dealing that was of benefit for the public users.[30] Chinese copyright law only regulates an exhaustive list of 12 fair dealings, but judicial practice adopts the

24 *Lion Laboratories Ltd v Evans* [1984] 2 All ER 417; *Initial Services Ltd v Putterill* [1968] 1 QB 396; *Attorney-General v Guardian Newspapers Ltd* [1988] 3 All ER 567.
25 *Unilever plc v Griffin* [2010] EWHC 899 (Ch), [2010] FSR 33.
26 Copyright Law of the United States (Title 17 of the United States Code) 2020, c 1, ss 107–12.
27 ibid s 107 states: (1) the purpose and character of the use, including whether such use is of a commercial nature or is for non-profit educational purposes; (2) the nature of the copyrighted work; (3) the amount and substantially of the portion used in relation to the copyrighted work as a whole; (4) and the effect of the use upon the potential market for or value of the copyrighted work.
28 Committee on the Judiciary, *Copyright Law Revision: Report together with Additional Views* (HR No 94–1476, 1976) 66.
29 Kurt Saunders, *Intellectual Property Law: Legal Aspects of Innovation and Competition* (St Paul MN, West Academic Publishing 2016) 406–7.
30 *Wang Xin v Google Inc & Beijing Gu Xiang Information Technology Co Ltd* (2011) Yi Zhong Min Chu Zi No 1321.

notice from the Supreme People's Court in 2011,[31] that some special circumstances can amount to fair dealing, although they need to follow strict standards. *Wang's* case references the US theory of "transformative use" to judge fair dealings. Article 8 of the Notice of the Supreme People's Court states, that to determine the legality of alleged infringement under the special circumstance, the courts need to consider: the nature and purposes of use, the nature of works used, the quantity and quality of the part of works used and the impact of use on potential markets or values.[32] The intermediate court conceded Google Library's view function neither conflicted with the normal exploitation of the claimant to her novel in the marketplace, not unreasonably prejudiced the claimant's legitimate interest.[33] Thus, Google's provision of a digital version of the novel to the public could, in theory, constitute fair dealing. However, the Court concluded that its digital reproduction of the novel infringed the claimant's copyright because normal exploitation includes the copyright owner's full control of her rights to authorise others to reproduce her work.[34] Accordingly, Google's reproduction of the novel without the claimant's permission would interfere with the claimant's normal exploitation of the work and unreasonably prejudice her legitimate interest, since it may jeopardise the market value of her novel.[35] In the appeal, the Beijing People's High Court determined that Google lacked sufficient evidence to prove its reproduction constituted "transformative use" to satisfy the defence of fair dealing. Therefore, Google lost this case in China.[36]

However, in a similar situation, the courts in the United States gave an opposite judgment and ruled in favour of Google by assessing the four factors of fair use.[37] In *Wang's* case, the intermediate court confirmed the ultimate goal of Chinese copyright law was to protect the public interest, and that protecting the author's copyright is the ultimate goal. However, it is disappointing that the court focused on how Google Library affected the copyright owner's economic interest, rather than analyse fair dealings from a perspective of achieving the public interest. In the appeal, the High Court gave neither an interpretation on whether Google's use of the novel could be treated as a fair dealing belonging to the special circumstances regulated by the Notice of the Supreme Court, nor test factors regulated in the

---

31 最高人民法院印发《关于充分发挥知识产权审判职能作用推动社会主义文化大发展大繁荣和促进经济自主协调发展若干问题的意见》的通知 (Notice of the Supreme People's Court on Issuing the Opinions on Issues concerning Maximizing the Role of Intellectual Property Right Trials in Boosting the Great Development and Great Prosperity of Socialist Culture and Promoting the Independent and Coordinated Development of Economy) (Notice of the Supreme People's Court) 2011, art 8.

32 ibid.

33 *Wang Xin* (n 30).

34 ibid.

35 ibid.

36 *Wang Xin v Google Inc & Beijing Gu Xiang Information Technology Co Ltd* (2013) Gao Min Zhong Zi No 1221.

37 *Authors Guild v Google Inc* 954 F Supp 2d 282, 288 (SDNY 2013); *Authors Guild v Google Inc* 804 F 3d 202, 208 (2d Cir 2015).

Notice. Instead, it required Google to provide evidence, and because of the failure to provide sufficient evidence, it rejected Google's defence. It is further argued that the High Court's decision was summary, as it could have determined whether such use refers to transformative use when considering a wider interest of the public.

In a copyright context, the term "copyright limitations and exceptions" applies to identify what kind of use by the public is allowed instead of using other terms such as users' rights or rights of the public. The term "rights" only links with the use made by copyright owners and authors of works, whereas the action of use made by the public is not expressly recognised as a kind of right (apart from some limited and exceptional cases). In other words, public interest space is significantly reduced from the outset when detailing the regulations and in balancing the relationship between the individual and the public interest. Furthermore, the regulation of limitations and exceptions is intended to reduce the scope of copyright holders' rights and interests, treated as damage to right holders. Therefore, national copyright laws only allow very limited actions of use made by the public. While the feature of public interest in a work (an information resource in nature) has been significantly underestimated, there is no doubt that the design of copyright law contains a structural deficiency – stronger protection of individual copyright owners and less protection of the public interest.

Flexibility in educational use

Because of COVID-19, a question of whether permitted acts cover the use of a work in a digital environment for educational purposes highlights the unbalanced conflict between copyright owners and the public users. For example, there is controversy as to how educators use audio-visual contents during online delivery of a course and whether existing exceptions and limitations could apply to the online teaching approach.[38] Unlike the CDPA in the UK, which provides a series of exceptions and limitations specifically towards education,[39] Chinese copyright law offers a more restricted scope in this area.[40] The chapter will now

---

38 Playing a film in class may be qualified as a permitted activity (performing, playing or showing work in course of educational activities under section 34 of the CDPA). This means it would not infringe the public performance rights under section 19 of the CDPA. Nevertheless, doing the same act in an online environment would perhaps be an infringement by communication to the public under section 20 of the CDPA since section 34 does not cover the communication rights.

39 Sections 32–36A of the CDPA embraces details on exceptions to education. The CDPA also covers other exceptions being relevant to educational use, including fair dealing for research and private study, criticism, review or quotation, text or data analysis for non-commercial research, and caricature, parody or pastiche (sections 28B – 30A), the libraries and archives provisions (sections 41–42A), and exceptions for users with a disability (sections 31B and 31BA).

40 Chinese copyright law does not embrace caricature, parody or pastiche which are covered in the CDPA in the UK copyright reform in 2014. Besides, article 22(8) of Copyright Law 2010 clears that it only allows a library or archive to reproduce a work in its collections for the purposes of the display, or preservation of a copy, of the work.

explore Articles 22 and 23 in Copyright Law 2010,[41] the provisions covering educational use.

Article 22: fair dealings

While article 10(2) of the Berne Convention allows member states to 'permit the utilization, to the extent justified by the purpose . . . provided such utilization is compatible with fair practice,'[42] current copyright law only allows translation or reproduction for the purpose of educational use in a small quantity of copies.[43] Chinese judicial practice attempted to take a more liberal approach to interpret article 22(6), and allowed an adaptation of a novel to a screenplay, declaring that a short film based on the script was fair use for the purpose of education in a film academy institution.[44] However, with such limitations, current copyright law excludes the application of fair dealings to the online teaching provided by educational institutions, because it belongs to communication through the network, which is not covered in article 22. The Copyright Law 2020 extends permitted uses to adaptation, compilation and broadcasting, but these uses must be for classroom teaching or scientific research, and must be used by teachers or scientific researchers.[45] To some extent, added provisions of broadcasting may fix some of the issues in the 2010 version, depending on the interpretation of the term "broadcasting".

Furthermore, Chinese judicial practice strictly determined "classroom teaching" as in-person teaching in the classroom of an educational institution.[46] Therefore, alternative ways of teaching such as broadcasting, television and distance teaching were defined as non-classroom teaching and therefore did not attract article 22(6). In the United States, the copyright law exempts from infringement

41 Copyright Law 2010, art 22. Article 23 of the Copyright Law 2010 is renumbered as article 25 in the Copyright Law 2020.
42 Berne Convention, art 10(2).
43 Copyright Law 2010 is the law implemented during the pandemic that Chinese educational institutions deliver online teaching. Article 22(6) states translation, or reproduction in a small quantity of copies, of a published work for use by teachers or scientific researchers, in classroom teaching or scientific research, provided that the translation or reproduction shall not be published or distributed.
44 'Beiying Audio and Video Recording Company v Beijing Film Academy (Copyright Infringement to the Right to Exclusive Use of Works)' (中华人民共和国最高人民法院公报 (*Gazette of the Supreme People's Court of the PRC*)) <http://gongbao.court.gov.cn/Details/18365311f17c79b67f606e601b770e.html> accessed 3 March 2021.
45 Copyright Law 2020 (China), art 24(3).
46 *National Radio and Television Administration CCTV-6 v China Education Network Television* (2006) Hai Min Chu Zi No 8877. Beijing Haidian District People's Court states that the term "classroom teaching" in article 22(6) shall point at face-to-face teaching only and shall not apply to broadcasting education, teleteaching and correspondence education. Therefore, even if the defendant's broadcasting is use for educational purposes, it still does not fall in the 12 circumstances provided in article 22. The judgement is upheld by the Beijing No 1 Intermediate People's Court.

'performance or display of a work by instructors or pupils in the course of face-to-face teaching activities'.[47] Furthermore, the phrase "face-to-face teaching activities" under section 110 shall 'embrace instructional performances and displays that are not "transmitted," '[48] and the performance or displaying should be 'in the course of instructional activities other than educational broadcasting'.[49]

In the UK, it appears the copyright system provides much clearer rules for in-person classroom teaching, but not explicitly for online teaching. The non-explicitly rule in this regard means that if a teacher plays a film during an in-person classroom this would constitute educational use under section 34 of the CDPA,[50] without an infringement of the public performance rights owned by copyright holder.[51] Yet doing so during online teaching would constitute an infringement to copyright owner's communication rights, not covered by section 34.[52] In 2014, a new exception of fair dealing for the purpose of illustration for instruction was introduced in the CDPA,[53] which can perhaps remedy the issue in section 34. The CDPA does not define the phrase "illustration for instruction" and this offers the possibility to cover non-traditional teaching models including online teaching. Although there has been a narrow interpretation of this phrase,[54] the UK government's attitude during the pandemic is positive in supporting section 32 in covering online teaching.[55]

However, although presently courts would not treat all non-physical teaching as non-classroom teaching, its determination standards on fair dealing are still very rigid. The Chinese courts reference the US courts' fair use test-approach to determine if a use refers to the fair dealings. Chinese courts look step-by-step to determine whether a use satisfies all factors required in the US fair use doctrine at the same time, including non-commercial use, classroom teaching purpose, use for teachers only, a small quantity of copies and uses, and non-negative impact to original works in its market value. In *Beijing Sanmianxiang Copyright Agency v Ankang Municipal Committee Party School*,[56] the Supreme Court stated that although the defendant restricted its use of works into a small number of teaching

47 Copyright Act 1976 (US), s 110(1).
48 Committee on the Judiciary (n 28) 81.
49 ibid.
50 CDPA, s 34.
51 ibid s 19.
52 ibid s 20.
53 ibid s 32.
54 The Intellectual Property Office provides an illustration to the changes in the CDPA in 2014 that it allows copying of works in any medium if the work is used 'solely to illustrate a point' and such use is minor use. Intellectual Property Office, 'Exceptions to Copyright: Education and Teaching' (October 2014) <https://assets.publishing.service.gov.uk/government/uploads/system/uploads/attachment_data/file/375951/Education_and_Teaching.pdf> accessed 23 February 2021.
55 Letter from Amanda Solloway (Parliamentary Under Secretary of State – Minister for Science, Research and Innovation) to David Prosser on 23 April 2020.
56 (2009) Min Shen Zi No 1425.

staff by taking some restrictive measures, and such use was for non-commercial use, its insufficient technical measures resulted in a short-term transmission to unspecified internet users. This, in the Court's view, expanded the dissemination of the works and thus exceeded the purpose of internal use. Consequently, the defendant had to bear the liability of infringement. The number of users and transmission scope are also main factors in determining fair dealing. If these factors are not achieved, even if the use is for internal and non-commercial use, without obtaining profit from such use, this would not substantially influence the court's determination on fair use.

Article 22 of the Copyright Law 2010 provides an exhaustive list of fair dealings (12 circumstances) with neither general regulations on what a fair dealing/ use is, nor any miscellaneous provisions for special circumstances. Therefore, if any reasonable use during the pandemic falls outside of the 12 circumstances, it would be an infringement. Because the inflexibility of article 22 has been largely criticised in practice, the 2020 version adds a general restriction, which explicitly states that all permitted uses in article 22 must neither affect normal exploitation of the work, nor unreasonably damage the legitimate interest of copyright owners.[57] Furthermore, it adds a miscellaneous provision besides the 12 circumstances,[58] which changes the closed exhaustive list to a semi-opened model. However, since the court took a rigid fair use test approach, in practice there is little space to apply for miscellaneous provision in version 2020, although this provision has been added literally.

Another issue is that despite the Copyright Law 2010, 2020 or the Regulation on the Protection of the Right of Communication through Information Network (Regulation 2006)[59] – implemented to respond to copyright issues in the digital environment – they all restrict the permitted use of the works to teachers instead of students. It should be noted that the purpose of the educational exception should be making works accessible to students through guidance and instructions from the teachers. If these works are accessible only to teachers, the education exception misses its point. With the lockdown and social distance policy, there is a need for many students to access digital materials. In this case, the provisions hinder students in accessing those copyrighted works for the purpose of classroom

---

57 The added general restriction in principle is from the Notice of the Supreme People's Court in 2011 and the Notice has been referenced by many courts in their judgements. However, it is originally from article 21 of the Regulations for the Implementation of the Copyright Law of the People's Republic of China in 2013.

58 Copyright Law 2020, art 24(8): other circumstances regulated by legislation and administrative regulations.

59 Regulation on the Protection of the Right to Network Dissemination of Information 2006 (amended 2013), art 6: another person's work may be made available through information network without permission from, and without payment of remuneration to, the copyright owner when a small quantity of copies of a published work are made available to a small number of teachers or scientific researchers for the purpose of classroom teaching or scientific research.

teaching and learning. In addition, both the 2010 and the 2020 version allow the use of a published work if it falls into an appropriate quotation and for the purposes of introducing, illustrating or commenting on this work.[60] In other words, if a teacher uses a small proportion of work to assist their online teaching, such as referencing a few exercise questions in a mathematic exercise book to illustrate certain principles in mathematic teaching, article 22(2) applies. Nevertheless, if a teacher explains most or all questions and answers of an exercise book during online teaching, then it is difficult to prove such use is for the purpose of introducing or commenting on the exercise book. Furthermore, the phrase "appropriate quotation" in article 22(2) raises an issue of whether using all or substantial parts of that work would qualify as an appropriate quotation. It seems "appropriate quotation" constitutes an insignificant or insubstantial part of use. Without clear regulation, teachers explaining exercise questions and answers in the exercise books would result in at least a substantial part of the use of a work, and such use may not be able to apply article 22(2).

Article 23: statutory licence

The Copyright Law 2020 made changes to the statutory licencing of textbooks. It removes the phrase "nine years" from compulsory education to provide the possibility of applying a statutory licence to textbooks for high school education, while the government decides to extend compulsory education to high school level. It also deletes the phrase "except where the authors have declared in advance the use thereof is not permitted" to enhance the statutory licence,[61] and extends the scope of the statutory licence to graphical works.

The 2006 Regulations also provides two new statutory licencing provisions. Article 8 of the Regulations is similar to article 23 of both 2010 and 2020 versions, but extends article 23 to the digital environment as it is for online distance education.[62] The Regulations allow the use of a copyrighted work to produce courseware for implementing nine-year compulsory education or the national education plan. They also made such courseware available to registered students

---

60 Copyright Law 2010, art 22(2); Copyright Law 2020, art 24(2): appropriate quotation from a published work in one's own work for the purposes of introduction to, or comments on, a work, or demonstration of a point.

61 Copyright Law 2010, art 23: In compiling and publishing textbooks for implementing the nine-year compulsory education and the national educational program, parts of published works, short written works, music works or single copies of works of painting or photographic works may be compiled into textbooks without the authorization from the authors, except where the authors have declared in advance the use thereof is not permitted, with remuneration paid according to the regulations, the name of the author and the title of the work indicated and without prejudice to other rights enjoyed by the copyright owners according to this Law . . . The above limitations on rights shall be applicable also to the rights of publishers, performers, producers of sound recordings and video recordings, radio stations and television stations.

62 Regulation 2006, art 8.

through information network by distance education institutions, without the need for permission from the copyright owner or providing payment of remuneration.[63] While educational institutions produce courseware for online teaching purpose, there is no doubt that such producing belongs to the previously mentioned legally allowed use of copyrighted work – as such courseware producing activities implement compulsory education or the national education plans. However, article 8 has its limitations. Firstly, it borrowed from the Technology, Education and Copyright Harmonization Act 2002 (TEACH Act) in the United States,[64] and limits its applicable group to distant-educational institutions only. Distant-educational institutions in China are those specially approved institutions and they normally do not cover most educational institutional activities with traditional in-person teaching models. These narrow provisions in the TEACH Act would mean that most educational institutions cannot apply under this Act during the pandemic. This is because it is difficult to achieve what TEACH Act required 'the transmission is made solely for, and . . . reception [to] . . . students officially enrolled in the course for which the transmission is made'.[65] Furthermore, the pandemic means that many educators have to shift from face-to-face teaching to online modules. Therefore, some materials need to be adjusted to fit the online teaching approach. While the TEACH Act requires that 'the transmitting body or institution . . . provides information materials . . . promotes compliance with, the laws of the United States relating to copyright',[66] it does not appreciate that during an emergency like the COVID-19 pandemic that institutions may face difficulty in producing materials if they do not already have in place materials and policies that promote copyright compliance. Unfortunately, article 8 of the Regulations does not consider the limitation of the TEACH Act, and worse, it is more restrictive than the TEACH Act, since it requires remuneration to the copyright owner, whereas the TEACH Act allows free use.

Secondly, article 26 of the Regulations defines the right of communication through information network as:

> the right to make available to the public a work, performance, or sound or video recording, by wire or by wireless means, in such a way that members of the public may access the said work, performance, or sound or video recording from a place and at a time individually chosen by them.[67]

This means such broadcasting cannot be a live broadcast. Therefore, educational institutions could only provide pre-recorded lectures and resources, but not be

---

63   ibid. While the Copyright Law 2020 removes the phrase "nine years", it can predict that the Regulation 2006 would make the same changes to respond to the changes of the Copyright Law 2020.
64   Technology, Education and Copyright Harmonization Act (US) 2002.
65   ibid s 1(b2)(C).
66   ibid s 1(b2)(D).
67   Regulation 2006, art 26.

able to broadcast copyrights works to students during live session. Article 8 is thus not able to guarantee a smooth delivery of teaching during the pandemic, especially for those whose broadcasting copyright works are necessary for live teaching. Accordingly, many needs from the public (students) in obtaining knowledge through educational institutions during the pandemic will be artificially hindered.

Another statutory licencing provision contained in the Regulations refers to making available published works to the public in rural areas for the purpose of aiding poverty-stricken areas (such as cultivation and breeding, prevention and treatment of diseases, and prevention and reduction of disasters). This provides that the copyright owners are notified and remunerated by the network service provider. However, in practice it is too restrictive in its application. Article 9 states the provider shall 'announce the title of the work to be made available and the name of its author as well as the rates of remuneration to be paid'[68] before providing works. Further, they shall not make works available if the copyright owner objects within 30 days from the announcement date. After 30 days without objection, the provider shall make available works with remuneration; and even after this work has been provided, the provider shall immediately delete works if any objection of the copyright owner is raised and must pay relevant remuneration.[69] If the provider fails to do so, they must bear liabilities and punishments. Such provision will largely discourage others to be engaged in charity activities, considering their complexity and extremely restrictive nature. This fails to sufficiently consider the larger interest of the public in most rural areas.

Post-COVID considerations

Compared with many other countries in the world, China has at present effectively controlled COVID nationally. Most Chinese can work and enjoy their normal life, although a small number of areas may suffer re-lockdown due to imported cases or increased cases locally. Nevertheless, the COVID-19 crisis brings us a much clearer view that existing copyright law does not respond well to public crises or guarantee a larger interest of the public as is desirable. Because of its wider impact on almost all sectors in the country, and its negative affect on every single individual, such an incident is no longer a separate and simple public health incident but also affects social security and peace, economics and trade, and all human values. Therefore, COVID-19 is more like a serious public crisis affecting all people. COVID-19 is confirmed by WHO as a pandemic. In other words, the public health incident resulting from COVID not only impacts on single or several countries, but the whole world. While those policies on lockdown, social distancing and travel bans are applied to prevent the virus from spreading for a larger public health interest, threatening individual rights such as freedom of movement becomes reasonable and acceptable to most of the public.

68   ibid art 9.
69   ibid.

A long as the public interest refers to a public health nature, it seems easier to justify its importance to large groups, to obtain a wider social recognition, and justify a lawful sacrificing of individual's rights. Many countries provide compulsory licences for the purpose of a public health problem or national special situations.[70] Because of the COVID pandemic, some countries even add new laws or regulations to fix issues or potential issues in existing laws in responding to the COVID-19 impact in the public health areas.[71]

Chinese patent law clearly states '[w]here a national emergency or any extraordinary state of affairs occurs, or public interests so require, the patent administration department . . . may grant a compulsory license for exploitation of an invention patent'.[72] Further, article 50 states '[f]or the benefit of public health, the patent administration department . . . may grant a compulsory license for manufacture of the drug'.[73] However, the public interest in obtaining information and knowledge (normally covered by the copyright area), is not given an equal status as that of the public interest in obtaining health (normally covered by the patent area). Most countries' patent laws regulate compulsory licences to patented medicines, but the copyright law provides neither similar provision nor even general principles in responding to national emergencies or special situations.

Nevertheless, the COVID pandemic proves that a serious public health crisis also largely affects other aspects of the public interest. To save life, everyone is restricted to staying at home. Therefore, obtaining information and knowledge is significantly reduced from multiple approaches (in-person activities such as gathering information in libraries, visiting exhibitions and museums, attending an in-person workshop, on-campus class, blended activities and online activities) to a single approach of online activities. Even where such reduction results from understandable artificial restrictions, it is unavoidable that the public interest in obtaining knowledge and information has been significantly restricted and limited, particularly considering that existing copyright law in benefiting the public interest is not friendly.

70   In the UK, section 128A of the Patent Act 1977 (as amended) provides a compulsory pharmaceutical licence for a public health problem. Sections 55–59 of the Act allows government departments to use a patent without licence; In Australia, sections 163–170 Patents Act 1990 and sections 94–105 Designs Act 2003 provides Crown use in emergencies which allow governments or any person authorised by the governments to exploit a patented invention or a registered design without the consent of the right holders.
71   Jordana Sanft and others, 'Governmental Use of Patented Inventions During a Pandemic: A Global Survey' (*Norton Rose Fulbright*, 16 April 2020) <www.nortonrosefulbright.com/-/media/files/nrf/nrfweb/knowledge-pdfs/governmental-use-of-patented-inventions-during-a-pandemic-guide.pdf?la=en-ca&revision=> accessed 8 March 2021.
72   Patent Law of the People's Republic of China 2008, art 49. China passed the fourth amendment of the patent law in October 2020 and it will be effective on 1 June 2021. Article 49 of the Chinese Patent Law 2008 is renumbered as article 54 in the fourth amended version.
73   ibid art 50. Article 50 is renumbered as article 55 in the fourth amended version of the patent law.

While educational and public libraries are closed, educators and students must rely on the online accessing approach to support teaching and learning. They may have to select alternative e-materials to replace physical ones without electronic versions, and they must get permission of copyright owners first and use them later under the copyright system. COVID-19 has been unpredictable, but radically changed the way that the public obtains knowledge and information in a very short time, exposing the fact that existing facilities are not able to respond effectively in such a short period. Consequently, it is possible that educators cannot find copyright owners or cannot get authorisation quickly during their teaching period. Hence, relying on exceptions and limitations provided in the copyright system to use these alternative materials is an important approach to guaranteeing the smooth delivery of education and in minimizing the disruption of teaching and learning. It is disappointing that even though the 2020 version was discussed and amended during the pandemic, legislators failed to sufficiently consider a large group of the public who would rely heavily or solely on the online education model to obtain knowledge and information, and who did not perhaps sufficiently predict COVID-19. Although the Copyright Law 2020 version has extended permitted use of copyrighted works, it does not cover all educational uses during the pandemic; although they should, without doubt, be covered. While the 2020 version is not implemented until June 2021, the current 2010 version provided more restrictive provisions during the pandemic, including both aspects of fair use and compulsory licence.

Considering this, it is perhaps necessary to consider introducing a compulsory licence for the public interest in copyright law. It is indeed possible to reference compulsory licence regulation for the public interest purpose provided in patent law. In the copyright context, the compulsory licence for the public interest can be understood as regulation taken for the purpose of guaranteeing a larger interest of the public in an emergency or a special situation. The purpose of such compulsory licence design is to guarantee that knowledge and information could achieve free movement, exchange and communication during an extreme situation such as COVID. With this compulsory licence, individual users do not need to get the copyright owners' permission first before the use of a work. This would avoid the situation where users neither rely on exceptions and limitations nor are able to contact copyright owners for authorisation in extreme situations. Through this compulsory licence, the government could respond efficiently and immediately, guaranteeing the necessary use of copyrighted works in time to be beneficial for large groups of the public. This could also resolve the issue that certain use is not covered in exceptions and limitations, and allow such use for the benefit of the larger interest of the public.

Furthermore, the term "public interest" in this compulsory licence should be restricted to the circumstance of an emergency or special situation. This is to ensure such compulsory licences would not be abused and further damage copyright owners' rights. The public interest purpose along with the circumstance of an emergency or special situation would offer such compulsory licences. In other words, only if a region or country is identified by the government as an emergency or special situation will compulsory licences for the public interest apply. The term "public interest" is not limited to a specific aspect of the public interest. However, considering that the compulsory licence would restrict copyright owner's rights in authoring use of their works, and the approach of such use, the term "public interest" should be restricted in necessary areas such as education and emergency aids.

The application areas for this compulsory licence would be limited in the areas with the highest level of emergency identified by the national government. The use also be for non-commercial and non-profitable use, and the applicable works should be already published works. To minimise damage rights of copyright owners, the author suggests that the license only covers those works published at least three years from the first date of publishing. Considering that digitalisation and internet would be transmitted to the areas not being in the highest level of emergency, such as no-lockdown areas, it could consider some possible technical measures to restrict compulsory licenced works to be used only in the areas with an emergency. The national government could guide institutions and organisations as to these measures.

The starting point of the allowed period of use for this licence must be after the emergency or special situation exists. The author would suggest using the date announced by the relevant government bodies as the starting date of emergency, and the date of release of that emergency to calculate the permitted time of use. While the works relate to special contents like the COVID-19 guidance book, it would not consider setting a time limit or area restriction to use. It is noticeable that the payment to copyright owners is a prerequisite for this compulsory licence, which is in line with other compulsory licence systems. The licence payment fee could reference the statutory licence payment provision regulated by the relevant State Copyright Administrations.[74] The compulsory licence fee for the public interest should be affordable by both the national finance department and the local government's financial development in the emergency, with an agreed proportion of payment.

Conclusion

While this chapter has been completed, COVID-19 has been well controlled in China, although there are some regions in China in an in-and-out or re-emergent

74　使用文字作品支付报酬办法 (Measures for Paying Remuneration for the Use of Written Works) 2014 (*The Central People's Government of the People's Republic of China*, 2014) <www.gov.cn/gongbao/content/2014/content_2792659.htm> accessed 8 March 2021; 教科书法定许可使用作品支付报酬办法 (Measures for Paying Remunerations to Works Legally Permitted to Be Used in Textbooks) 2013 (*National Copyright Administration*, 29 October 2013) <www.ncac.gov.cn/chinacopyright/contents/12232/353523.shtml> accessed 8 March 2021; 录音法定许可付酬标准暂行规定(Interim Provisions on the Remuneration Standards of Statutory License for Sound Recordings) 1993 (*National Copyright Administration*, 10 January 2007) <www.ncac.gov.cn/chinacopyright/contents/12232/353517.shtml> accessed 8 March 2021.

re-lockdown situation because of imported cases or suddenly increased number of local cases in particular regions. Most other countries still suffer from the pandemic. Countries such as the UK and Israel have started, or are halfway through, the vaccine jab process. The whole world will, hopefully, be back to normal in a predictable time. However, there are various questions that human beings need to consider in the post-COVID age, one of which is to re-examine the applicability of existing laws in responding to any large-scale public crisis. In the copyright context, the COVID-19 situation has already proved that the existing copyright laws in China do not effectively fit a larger interest of the public. This is despite its narrow restriction in provisions referring to the public interest or other copyright provisions responding to an emergency or special situation. While the public users must wait for relevant bodies' generosity in allowing use notice, or temporary administrative measures to avoid copyright infringement, these are normally time-consuming. Furthermore, such temporary measures/notices during a short time preparation would often result in them not covering all justifiable uses; and interpretations may not be clear, or conflict with existing rules. Moreover, the longer the pandemic lasts, the more necessary it is to consider suitable legal provisions in responding to public needs. Once the legally defined situation exists, the provisions could apply immediately; public users do not have to worry about any misunderstanding of those temporary measures/notices, or whether they constitute an infringement. From the governmental perspective, the government could reference these comprehensive provisions to immediately respond to large public crises, instead of further considering any temporary interpretation to those unfit provisions.

In general, a compulsory licence for the public interest is a preferred approach to restrict copyright owners' rights for the purpose of protecting a larger interest of the public in an emergency or special situation. This compulsory licence also links with a country's national interest. This compulsory licence is not designed for common use, but in responding to any unpredictable public incident negatively affecting all individuals of the country as a whole, or at least a large group of the public in large regions. It is not intended to replace any existing copyright provisions, but to provide flexibility and the possibility of a timely response to suit public interest needs.

Bibliography

Attorney-General v Guardian Newspapers Ltd [1988] 3 All ER 567.
Authors Guild v Google Inc 954 F Supp 2d 282, 288 (SDNY 2013).
Authors Guild v Google Inc 804 F 3d 202, 208 (2d Cir 2015).
Beijing Sanmianxiang Copyright Agency v Ankang Municipal Committee Party School (2009) Min Shen Zi No 1425.
'Beiying Audio and Video Recording Company v Beijing Film Academy (Copyright Infringement to the Right to Exclusive Use of Works)' (中华人民共和国最高人民法院公报 *(Gazette of the Supreme People's Court of the PRC)*) <http://gongbao.court.gov.cn/Details/18365311f17c79b67f606e601b770e.html> accessed 3 March 2021.

Berne Convention for the Protection of Literary and Artistic Works (adopted 9 September 1886, entered into force 5 December 1887).

Cade A, Talas T and Klimis S, 'Crown Use of Intellectual Property Rights in Australia' (*Ashurst*) <www.ashurst.com/en/news-and-insights/legal-updates/crown-use-of-intellectual-property-rights-in-australia/> accessed 3 March 2021.

Canadian Association of Research Libraries, 'CARL Statement on Optimal Equitable Access to Post-Secondary Learning Resources During COVID-19' <www.carl-abrc.ca/wp-content/uploads/2020/03/CARL_statement_optimal_equitable_access_COVID19.pdf> accessed 3 March 2021.

Chen SL, 'Safeguarding Online Teaching from Copyright Risks During the Pandemic' (*Speedy Report (Kandian Kuaibao), Shanghai*, 11 March 2020).

Committee on the Judiciary, 'Copyright Law Revision: Report together with Additional Views' (HR No 94–1476, 1976) 66.

Copyright Act 1976 (US).

Copyright Law of the People's Republic of China 2010.

Copyright Law of the People's Republic of China 2020.

Copyright Law of the United States (Title 17 of the United States Code) 2020.

'COVID-19: Copyright and Licensing Tips for Online Teaching' (*Imperial College London*) <www.imperial.ac.uk/admin-services/library/learning-support/copyright-guidance/copyright-for-lecturers/tips-for-online-teaching/> accessed 3 March 2021.

Feng XQ, '著作权法目的与利益平衡论 (The Goal of Copyright and the Theory of Rights Balance)' (2004)2 *Science Technology and Law* 86–87.

Feng XQ, 'Research on the Theory of Balancing of Interests in Copyright Law' (2008)22 *Journal of Hunan University (Social Sciences)* 6, 113.

Initial Services Ltd v Putterill [1968] 1 QB 396.

Intellectual Property Office, 'Exceptions to Copyright: Education and Teaching' (October 2014) <https://assets.publishing.service.gov.uk/government/uploads/system/uploads/attachment_data/file/375951/Education_and_Teaching.pdf> accessed 23 February 2021.

录音法定许可付酬标准暂行规定 (Interim Provisions on the Remuneration Standards of Statutory License for Sound Recordings) 1993 (*National Copyright Administration*, 10 January 2007) <www.ncac.gov.cn/chinacopyright/contents/12232/353517.shtml> accessed 8 March 2021.

Lee H, 'Intellectual Property and Copyright in Course Materials During COVID-19 Remote Teaching: Information and Language for Instructors' (*US Santa Cruz*, 19 March 2020) <https://news.ucsc.edu/2020/03/intellectual-property-and-copyright-in-course-materials-during-covid-19-remote-teaching.html> accessed 3 March 2021.

Letter from Amanda Solloway (Parliamentary Under Secretary of State – Minister for Science, Research and Innovation) to David Prosser on 23 April 2020.

Lion Laboratories Ltd v Evans [1984] 2 All ER 417.

使用文字作品支付报酬办法 (Measures for Paying Remuneration for the Use of Written Works) 2014 (*The Central People's Government of the People's Republic of China*, 2014) <www.gov.cn/gongbao/content/2014/content_2792659.htm> accessed 8 March 2021.

教科书法定许可使用作品支付报酬办法 (Measures for Paying Remunerations to Works Legally Permitted to Be Used in Textbooks) 2013 (*National*

Copyright Administration, 29 October 2013) <www.ncac.gov.cn/chinacopyright/contents/12232/353523.shtml> accessed 8 March 2021.

National Radio and Television Administration CCTV-6 v China Education Network Television (2006) Hai Min Chu Zi No 8877.

最高人民法院印发《关于充分发挥知识产权审判职能作用推动社会主义文化大发展大繁荣和促进经济自主协调发展若干问题的意见》的通知 (Notice of the Supreme People's Court on Issuing the Opinions on Issues concerning Maximizing the Role of Intellectual Property Right Trials in Boosting the Great Development and Great Prosperity of Socialist Culture and Promoting the Independent and Coordinated Development of Economy) (Notice of the Supreme People's Court) 2011, art 8.

Okediji LR, 'The International Copyright System: Limitations, Exceptions and Public Interest Considerations for Developing Countries' (2006) ix <https://unctad.org/system/files/official-document/iteipc200610_en.pdf> accessed 2 February 2021.

Patent Law of the People's Republic of China 2008.

Phillips J, 'The Berne Convention and the Public Interest' (1986)11 *Columbia-VLA Journal of Law & the Arts* 165, 169.

'Public Statement of Library Copyright Specialists: Fair Use & Emergency Remote Teaching & Research' (*Infojustice*, 13 March 2020) <https://infojustice.org/archives/42126> accessed 3 March 2021.

Regulation on the Protection of the Right to Network Dissemination of Information 2006 (amended 2013).

Sanft J and others, 'Governmental Use of Patented Inventions During a Pandemic: A Global Survey' (*Norton Rose Fulbright*, 16 April 2020) <www.nortonrosefulbright.com/-/media/files/nrf/nrfweb/knowledge-pdfs/governmental-use-of-patented-inventions-during-a-pandemic-guide.pdf?la=en-ca&revision=> accessed 8 March 2021.

Saunders K, *Intellectual Property Law: Legal Aspects of Innovation and Competition* (St Paul MN, West Academic Publishing 2016) 406–7.

Story A, ' "Balanced" Copyright: Not A Magic Solving Word' (2012) 34(8) *European Intellectual Property Review* 493, 494–95.

Technology, Education and Copyright Harmonization Act (US) 2002.

Trosow S and Macklem L, 'Fair Dealing and Emergency Remote Teaching in Canada' (*Infojustice*, 24 March 2020) <https://infojustice.org/archives/42120> accessed 3 March 2021.

Unilever plc v Griffin [2010] EWHC 899 (Ch), [2010] FSR 33.

Wang CJ, '网络时代著作权相关利益再平衡研究 (Research on Re-Balanced Interest in Copyright During the Internet Age)' (2017) 23 *China Publishing Journal* 44–48.

Wang Xin v Google Inc & Beijing Gu Xiang Information Technology Co Ltd (2011) Yi Zhong Min Chu Zi No 1321.

WIPO, 'Guide to the Berne Convention for the Protection of Literary and Artistic Works (Paris Act, 1971)' (1978) 58 <www.wipo.int/edocs/pubdocs/en/copyright/615/wipo_pub_615.pdf> accessed 2 February 2021.

WIPO Copyright Treaty 1996 (adopted 20 December 1996, entered into force 6 March 2002) WCT Preamble.

Yang Y, '著作权法中损害公共利益的认定研究 (Research on Determination of Public Interest Damage in Copyright Law)' (2016) 5 *China Copyright* 13–17.

Yuan B, '细说著作权之"合理使用"不是"任性使用" (Copyright "Fair Use" Is Not "Abuse")' *China Press Publication Radio Film and Television Journal* (Beijing, 18 May 2017) 5.

Zhang YM and Li YF, 知识产权法学 (*Intellectual Property Law*) (2nd edn, Beijing, Law Press China 2011) 158.

Part II

Contracts and mediation in the post-COVID-19 market arena

5 The global impact (both challenges and opportunities) of COVID-19 on rights and justice

Juha Karhu

Introduction

There is always reason to expect that unexpected things happen. This old wisdom, enhanced by for example Ancient Greek philosophers, reveals one of the many mysteries of unexpected events intervening in the normal chain of events.

What if the initial conditions and circumstances contemplated and relied on by the parties to a long-term contract unexpectedly change? There are several legal perspectives to construct the problem of unexpected changes in the circumstances to the commercial arrangements adopted by business parties. In Western legal tradition, the perspectives challenging the supremacy of the strict binding force of contract (*pacta sunt servanda*) boil down to two main doctrines: *force majeure* doctrines and changed circumstances doctrines. In certain jurisdictions like most European Union (EU) member states, including Germany, France, Italy and Spain, and all of the Nordic countries, both a general *force majeure* doctrine and several changed circumstances doctrines may be available, capable of excusing or modifying the parties' performance. However, it is important to emphasise that there are profound variations in national legal traditions. For example, it is well-known that the common law of contract does not need to distinguish between these two doctrines – because neither of them is recognised as independent doctrines under the common law of contract. Notwithstanding, common law contains specific but normally extremely narrowly constructed exceptions, such as impossibility, frustration and impracticability to the strict adherence to the contract.[1]

In this chapter, the author selects some variants and applications of *force majeure* and changed circumstances doctrines, and analyse what kind of more concrete legal "hooks" these perspectives offer in order to provide legal relief because of circumstances such as the COVID-19 pandemic. The author's general aim is to show the strengths but also weaknesses in *force majeure* and changed

---

1 See for example Klaus Peter Berger and Daniel Behn, 'Force Majeure and Hardship in the Age of Corona: A Historical and Comparative Study' (2019–2020)6 *McGill Journal of Dispute Resolution* 78.

DOI: 10.4324/9781003176848-8

circumstances doctrines when dealing with unexpected events in commercial law contexts, keeping in mind that commercial arrangements between two parties are often elements in and related to wider overall arrangements.

However, this will not be the whole story. The author wants to use the COVID-19 outbreak as an occasion and an incentive to develop and propose a new doctrine – the "Black Swan doctrine/contract" – to better meet the challenges of our epoch of globalisation and complex business networks such as global value chains (GVC). Black Swan doctrines would in general be constructed by respecting the extreme unexpected nature of occasions like the COVID-19 pandemic instead of, as in "Mediocristan",[2] analysing them legally as something fitting the normal scales (the "business as usual" attitude). This new doctrine could better combat the business consequences of the COVID-19 pandemic without falling into the weaknesses of the old doctrines, whilst preserving some of their strengths.

This chapter is structured as follows.[3] The author analyses some variants of these three doctrines – *force majeure*, changed circumstances and the Black Swan doctrine/contract – each in their own sections. *Force majeure*, or the Act of God, is a *suspension reaction*, whereas changed circumstances is a *modification reaction*. The new Black Swan doctrine is needed, because there is no clear-cut line between the two existing doctrines, or any generally accepted solution to the problem of which one of the two should prevail in cases of tension between them. Moreover, the Black Swan doctrine shifts the focus to *survival and coping*. The Black Swan doctrine is required because common commercial distress calls for a framework orienting towards and generating incentives to actions that, even if taken unilaterally, fulfil the criterion of appropriateness. The complexity of GVC as paradigmatic instances of the modern global economy requires the availability of a variety of means, or principles, to act (or not to act). The crucial consequence and testing ground will be how the new doctrine strengthens and widens the general duty to mitigate in commercial contexts. On a general level, Black Swan doctrines offer a mechanism to balance the growing legal systematic weight of private self-determination and private ordering against global needs and interests (often rounded up as corporate social responsibilities).

Force majeure doctrines (including impossibility)

Force majeure is an event or occasion that occurs after the conclusion of the contract, and which is beyond the control of the parties, something that the parties could not or should not foresee at the time when the contract was made,

---

2   Nassim Taleb's term for a society which relies on the general validity of the Gaussian statistical curve and does not recognize extremely unexpected events as phenomena of their own. Nassim Taleb, *The Black Swan: The Impact of the Highly Improbable* (2nd edn, New York, Random House Trade 2010) 49.

3   An excellent analysis following similar structure is Berger and Behn (n 1) focusing on English law.

and which makes the execution of the contract impossible or excessively burden-some.[4] All of these criteria must be fulfilled, all are evaluated separately case by case. The time horizon of the evaluation is normally simple because the conclusion of business contracts is bound to the date of the signing of the deal.

The control criterion is clearly fulfilled in cases of natural disasters like floods, draughts, earthquakes and human related events such as wars, civil riots and terrorist attacks, but may prove difficult in cases of rapid market changes or, for example, global shortage of components. Very often, distressful commercial situations can be expected and therefore should be met with appropriate and sustainable legal design of the business relations, through planning and organisation of mutual interaction, including change of information and constant monitoring. This leads sometimes to a vigilant company taking out insurances to manage the risk.[5]

War can be the cause of an export ban, acting as the direct cause for impossibility of performance (*impossibilium nulla obligatio est*). Similarly, the COVID-19 pandemic often influences business relations through measures taken by governments and other public authorities to combat the pandemic. It is an open legal question as to what extent such measures are immediate and concrete enough to the pandemic to be also considered as a *force majeure* event caused by the pandemic. During COVID-19, lockdowns are typically immediate measures against the pandemic, whereas various recommendations for the public at large are more open to interpretation.[6] Final argumentation must be carried out case by case.

The foreseeability criterion is open to several interpretations. Again, unforeseeability can be established only on individual basis. For example, a private individual building her family home with all necessary public permissions is not expected to take into account some very improbable natural disasters such as extraordinary flooding. However, the same level of improbability may not excuse municipal public bodies making long-term plans for building sites in the locality. Climate change is one of our great challenges in this respect, and it is clear that now much more "extraordinary" possibilities must be taken into account by everyone than some decades ago. After the COVID-19 pandemic, the risk of similar pandemics is not any more unforeseeable.

4   Berger and Behn (n 1) 90.
5   See in general of the role of insurance in natural disasters: Thomas Thaler and Thomas Hartmann, 'Justice and Flood Risk Management: Reflecting on Different Approaches to Distribute and Allocate Flood Risk Management in Europe (2016)83 *Natural Hazards* 129–47 <https://doi.org/10.1007/s11069-016-2305-1> accessed 19 May 2021.
6   In the case of Finland see for example Government Communications Department, 'Government Updates Policies on Border Issues, Remote Working and Recommendations for Persons Over 70 Years of Age' (*Finish Government*, 23 June 2020) <https://valtioneu-vosto.fi/en/-/10616/government-updates-policies-on-border-issues-remote-working-and-recommendations-for-persons-over-70-years-of-age> accessed 19 May 2021.

The last criterion of *excessive burdensome* is a descendant of Roman Law institution of *laesio enormis*.[7] In Roman Law, it was used as an exceptional excuse in situations where the burden of fulfilling the duties would mean exhausting one's resources to an unbearable extent, thus ruining the economy of one's household.[8] Again, the level of what can be tolerated because of the inherent risk-taking involved in commercial arrangements is different in various legal systems and depending on the business branch in question. For example, the price and value of land in real estate sales has been historically treated differently in different cultures when deciding on the unfairness of the sale.[9] Concretely, this criterion sets an ultimate limit for how much of the overall losses a business party to a contractual arrangement must bear alone.[10] One way to draw this ultimate line could be a law and economics' perspective on effective breach, developed for situations where it is more effective to break the contract and pay damages than to fulfil the contract as agreed. Notwithstanding, there is no doubt that we are speaking of substantial losses before this criterion is fulfilled to the extent that is required in *force majeure*. Typically, all the normal means and most of the other extraordinary means must also be exhausted before *force majeure* can step in because *force majeure* is closely related to the temporal or final impossibility on the side of the debtor.[11]

Among these four conjunctive criteria the last two – foreseeability – (often leading to a duty of the court to take a complex variety of circumstances into account) – and excessive burdensome, leading to the need to weigh known risks and unexpected losses – are generally most widely open for interpretations.[12] These two criteria are also the reason for the overlap between the doctrines of *force majeure* and changed circumstances.[13] It is therefore no surprise that in international trade model norms such as the Convention on International Sale of Goods (CISG), it is precisely these two criteria that are made more concrete by reference to either causes or consequences of the action, or both, ('a party is faced with genuinely unexpected and radically changed circumstances in truly

---

7   James Gordley, *The Philosophical Origins of Modern Contract Law* (Oxford, OUP 1991) 64, 94. See also Andrea Perrone, 'The Just Price Doctrine and Contemporary Contract Law: Some Introductory Remarks' (2013) 3 *Orizzonti del diritto commerciale* 1.

8   Raymond Westbrook, 'The Origin of *laesio enormis*' (2008)55 *RIDA* 40.

9   ibid.

10   Perrone (n 7) 11.

11   Berger and Behn (n 1) 101 making a reference to *Canary Wharf (BP4) T1 Ltd v European Medicines Agency* [2019] EWHC 335 (Ch) at paras 22 and 28 where Brexit was not considered to make a lease contract for European Union agency headquarter offices frustrated.

12   Berger and Behn (n 1) 111 (on foreseeability) and 128 (on excessive burdensome).

13   A simple answer to this overlap would be to say that the doctrine of changed circumstances is considered a concrete variant of *force majeure* doctrines. This is how for example the Nordic Sales Laws essentially imitating CISG combine these two doctrines in their Section 27 providing sellers liability to pay damages in situation of delay.

exceptional cases').[14] The key idea here is that a comparison is made between the normal chain of events as they were contemplated by the parties, and the extraordinary circumstances which occurred instead of the normal ones. It is imperative for legal relief on the basis of *force majeure* that the effective factor causing the out-of-joint development of circumstances is outside the control of the parties.[15] In the CISG model, liability becomes a control liability because a party to a business arrangement is liable only insofar as the disturbance was such that the party could expect it or could have, with reasonable costs, taken precautionary measures to avoid the disturbance, or where the party could easily mitigate the consequences of the disturbance.[16] Thus, one could even go so far as saying that *force majeure* and control liability are the different faces of the same legal coin.[17]

The legal effects of *force majeure* are normally and logically that the reciprocal rights and duties affected by *force majeure* are suspended until the situation normalises again. After the normalisation, the parties fall back to their original arrangement, with the same contract positions established when the arrangement was originally made. There is a kind of rubber ball effect from non-normal back to normal. On the legal level, everything will be back once again as it was before the incident. The new commercial situation after the *force majeure* event contains the old normal in legal respects: the legal rights and duties are re-installed as they were before the incident.[18] In special cases where the *force majeure* factor makes the whole contract impossible, relief can be given of the duties.[19] In some jurisdictions, a party can in such situations ask for a judgment of relief by a court if the contract is not terminated voluntarily.[20]

---

14   Berger and Behn (n 1) 89 referring to Alejandro M Garro, 'Exemption of Liability for Damages under Article 79 of the CISG', CISG-AC Opinion No 7 on Article 79 of the CISG (2007) at para 37. Because of open nature of the general doctrine, even after the clarifications in international conventions like CISG, business parties normally exclude CISG and other conventions and write their own contract terms on *force majeure*.

15   Berger and Behn (n 1) 98 (referring especially to the modern doctrine of subsequent impossibility).

16   Rodrigo Momberg Uriber, 'Change of Circumstances in International Instruments of Contract Law: The Approach of the CISG, PICC, PECL, and DCFR' (2011)15(2) *European Review of Private Law* 242.

17   CISG control liability is of course focused on liability towards one's contract partner and not for all the risks relating to the business activity.

18   Momberg Uriber (n 16) 243 with references to CISG application.

19   Berger and Behn (n 1) 97.

20   The Law Reform (Frustrated Contracts) 1943 Act gives an automatic discharge of contract in certain situations of unforeseeable impossibility which was caused without the fault of either party where the contract does not either expressly or impliedly allocate the risk of inability to perform to one of the parties. If the impossibility is only temporary a relief is possible only if performance in the new situation would be completely different to what the contract called for or purpose from both parties' view would be destroyed. However, the scope of application of the Act is very limited due to *Davis Contractors Ltd v Fareham UDC* [1956] AC 696 at 729. See also Code Civil articles 1351 and 1351-1. Article 1351 of the Civil Code provides that 'Impossibility of performance shall release the debtor to the

Because of the possibly severe effects of *force majeure*, parties to a business arrangement normally agree upon *force majeure*. Of course, this essentially changes the nature of the legal approach. The *force majeure* doctrine loses its immediate value, and *pacta sunt servanda* takes over. The move of subjugation of *force majeure* to *pacta sunt servanda* is locked and made irreversible by contractual clauses typical for business contracts, such as "entire agreement" and "no waiver", which function by certifying the decisive role of the final written contract document. Entire agreement clauses close the four corners of the contract to become the only basis for legal relations between the parties from all external factors (including contract negotiations). No waiver clauses close the four corners of the contract against any internal change causing one party to act in a way not normatively regulated in the contract (under the validity period of the contract). This idea of whole contract also has consequences in situations where despite *force majeure* some parts of the contract can be upheld, in which case they should be followed as normal and only those clauses specifically effected by *force majeure* are put on hold.

One must be very careful in claiming anything more specific about contractual *force majeure* clauses agreed upon by the business parties.[21] Commercial contracts contain various lists of events to be considered as *force majeure* under that specific contract, and there are numerous model clauses intended for various situations and various branches of business.[22] The content of these clauses is overwhelmingly dependent on the contract at hand and the business context; and the general *force majeure* doctrines offer only minor supplementary arguments.[23] The situation is complicated further by the fact that it is also typical that contractual *force majeure* clauses are used as tacit means for limitations of liability, by either including or not including certain events or modifying the consequences of the *force majeure* doctrine.[24]

Due to its unforeseen nature, it is doubtful whether COVID-19 could have been concretely named in such clauses in business arrangements made before

---

extent that it is due to force majeure and is definitive, unless the debtor has agreed to perform or has been given prior notice of default.' Article 1351-1 of the Civil Code provides that 'Where the impossibility of performance results from the loss of the thing due, the debtor who has been put in default shall nevertheless be discharged if he proves that the loss would have occurred in the same way if the obligation had been performed.'

21 Same holds for how to apply contracts in COVID-19 circumstances even from non-*force-majeure* perspective. See for example in insurance English Supreme Court 15 January 2021 Hilary Term [2021] UKSC 1.

22 Hubert Konarski, 'Force Majeure and Hardship Clauses in International Contractual Practice' (2003)4 *International Business Law Journal* 405.

23 ibid.

24 For example, in touristic commerce between large global firms and small local travel enterprises *force majeure* clauses can be unilateral in including or excluding certain occasions totally outside the control of the parties like the prevalence of snow at the holiday resort, and thus actually affecting the risk position of the business parties in cases of exceptional seasonal weather conditions.

2020.[25] More probably, a reference relevant to COVID-19 is phrased as "epidemic" or "pandemic". At the latest, after the declaration made on 11 March 2020 by the Word Health Organisation (WHO) that COVID-19 is a pandemic,[26] there should be no real room for general counter arguments that contract clauses referring to epidemic or pandemic encompass COVID-19 pandemic.

Even if the parties are free to agree upon *force majeure* terms, there is at least one situation where the *force majeure* doctrine could strike back. If in a commercial contract under English law (or for that matter a US state law), epidemic or pandemic has not been mentioned as a *force majeure* event, or the *force majeure* consequences of pandemic have been totally blocked, how would a foreign court or an execution authority judge the possible arbitration award in the execution phase? More concretely, would a court in a country accepting the *force majeure* doctrine as one of the fundamental institutions of its commercial law view such an arbitration award against *ordre public* or public policy? In other words, would there be a possibility and risk that Article III of the Convention on the Recognition and Enforcement of Foreign Arbitral Awards in 1958[27] would it be invoked against such an award?

The author believes such a possibility is real. For example, under Chinese contract law, and included in the Civil Code of the People's Republic of China (Chinese Civil Code 2020), there are statutory norms on *force majeure*. Moreover, in its earlier declaration the Supreme People's Court has stated that the SARS pandemic was a *force majeure* under Chinese contract law, which standpoint was renewed concerning COVID-19.[28] In China, a semi-public organisation, the China Council for Promotion of International Trade, even issued certificates on the *force majeure* character of COVID-19 to enable businesses to be legally safe when making their demands to their foreign business partners.[29] A foreign

---

25 Matthew Jennejohn and others, 'COVID-19 as a Force Majeure in Corporate Transactions' in Pistor K (ed), *Law in the Time of COVID-19* (New York, Columbia Law School 2020) 141 <https://scholarship.law.columbia.edu/faculty_scholarship/2645> accessed 19 May 2021.

26 Tedros Adhanom Ghebreyesus, 'WHO Director-General's Opening Remarks at the Media Briefing on COVID-19–11 March 2020' (*WHO*, 11 March 2020) <www.who.int/director-general/speeches/detail/who-director-general-s-opening-remarks-at-the-media-briefing-on-covid-19–11-march-2020> accessed 19 May 2021.

27 Article III provides that the recognition and enforcement of foreign arbitral awards shall be granted 'in accordance with the rules of procedure of the territory where the award is relied upon'.

28 Circular of the Supreme People's Court on Issuing the Guiding Opinions (II) on Several Issues concerning Proper Trial of Civil Cases Related to the COVID-19 Epidemic According to the Law, dated 15 May 2020. See for example Qiao Liu, 'COVID-19 in Civil or Commercial Disputes: First Responses from Chinese Courts' (2020) 8 *The Chinese Journal of Comparative Law* 487 <https://academic.oup.com/cjcl/article/8/2/485/5899311> accessed 8 June 2021.

29 Since January 2020 the China Council for the Promotion of International Trade has issued more than 5600 certificates attesting force majeure on behalf of companies that have failed to comply with the obligations of international contracts, allegedly due to COVID-19.

arbitration award blocking the Chinese business party in invoking *force majeure* because of COVID-19 would clearly be against this line of established legal reasoning, containing the protection of important social policy in relation to a means of fighting against a pandemic and mitigating its harmful effects on people and businesses.[30] At the very least, it would be over optimistic to think that the Chinese execution authorities would willingly enforce such arbitration awards.[31]

In the European context, *force majeure* is a doctrine normally seen as one of the main excuses for non-performance, and thus outside the private autonomy of the parties.[32] In this sense, the doctrine is setting limits as to the validity of contract and resembles other doctrines and norms guaranteeing a fair business framework, such as prohibition of fraud, mandatory contract law legislation and (other) *ordre public* norms.[33] However, the border between private autonomy and such a framework is not clear-cut. Thus, the author believes that the courts and execution authorities of EU member states would allow, and see as legally relevant, counter arguments on the grounds "against important public policy" and what the consequences would be of dismissing commercial contracts without "normal" *force majeure* possibility. In this weighing and balancing, a comparison could be made between the effects of the lack of *force majeure* possibility and the overall business setting agreed upon in the contract in question. If there is a substantial adverse effect (hardship) to one party due to the "missing" *force majeure* possibility, that is an argument in favour of applying the public policy exception. Even so, the systemic importance of accepting arbitral awards may easily outweigh this argument.

Changed circumstances doctrines (including hardship)

Changed circumstances refers to a situation where an emergence of a new circumstance or an essential change of a circumstance, which was unforeseeable and beyond the control of the parties, changes the risk positions of the parties under the contract in such a way that the purpose of the contract is frustrated and the contract becomes excessively burdensome to one party.[34] In such situations, many jurisdictions allow the contract to be modified, either through renegotiation

---

Laura Maria Franciosi, 'The Effects of COVID-19 on International Contracts: A Comparative View' (2020)51 *Victoria University of Wellington Law Review* 433.

30   New York Convention 1958, Article V 2(b).

31   See also on a general level Brandon M Boylan and others, 'US – China Relations: Nationalism, the Trade War, and COVID-19' (2021)14 *Fudan Journal of the Humanities and Social Sciences* 23–40 <https://doi.org/10.1007/s40647-020-00302-6> accessed 19 May 2021.

32   Giuditta Cordero-Moss, 'Limits to Party Autonomy in International Commercial Arbitration' (2014)1 *Oslo Law Review* 47.

33   There are also opposing views. For example, Marel Katsivela, 'Contracts: Force Majeure Concept or Force Majeure Clauses?' (2007)12 *Uniform Law Review* 101.

34   Berger and Behn (n 1) 115.

by the parties or by a judge in a court of law.[35] Exceptionally the whole contract can be terminated.[36]

This doctrine is not meant to excuse a party if the performance has become more onerous because the cost of performance has increased or because of the value in return has diminished, or similar flaws or normal risks in the business judgment made by the contract party claiming for the relief. The doctrine only applies in situations where it would be manifestly unjust to hold the party under duty to perform according to the original terms of the contract.[37] Moreover, there are similar requirements as in *force majeure*. For example, the change in question must have occurred after the time of conclusion of the contract, and the party under obligation did not take into account or assume, and could not reasonably have been expected to have taken into account or assume, the possibility or scale of the changed circumstance and its effect on the risk positions of the parties.[38] Lastly, in more modern versions of this doctrine, such as the French Code Civil article 1195, a supplementary criterion requires that there must have been renegotiations in good faith to achieve a reasonable and equitable adjustment by the parties before the judge has the authority to terminate or modify the contract.[39]

Contracts are always incomplete. There are always implied terms, conditions and understandings relating to change and non-change of the context besides the

---

35 For example, all the Nordic contract laws enable such a possibility. Ole Lando and others (eds), *Restatement of Nordic Contract Law* (Copenhagen, Djof Publishing 2016) 220.

36 In a Danish case (UFR 2002.1224) the part of an agreement made 1925 on royalty payments for a piece of music was considered unreasonable and therefore should be disregarded with respect to the period of following the commencement of the legal proceedings.

37 In this sense the English case *Davis Contractors Ltd v Fareham UDC* [1956] AC 696 at 729 represents a general attitude.

38 See *Canary Wharf (BP4) T1 Ltd v European Medicines Agency* [2019] EWHC 335 (Ch) at paras 35 and 244. The case dealt with the effects of Brexit where a lease agreement was alleged to be frustrated following Brexit. The lease was determined not to be frustrated either on the basis of purpose, or of supervening illegality, because the supervening event, Brexit, did not frustrate the underlying purpose of the contract, which was to rent headquarter offices in a European Union Member State. According to Berger and Behn (n 1) 102 this case did not even get close to reaching the high threshold to excuse performance, reinforcing just how seldom a frustration excuse is likely to succeed under English law unlike many Civil Law jurisdictions.

39 French Code Civil article 1195 provides that 'If a change in circumstances, unforeseeable at the time of conclusion of the contract, makes performance excessively onerous for a party who had not agreed to bear the risk, that party may request the other party to renegotiate the contract. It shall continue to perform its obligations during the renegotiation. If the renegotiation is rejected or fails, the parties may agree to terminate the contract, on the date and on the conditions they determine, or may request the court to adapt it by mutual agreement. If no agreement is reached within a reasonable time, the court may, at the request of one of the parties, revise or terminate the contract, on the date and under the conditions it shall determine'.

parties' explicit consent.[40] Therefore, a legally relevant change of circumstances requires that the commercial basis of the contract (when it was made) is substituted to an essential degree by new circumstances to the detriment of one party.[41] These new circumstances must lead to an outcome where the contract does not anymore fulfil the original reciprocity and contractual equivalence adopted by the parties.[42] The change causes an imbalance in the rights and duties of the parties in relation to the situation when the contract was made. This emerging cause must also be unforeseeable in the sense that neither party could reasonably have taken it into account when the contract was made.[43] Moreover, the change in the circumstance must not be the outcome of the activity of either party.[44] Lastly, there must not exist any other contract law means to remedy this imbalance.[45]

The doctrines of changed circumstances have a long legal history and therefore some of them have been discussed and developed under the Latin name of "*clausula rebus sic stantibus*".[46] The doctrine has its origin in Roman Law as well as in Canon Law, as these were understood (and constructed) in the Middle Ages and Early Modernity with reference to the idea that the circumstances must remain the same after a promise was given for the promise to be binding.[47] Contracts are binding only as long and as far matters remain the same as they were at the time of the conclusion of the contract. Obviously, there are numerous later variants of the *clausula* doctrine. One of the most influential in Germany and more widely for European development has been Bernhard Windscheid and his reading of Roman Law in "*Voraussetzungslehre*" emphasizing the importance of tacit presuppositions.[48] Presently, it is normal, except in common law contract, that a modern legal system contains some routes to react against an essential change of circumstance taking place after the conclusion of the contract.[49]

Unlike *force majeure* doctrines, changed circumstances doctrines focus on the contractual balance originally created by the commercial parties (i.e.) before the incident. The legal challenge in the application of the doctrines of changed

---

40   This is a theoretical statement. It finds support by philosophical perspective in hermeneutics, and by economic perspective in considerations of effectivity. See about the former Shahar Lifshitz and Elad Finkelstein, 'A Hermeneutic Perspective on Interpretation of Contracts' (2017)54 *American Business Law Journal* 519, and about the latter Oliver Hart and John Moore, 'Incomplete Contracts and Renegotiation' (1988)56 *Econometrica* 755.

41   Berger and Behn (n 1) 97.

42   ibid 128.

43   ibid 98.

44   As such, it would evidently be inside the control sphere of that party.

45   This means that other remedies than the doctrine of changed circumstances take priority. See for example Code Civil articles 1351 and 1351–1 (n 20).

46   See for example Pascal Pichonnaz, 'From *clausula rebus sic stantibus* to Hardship: Aspects of the Evolution of the Judge's Role' (2011)17(1) *Fundamina* 125 <https://hdl.handle.net/10520/EJC34434> accessed 19 May 2021.

47   Reinhard Zimmermann, *The Law of Obligations: The Roman Foundation of the Civilian Tradition* (Oxford, OUP 1996) 687.

48   Bernhard Windscheid, *Die Lehre des Römischen Rechts von der Voraussetzung* (*The Doctrine of Assumption in Roman Law*) (Düsseldorf, Buddeus 1850).

49   Berger and Behn (n 1) 115.

circumstances (including hardship) is to find a balance between respecting at the same time, on one hand, the binding force of contracts, and, on the other, the reasonable sharing of common and individual losses when unexpected changes happen to the fundaments of the mutual arrangement.[50] This challenge is reflected in the legislative provisions. There are several statutory provisions relating to changed circumstances such as article 1195 of the French Civil Code, section 313 of the German Civil Code (BGB), and some model laws such as DCFR III 1:110 and PECL 6.111.[51] I will presently consider two recent (in the sense of development of legal doctrines) variants of the traditional changed circumstances doctrine. The German *Geschäftsgrundlage* doctrine was originally developed and employed to combat the hyperinflation at the beginning of the twentieth century and is now established as a specific provision in the BGB.[52] Nordic contract law contains an important doctrine of general clause on unfairness.[53] These examples are provided to show the main reference points if this second main line to legally combat COVID-19 is chosen.

The doctrine of *Wegfall der Geschäftsgrundlage* was originally developed under the "*Treu und Glaube*" section 242 of the BGB (roughly, in English, good faith and fair dealing). It was also based on the case law of the 1920's dealing with the consequences of hyperinflation on business contracts. Now there is a new special section 313 of the BGB titled "*Störung der Geschäftsgrundlage*".[54] It provides that

if the circumstances which became the foundation of a contract have profoundly changed since the contract was entered into, and if the parties would not have entered into the contract or would have entered into it only with different contents if they had foreseen this change, adaptation of the contract may be claimed; given that, taking into account all the circumstances of the specific case, in particular the contractual or statutory distribution of risks, one of the parties cannot reasonably be expected to uphold the contract without alteration.[55]

---

50 ibid 87.
51 See also European Law Institute Principles for the COVID-19 Crisis Principle 13 Force majeure and Hardship. These principles address some of the most important legal issues arising in relation to the COVID-19 crisis offering guidance to European States.
52 Jens Prütting, *Wegfall der Geschäftsgrundlage als Antwort des Zivilrechts auf krisenbedingte Vertragsstörungen* (*Wegfall der Geschäftsgrundlage as a Private Law Answer to Contractual Commitments Effected by Crises*) (2020) 47 <www.nomos-elibrary. de/10.5771/9783748909279-47/wegfall-der-geschaeftsgrundlage-als-antwort-des-zivilrechts-auf-krisenbedingte-vertragsstoerungen-systemerwaegungen-zu-313-bgb-und-sachgerechter-einsatz-in-der-praxis> accessed 10 June 2021.
53 Lando and others (n 35) 154. referring to joint Nordic Act on Formation of Contract, Representation and Voidable Promises § 36.
54 Prütting (n 52).
55 Bundesministerium der Justiz und Verbraucherschutz (Federal Ministry of Justice and Consumer Protection) and Bundesamt für Justice (Federal Office of Justice), Translation provided by the Langenscheidt Translation Service <www.gesetze-im-internet.de/ englisch_bgb/englisch_bgb.html#p1146> accessed 10 June 2021.

If the adaptation of the contract is not possible, or one party cannot reasonably be expected to accept it, the disadvantaged party may withdraw from the contract or terminate the contract.

Section 313 of the BGB does not contain any requirement for *laesio enormis*, which means that the "*Störung der Geschäftsgrundlage*" doctrine stands alone in this respect. It is very likely that COVID-19 would satisfy the requirement of not being foreseeable, especially with reference to Robert Koch Institute's estimate published in January 2013 that a catastrophic pandemic like COVID-19 happens only once in a hundred or thousand years.[56] However, it remains to be seen to what extent a relief based on governmental Corona measures significantly restricting the usability of business property, such as prohibitions on hotels and restaurants (directly causing expenses such as rents becoming worthless), will be given under section 313 of the BGB, or more specific provisions dealing with the same situation.[57]

In Nordic countries, adjustment because of unfairness is based on the essentially similar sections 36 of the national Contracts Acts.[58] In its Finnish version, the general clause in section 36 of the Finnish Contracts Act (FCA) provides that if a contract term is unfair or its application would lead to an unfair result, the term may be adjusted or set aside. In determining what is unfair, regard shall be had to the entire contents of the contract, the positions of the parties, the circumstances prevailing at and after the conclusion of the contract, and to other factors. If the unfair term is such that it would be unfair to enforce the rest of the contract after the adjustment of the term, the remainder of the contract may also be adjusted or declared as terminated. It is specifically provided in subsection 36(3) of the FCA that a provision relating to the amount of consideration such as price shall also be deemed a contract term.[59]

Section 36 of the FCA requires an overall evaluation. In an adjustment reasoning no single circumstance can absolutely require or absolutely prevent the adjustment. When a claim of unfairness is made and directed to one term of the contract, a judge must always consider the interaction of that contract term with other terms.[60] Moreover, an overall evaluation means that not only the contract at hand is evaluated, but in situations where the contract is part and parcel of a larger arrangement other contractual and even non-contractual circumstances

---

56   Risikoanalyse Bevölkerungsschutz Bund: Pandemie durch Virus Modi-SARS (Risk Analysis by Civilian Population Protection League: Pandemic Caused by Virus of the SARS Type) (3 January 2013) 55 <http://dipbt.bundestag.de/doc/btd/17/120/1712051.pdf> accessed 19 May 2021.

57   Special amendments are made in the application statute of German Civil Code (EGBGB) in relation to lease agreements.

58   Lando and others (n 35) 154.

59   Finnish Contracts Act (228/1929) section 36, unofficial translation by Finnish Ministry of Justice available at <www.finlex.fi/en/laki/kaannokset/1929/en19290228_19990449.pdf> accessed 19 May 2021.

60   Lando and others (n 35) 155 for cases from Swedish, Danish, Norwegian, Finnish and Icelandic Supreme Courts applying section 36 of Nordic contracts acts.

can also become relevant. A party can be excused of the full demands of performance in situations where the foundation of the contract changes and randomly favours one party over the other.[61] However, normal market changes making the common business based on mutual contract more profitable or less profitable do not call for adjustment.[62] There is no doubt that section 36 of the FCA could be applied in commercial disputes relating to COVID-19 due to and to the extent that the pandemic is a circumstance occurring after the conclusion of the contract. Whether such application leads to an adjustment of the contract at hand is dependent on the facts of each case at hand.

A balanced outcome does not always mean that we consider a contractual term null and void. Fairness can very often be reached by settling a fair period for termination and/or considering the benefits the other party has already gained through the contract and/or losses that party would suffer if the contract is terminated.[63] Notwithstanding, in cases where changes impact on a long-term business contract at the beginning of the contract period, adjustment might be a better means to correct the situation. This is preferable to letting burdensome contract continue for long periods, causing incentives for the obliged party to make efforts to avoid them or a constant "race to the bottom" for the expenses of fulfilment.[64]

Changed circumstances doctrines perceive contracts as legal forms for cooperation. The cooperation nature of business contracts also means that in situations of unexpected change the cooperation must prevail alongside the contractual balance; or more exactly, the risk positions adopted by the parties in the overall arrangement must prevail.[65] Mitigation is a seminal duty to all involved in commercial activities.[66] In the Nordic context, mitigation is connected to a more general duty of loyalty, owed not so much to the other party but to the contract itself.[67]

---

61   Lando and others (n 35) 15.
62   Juha Pöyhönen, *Sopimusoikeuden järjestelmä ja sopimusten sovittelu* (*The System of Contract Law and the Adjustment of Contracts*) (Vammala, SLY 1988) 300; Juha Karhu, 'Review of Business Contracts/Finland' in Wais H and Pfeiffer T (eds), *Judicial Review of B2B Contracts* (Oxford, Hart Publishing 2021) 94.
63   For example, Law Reform (Frustrated Contracts) Act 1943 provides for an adjustment of rights and liabilities of parties to frustrated contracts.
64   In the Swedish case NJA 1983.332 it was considered unreasonable that a bank had a unilateral right to change the terms of a letter of credit to the detriment of a guarantor. Such unilateral contract clauses are also mentioned in the Government Bill for FCA § 36 as typical examples of unreasonable contract terms.
65   See on Nordic contract law Lars Erik Taxell, *Avtal och rättsskydd* (*Contract and Protection Under the Law*) (Turku, Åbo Akademi 1972). Taxell uses the term contractual equilibrium (*avtalsbalans*) to describe the risk positions adopted by the parties when concluding the contract.
66   Horia Ciurtin, 'A Hermeneutical Perspective Upon the "Mitigation of Damages" Principle: The Metamorphosis of a Concept in International Law' (2015)6 *Transnational Dispute Management* 1.
67   Lando and others (n 35) 85 stating that 'contracting parties are . . . expected to pursue the non-occurrence of detrimental events to a reasonable extent'.

If contracts are always seen to contain a speculative aspect, the gains and losses are allowed to fall on the contract parties randomly. Thus, it is again the unexpected nature of the events that is key: common characteristic in both *force majeure* and changed circumstances. However, unlike *force majeure*, the doctrine of changed circumstances focuses on the most important elements structuring and maintaining the common business activity in question. The German notion of "*Geschäftsgrundlage*" (foundation of the business deal) clarifies the point. Often these fundamentals are documented by the business parties by expressly stating them in the preamble of business arrangements (the so called "whereas" statements).[68] Very often these fundamentals are tacit and taken for granted by both parties. For example, in commercial leases it is a tacit assumption that the government does not prohibit the use of the rented premises.[69]

One important difference between *force majeure* and changed circumstances relates to effects. Changed circumstances call for a change of the contractual arrangement to meet again the originally adopted risk positions (possibilities of gain and losses under the arrangement). In COVID-19 we have witnessed that it is difficult to foresee the course and end of the pandemic. For dynamic businesses, it would therefore be of importance to find a substitute line of action instead of just waiting for things to normalise, as the application of *force majeure* calls for.

Force majeure and changed circumstances are meant to be used only after other possible remedies have been exhausted.[70] Yet what of their mutual order of priority? The author uses an example here from China. The Chinese Civil Code 2020 contains in its contract law chapter a special section on *force majeure*, but also on the basis of Supreme People's Court's interpretation on Chinese contract law (which is now part of Chinese Civil Code) the doctrine of changed circumstances is part of Chinese law.[71] Therefore, a question arises, which one of the two – *force majeure* and changed circumstances – should be applied in situations caused by COVID-19? It is not submitted that there is one answer on a general level. It is up to the parties to decide which relief they are arguing for and against, and for the Chinese courts to make a legal evaluation of the overall situation. Because of the overlapping requirements, but not overlapping effects, it is more the choice on the outcome – (only) delay or (also) modification – that is the crux of the

---

68   In a contract a whereas clause is an introductory statement that means "considering that" or "that being the case". The clause explains the reasons for the execution of the contract and, in some cases, describes its purpose. The "whereas" clause may properly be used in interpreting the contract. However, it is not an essential component for its operative provisions. See <https://law.jrank.org/pages/11290/Whereas.html> accessed 19 May 2021.
69   The author concurs with the opinion presented by a Finnish Law firm on COVID-19 situation in Finland at Waselius & Wist, 'Covid-19 And Its Impact on the Obligation to Pay Rent in Commercial Leases (*Waselius & Wist*, 30 March 2020) <www.ww.fi/news/2020/03/covid-19-and-its-impact-on-the-obligation-to-pay-rent-in-commercial-leases/> accessed 19 May 2021.
70   Code Civil articles 1351 and 1351-1 are illustrative in this respect (n 20).
71   Liu (n 28) 487.

question. When the pandemic takes longer to tackle, as with the COVID-19 pandemic, this question becomes more pressing, and China seems to have avoided this situation of a prolonged pandemic. Yet the open question of the priority between *force majeure* and changed circumstances remains one reason (although a minor one) to develop a new doctrine better adapted to the paradigm of new global crises.

Towards Black Swan doctrines

Black Swan is of course a reference – and an homage – to Nassim Taleb.[72] Black Swans are events so unthinkable with the logic of the terms used in normally constructed contractual arrangement that they fall wholly outside of the scale expected – unexpected; they are totally unexpected. Black Swans are not at all foreseeable, they have severe and extraordinary consequences, and they are explainable only in hindsight. One cannot exhaustively define Black Swans, one just knows them when they are happening and especially after they have happened. The subsequent concept besides Black Swan that the author needs to emphasise is that of the fragility of arrangements. The spirit of Black Swan doctrine is towards antifragile.[73] Thus, is there a way to treat Black Swans from the legal point of view without falling back to the tempting trap of "business as usual"?

To start with new ideas, we need a reference point in the prevailing doctrines to build upon, but also to react and to oppose. There must be a continuation and discontinuation at the same time, as in the German doctrine of "*Geschäfts-grundlage*". Even if *force majeure* and changed circumstances are both possible reactions to changes, the latter offers a wider perspective. In this sense, the Black Swan doctrine/contract is more a continuation of the changed circumstances doctrines than *force majeure*. This means that it is also the case that the foundation in legal sources for the Black Swan doctrine/contract is the same kind of statutory provisions than in the changed circumstances doctrines, for example section 242 of the BGB and section 36 of the FCA.

But there must also be something substantive ensuring its continuation. Here the duty to mitigate takes a key position.[74] It is clearly an important element both in *force majeure* and changed circumstances.[75] Respecting your contract

---

72 Taleb (n 2) xxi.
73 Nassim Taleb, *Antifragile: Things That Gain from Disorder* (New York, Random House Trade 2014) 349.
74 Ciurtin (n 66).
75 On the relation between mitigation and *force majeure* see Christian Twigg-Flesner, 'A Comparative Perspective on Commercial Contracts and the Impact of Covid-19 – Change of Circumstances, Force Majeure, or What?' in Pistor K (ed), *Law in the Time of COVID-19* (New York, Columbia Law School 2020) 155 <https://scholarship.law.columbia.edu/cgi/viewcontent.cgi?article=1239&context=books> accessed 8 June 2021. On the relation between mitigation and changed circumstances see Momberg Uriber (n 16) 242.

partner's distress by allowing delay without sanctions most probably minimises that partner's economic losses and other damage. Modifying and adjusting the contract to better fit the changed circumstances is done with the aim to balance the gains, but also losses, suffered by both parties. You need not sacrifice more than your partner benefits. Moreover, the duty to mitigate is reciprocal and it applies both to your own losses as well as losses of your partner. Further, it is a duty without upper limit, in the sense that if you can reach mitigation by minor efforts of your own, you should do it even if it hugely benefits only your contractual partner. The duty to mitigate is so strong that it can even transform an expense normally outside the scope of coverage, because it is too distant (indirect damage), to a compensable expense (direct damage) when the compensation is asked for an act with the aim of mitigation.[76] Last, but not least, the duty to mitigate resonates to common sense. Why should we lose more of our economic resources than is necessary?

A reference point to oppose the concept is also needed. In the Black Swan doctrine/contract, the basic concept of contract is a relational process instead of a fixed and compact document-based concept.[77] This relational process consists of three interrelated dimensions: personal scope, time and substantive content. Instead of dualities, the procedural concept of contract refers to scales and the ever-changing character of contract. This formulation shows the connection between the Black Swan doctrine and the doctrines of changed circumstances. In the relational conception of contract, the time dimension is more like periodisation in history than calendar time. The personal dimension resembles a stakeholder approach instead of sharp privity. The substantive content is defined not only narrowly and separately by the single contract in question alone, but with the view of the contract as a part of an overall arrangement, such as global value chain. In one expression, the relational conception of contract leans towards enhanced contextuality.[78]

What happens when the Black Swan doctrine/contract abandons the traditional conception of contract and replaces it by a relational conception? A shift of legal focus in commercial contexts is created, from the substance matter of the legal arrangement to the involved parties (including all the members of the value chain) and their survival; a key legal principle activated to preserve *pacta*

---

76 See for example Nordic Sales Laws section 67(3) providing that loss incurred by the injured party for mitigation of loss shall not be considered indirect loss. This outcome is in line with CISG article 79.

77 Block chain technology makes this mistake even worse; instead of smart contracts we get even more "stupid" contracts. For an analysis and criticism of smart contracts with an emphasis to move to smart contracting see Maria Claudia Solarte Vasquez, *Smart Contracting for the Proactive Governance of Digital Exchange* (Tallinn, Tallinn University of Technology 2019) 37.

78 See also Andrew Hutchison, 'Relational Theory, Context and Commercial Common Sense: Views on Contract Interpretation and Adjudication' (2017) 134 *South African Law Journal* 296.

sunt servanda, as much as it is possible, is the duty of loyalty.[79] Yet it is not loyalty directly towards the other parties, but foremost towards the arrangement itself.[80] The duty of loyalty becomes an advanced duty to communicate, to keep all involved parties on the same map. When it comes to harm, the duty of loyalty becomes a duty to mitigate the overall damage as much as possible and is reasonable.[81] So, instead of formal emphasis, as *force majeure* or substantial emphasis, as changed circumstances, the Black Swan doctrine places its emphasis on procedures such as negotiations, discussions and the sharing and mitigation of harmful effects, to allow coping and healing.

Legal doctrines are built, besides a network of basic legal concepts, with legal principles. Legal principles set normative goals for the activities. The author has already mentioned the significance of the duty of loyalty to the Black Swan doctrine/contract. The duty of loyalty could in addition be seen as the principle of loyalty. The other principles of Black Swan doctrine/contract can be grouped in three headings: resilience principles, agility principles and creativity principles.

Resilience principles guide the actions of coping. Black Swan events destroy the old normal, and commercial activities affected by this destruction need legal backing for their efforts of economic survival. These efforts can be adjusted to the situation at hand. Sometimes the best move is to wait and see and react only after one can recognise some logic in the Black Swan event. Time is not always money, and short-termism is not the norm. However, resilience does not set passivity as the new norm either. Similar to chess, even if you do not have a single overall strategy, you still can set some interim short-term goals to improve your position. Thus, situation sensitivity is still needed.

Agility principles are compatible with the relational understanding of contract. In Black Swan situations, one needs to have capacity to seize all small opportunities. Instead of the normal accountant type of calculative rationality, smart rationality takes over.[82] Smart rationality is a key resource in surviving in situations of crisis. It functions by constantly readjusting the activities on changes and emerging possibilities. The future, and at least the near future, is not going to look like

---

79 References to the duty of loyalty has become almost a legal fashion in the Nordic countries during the last decades. See for example Lando and others (n 35) 82, 181.

80 This important distinction between loyalty towards your contract partner and the loyalty towards the contract itself is emphasised by Tuomas Lehtinen, *Kansainvälisen kaupan liikesopimus ja remburssi* (*Business Contract in International Trade and Letter of Credit*) (Vammala, SLY 2006) 81.

81 Momberg Uriber (n 16) 242.

82 Smart rationality was recognized when making empirical research on how single mothers could survive in the slums of New Delhi. The presupposition was that poor people cannot be rational because of the constant urgent needs. The outcome of the research was quite the contrary. These women were fully capable of rational decision making but they also possessed an extra capacity to quickly – and rationally! – adapt to changes in the environment. Inspiration for the studies was Amartya Sen, 'Rationality and Social Choice' (1995) 85 *The American Economic Review* 1–24.

the old normality, and focus should be on the immediate consequences that can be known, instead of trying to calculate the distant future. Non-flexible contracts create in unforeseeable emergency situations random outcomes because the parties could not have taken into account such situations in their risk calculations when the contract was made. Norms should be adapted to the changing reality and not vice versa.

Creativity principles as legal principles support 'out of the box' measures. Instead of simply minimizing losses, the legal framework for Black Swan events should support efforts, even unsuccessful ones, to create new business models. If restaurants cannot serve at their location, they perhaps can make business by take-away services. If holiday resorts cannot receive physical tourists, then perhaps virtual travel is an option. The COVID-19 pandemic has shown the possibilities of carrying out activities normally done by physical presence over the internet.[83] Similarly, as you can transform an indirect loss to a direct one by taking action to mitigate, you are allowed according to these creativity principles to modify your business outside the normal business scope.

There are two important characteristics of the Black Swan doctrine/contract as it has been composed here. First, the doctrine aims at activating the contract partners and other stakeholders to go forward instead of giving them incentives to go back and stick to the original contractual document. It is important to know what to do now in co-operation with your business partner instead of asking how the original contract should be applied. The Black Swan doctrine's perspective and holding point is the future not the past. This is of course to rely profoundly on human experience of Black Swans and common sense. Secondly, there is no sense in blaming somebody for the occurrence of the Black Swan event – even if some Black Swans have their origin in human interaction and human societies. Notwithstanding that, the time should not be wasted in looking for guilt.

Legal tools of *force majeure*, and essentially also those of changed circumstances, work by offering final legal outcomes because the law's role is expected to be expanded to solve the conflicts. But there is no permanent or static way to solve Black Swan situations by rules given before the event. Therefore, the tools offered by the Black Swan doctrine/contract are really only tools enabling the commercial actors to work out the outcomes for themselves. Law deals the cards but does not play the game. Law is more oriented to supporting the management of crisis than giving final solutions.[84]

---

83 For example, the Finnish government has repeatedly given a recommendation to arrange possibilities for remote working. Government Communications Department (n 6).

84 This conclusion is a bricolage of various tendencies. Among them the move from traditional governance to collaborative governance, the move from pure private ordering to sustainable and responsible self-regulation, the move from legal rules as direct norms of behaviour to norms accommodating and facilitating activity, and the move from the dominance of Western legal cultures to more balanced basis of legal traditions in the world.

Concluding thoughts

Pandemics like the one caused by COVID-19 call for measures enabling business partners to deal with the situation. These measures have been, and are stemming, from two separate legal intellectual sources: *force majeure* and changed circumstances (*clausula rebus sic stantibus*). But *rigor commercialis* and strict *pacta sunt servanda* seem to take a strong systematic grip as the main rule. A more frequent review of business contracts because of COVID-19 pandemic does not receive much support among contract lawyers, even if it is widely admitted that the COVID-19 situation is unexpected and causes many businesses unbearable losses. Variations between different legal cultures are smaller than expected, and even in Europe and China, at least in theory, legal reliefs by *force majeure* and changed circumstances are seen only very exceptionally as having significant roles.

This mainstream contract law attitude almost seems to be contrary to the measures taken by states. States worldwide consider COVID-19 as an emergency situation requiring extraordinary measures. Moreover, individuals are sharing the burden of limitations to their normal lives. However, in business, gains and losses caused by COVID-19 are allowed to fall randomly. Law, including contract law, seems neither to offer any effective tools, nor an attitude to change this randomness. Business as a whole is benefitting from globalisation, and globalisation is the key reason why COVID-19 pandemic causes the losses. Even a basic sense of justice seems to require that losses to businesses are shared by the whole business community, and in accordance with some non-random criteria.

What is needed is a change in contract law attitude towards a more balanced outcome when weighing between strict adherence to contract and flexibility in special situations. *Pacta sunt servanda* does not need to become formalism, and changed circumstances can be more strongly taken into account by emphasizing the contractual bond between the parties. To adapt the contract to changed circumstances is in many cases in an overall evaluation that is both less expensive and more effective than strict adherence to the original contract.

Lastly, there also some lessons of COVID-19 for the general ideas concerning contracts as a means of self-determination. Patrick Selim Atiyah analysed in "The Rise and Fall of Freedom of Contract" the economic, social and cultural background of the development of contractual private autonomy in 18th and 19th Century England.[85] One key finding was that in its early period contractual freedom was internally related to the concept of a gentleman. However, the defects of unlimited contractual freedom became obvious when this bond was broken, and the notion "gentlemen's agreement" became a curiosity with no legal significance.[86] The fall of freedom of contract was caused by the social defects of the time. After the fall, around the middle of the 20th Century, freedom of

85 Patrick Selim Atiyah, *The Rise and Fall of Freedom of Contract* (Oxford, OUP 1979).
86 ibid 412.

contract has risen again especially backed by the principle of self-determination.[87] The author believes that now is the time to again emphasise the defects of unlimited freedom of contract. But, instead of longing back to ideas like the gentleman, we should find internal routes for the influence of social and cultural values in contract practices. The Black Swan doctrine/contract is designed to be one such path by widening the scope of proactive measures matching the need to survive and learn to cope with these new kinds of crises.

Bibliography

Atiyah PS, *The Rise and Fall of Freedom of Contract* (Oxford, OUP 1979).

Berger KP and Behn D, 'Force Majeure and Hardship in the Age of Corona: A Historical and Comparative Study' (2019–2020) 6 *McGill Journal of Dispute Resolution* 78.

Boylan BM and others, 'US – China Relations: Nationalism, the Trade War, and COVID-19' (2021)14 *Fudan Journal of the Humanities and Social Sciences* 23–40 <https://doi.org/10.1007/s40647-020-00302-6> accessed 19 May 2021.

Calliess GP and others, 'Law, the State, and Private Ordering: Evolutionary Explanations of Institutional Change' (2008)9 *German Law Journal* 397–410.

Ciurtin H, 'A Hermeneutical Perspective Upon the "Mitigation of Damages" Principle: The Metamorphosis of a Concept in International Law' (2015)6 *Transnational Dispute Management* 1–19.

Cordero-Moss G, 'Limits to Party Autonomy in International Commercial Arbitration' (2014)1 *Oslo Law* Review 47–66.

Franciosi LM, 'The Effects of COVID-19 on International Contracts: A Comparative View' (2020)51 *Victoria University of Wellington Law Review* 413–38.

Garro AM, 'Exemption of Liability for Damages under Article 79 of the CISG', CISG-AC Opinion No 7 on Article 79 of the CISG (2007) at para 37.

Gordley, J, *The Philosophical Origins of Modern Contract Law* (Oxford, OUP 1991).

Government Communications Department, 'Government Updates Policies on Border Issues, Remote Working and Recommendations for Persons Over 70 Years of Age' (*Finish Government*, 23 June 2020) <https://valtioneuvosto.fi/en/-/10616/government-updates-policies-on-border-issues-remote-working-and-recommendations-for-persons-over-70-years-of-age> accessed 19 May 2021.

Hart O and Moore J, 'Incomplete Contracts and Renegotiation' (1988) 56 *Econometrica* 755–85.

Hutchison A, 'Relational Theory, Context and Commercial Common Sense: Views on Contract Interpretation and Adjudication' (2017) 134 *South African Law Journal* 296–326.

Jennejohn M, Nyarko J and Talley EL, 'COVID-19 as a Force Majeure in Corporate Transactions' in Pistor K (ed), *Law in the Time of COVID-19* (New York, Columbia Law School 2020) 141 <https://scholarship.law.columbia.edu/faculty_scholarship/2645> accessed 19 May 2021.

---

87 See for example Gralf-Peter Calliess and others, 'Law, the State, and Private Ordering: Evolutionary Explanations of Institutional Change' (2008)9 *German Law Journal* 397.

Karhu J, 'Review of Business Contracts/Finland' in Wais H and Pfeiffer T (eds), *Judicial Review of B2B Contracts* (Oxford, in Print by Hart Publishing 2021) 85–106.

Katsivela M, 'Contracts: Force Majeure Concept or Force Majeure Clauses?' (2007)12 *Uniform Law Review* 101–19.

Konarski H, 'Force Majeure and Hardship Clauses in International Contractual Practice' (2003) 4 *International Business Law Journal* 405–28.

Lando O and others (eds), *Restatement of Nordic Contract Law* (Copenhagen, Djof Publishing 2016).

Lehtinen T, *Kansainvälisen kaupan liikesopimus ja remburssi (Business Contract in International Trade and Letter of Credit)* (Vammala, SLY 2006).

Lifshitz S and Finkelstein E, 'A Hermeneutic Perspective on Interpretation of Contracts' (2017)54 *American Business Law Journal* 519–79.

Liu Q, 'COVID-19 in Civil or Commercial Disputes: First Responses from Chinese Courts' (2020) 8 *The Chinese Journal of Comparative Law* 485–501 <https://academic.oup.com/cjcl/article/8/2/485/5899311> accessed 8 June 2021.

Momberg Uriber R, 'Change of Circumstances in International Instruments of Contract Law: The Approach of the CISG, PICC, PECL, and DCFR' (2011)15(2) *European Review of Private Law* 233–66.

Perrone A, 'The Just Price Doctrine and Contemporary Contract Law: Some Introductory Remarks' (2013)3 *Orizzonti del diritto commerciale* 1–16.

Pichonnaz P, 'From *clausula rebus sic stantibus* to Hardship: Aspects of the Evolution of the Judge's Role' (2011)17(1) *Fundamina* 125–43 <https://hdl.handle.net/10520/EJC34434> accessed 19 May 2021.

Pöyhönen J, *Sopimusoikeuden järjestelmä ja sopimusten sovittelu (The System of Contract Law and the Adjustment of Contracts)* (Vammala, SLY 1988).

Prütting J, '*Wegfall der Geschäftsgrundlage als Antwort des Zivilrechts auf krisenbedingte Vertragsstörungen (Wegfall der Geschäftsgrundlage* as a Private Law Answer to Contractual Commitments Effected by Crises)' (2020) 47–72 <www.nomos-elibrary.de/10.5771/9783748909279-47/wegfall-der-geschaeftsgrundlage-als-antwort-des-zivilrechts-auf-krisenbedingte-vertragstoerungen-systemerwaegungen-zu-313-bgb-und-sachgerechter-einsatz-in-der-praxis> accessed 10 June 2021.

Sen A, 'Rationality and Social Choice' (1995)85 *The American Economic Review* 1–24.

Solarte Vasquez M, *Smart Contracting for the Proactive Governance of Digital Exchange* (Tallinn, Tallinn University of Technology 2019).

Taleb N, *The Black Swan: The Impact of the Highly Improbable* (2nd edn, New York, Random House Trade 2010).

Taleb N, *Antifragile: Things That Gain from Disorder* (New York, Random House Trade 2014).

Taxell L, *Avtal och rättsskydd (Contract and Protection Under the Law)* (Turku, Åbo Akademi 1972).

Thaler T and Hartmann T 'Justice and Flood Risk Management: Reflecting on Different Approaches to Distribute and Allocate Flood Risk Management in Europe' (2016)83 *Natural Hazards* 129–47 <https://doi.org/10.1007/s11069-016-2305-1> accessed 19 May 2021.

Twigg-Flesner C 'A Comparative Perspective on Commercial Contracts and the Impact of Covid-19 – Change of Circumstances, Force Majeure, or What?' in Pistor K (ed), *Law in the Time of COVID-19* (New York, Columbia Law School 2020)

155–65. <https://scholarship.law.columbia.edu/cgi/viewcontent.cgi?article=123 9&context=books> accessed 19 May 2021.

Vasquez CSM, *Smart Contracting for the Proactive Governance of Digital Exchange* (Tallinn, Tallinn University of Technology 2019).

Westbrook R, 'The Origin of *laesio enormis*' (2008)55 *Revue internationale des droits de l'antiquité RIDA* 39–52.

Windscheid B, *Die Lehre des Römischen Rechts von der Voraussetzung* (*The Doctrine of Assumption in Roman Law*) (Düsseldorf, Buddeus 1850).

Zimmermann R, *The Law of Obligations: The Roman Foundation of the Civilian Tradition* (Oxford, OUP 1996).

6 Mediation as a key conflict resolution system to address the increase in litigation as a result of COVID-19

Geraldine Bethencourt Rodríguez

Introduction

Since the early nineties alternative dispute resolution methods have been seen as the most appropriate way of resolving certain disputes in the European Union, both by facilitating a more satisfactory resolution and by preventing the excessive judicialisation that has led to the collapse of the court system.[1] Despite the state of the justice system and the merits of alternative dispute resolution systems, the reality before COVID-19 was that insufficient progress had been made and that these mechanisms had not been consolidated to the extent that was expected and desired. Thus, with regard to mediation, Fernández rightly states that it has not ended up permeating legal practice, despite the efforts made by many professional groups to adapt and raise its awareness.[2]

The serious situation in which the courts found themselves was exacerbated by the pandemic, and an intense debate began on the need to invest in and promote these alternative dispute resolution mechanisms. The need for a rapid response to many legal conflicts was not a one-off issue in 2020, as the COVID-19 pandemic will lead to an economic crisis that will result, as it did in 2008, in a large number of legal conflicts in all areas. The cost of dealing with such conflicts through the courts, especially in a context of economic crisis, is well-known to all. It is in this context that mediation needs to be established as an alternative method of conflict resolution; as a procedure that allows the best solution to be reached, always

---

1 Carolina Macho Gómez, 'Origin and Evolution of Mediation: The Birth of the "ADR Movement" in the United States and Its Expansion to Europe' (2014) *LXVII Civil Law Yearbook* 931–96; Carlo Pilia, *Aspects of Mediation in the European Level* (Madrid, Reus 2019) 15–79. See also Gema Vallejo Pérez, *Alternative Methods of Conflict Resolution in Roman Law: Special Reference to Mediation* (Madrid, Dykinson 2018) 21.

2 Along these lines, Fernández argues that confusion persists between the different conflict management systems. And there is distrust towards the mediation process when the results do not correspond to the expectations, conditioned by the idea, sometimes erroneous, of what mediation really is V Rosalía Fernández, 'Mediation can be a very timely response to the increase in litigation after the Covid' (*General Council of Spanish Lawyers*, 16 June 2020) <www.abogacia.es/actualidad/entrevistas/10-preguntas-a/rosalia-fernandez-alayamagistrada-de-la-audiencia-provincial-de-las-palmas-y-presidenta-de-gemme-la-mediacion-puede-ser-una-respuesta-muy-oportuna-al-aumento-de-litigiosidad-tras-el-covid/> accessed 20 May 2021.

DOI: 10.4324/9781003176848-9

taking into account the interests of the parties, and moving disputes more quickly and economically than through the traditional courts.

Thus, with the increase in conflicts and, consequently in court proceedings as a result of the pandemic, mediation may be an appropriate response in a number of cases. The desired scenario is for the parties to understand that mediation is the best solution for resolving their disputes and, therefore, for them to go voluntarily to extrajudicial mediation and not wait for a referral to occur.

Taking as a premise the desirable scenario for conflict resolution, the aim of this chapter is first to analyse the current situation of the activity of judicial bodies in order to explain and highlight the need for more flexible methods of conflict resolution. Secondly, it will analyse mediation as a voluntary dispute resolution procedure with multiple advantages, particularly useful in the current context of conflict resolution.

Judicial activity of the Spanish judicial bodies: evolution and future perspectives

Knowing the data of the judicial activity of the Spanish judicial bodies is essential in order to understand, on the one hand, the situation that existed before the pandemic, and, on the other hand, the impact of COVID-19 on conflict resolution. The ultimate objective is to demonstrate the need to promote alternative dispute resolution mechanisms.

The trend in the number of cases brought before the courts

In Spain, the litigation rate (number of cases filed per 1,000 inhabitants) has been historically high. In 2019, the number of new cases registered with Spanish judicial bodies was 6,279,302, which is 4.8% more than in 2018. At the national level, the litigation rate during the 2019 financial year was 133.5 cases per 1,000 inhabitants.[3]

The increase in litigation has not occurred in any particular jurisdiction; all jurisdictions have experienced an increase in the number of new cases. However, the civil and social courts have seen the greatest increase. According to data published by the General Council of the Judiciary, the number of cases filed in 2019 by jurisdiction were as follows: in the Civil Court, 2,384,147 new cases were registered, representing an increase of 7% compared to 2018; in the Social Jurisdiction 432,489 new cases were registered, which represents an increase of 6.5% compared to 2018; 3,213,114 new cases were registered in the criminal jurisdiction, representing an increase of 1.9% compared to 2018, and 249,367 new cases were registered in the Administrative Court, representing an increase of 19.7% compared to 2018.[4]

---

3   General Council of the Judiciary, 'Activity of Judicial Bodies' (*Judicial Statistics, Affairs Series*) <www.poderjudicial.es/cgpj/es/Temas/Estadistica-Judicial/Estadistica-por-temas/Actividad-de-los-organos-judiciales/Juzgados-y-Tribunales/Series-estadisticas-de-actividad-de-los-organos> accessed 2 April 2021.

4   ibid.

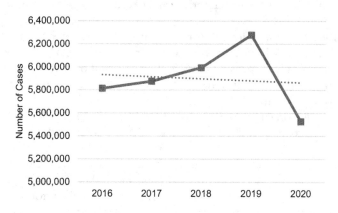

Figure 6.1 The trend in the number of cases brought before the courts

Source: Authors' own compilation based on data from the General Council of the Judiciary.

The year 2020 was marked by the pandemic, and data published in March 2021 by the General Council of the Judiciary shows the consequences that the confinement and suspension of judicial activity resulting from the health crisis had on the functioning of the courts and tribunals during that year. Thus, during 2020, a total of 5,526,754 cases were registered in Spanish courts, a figure that shows a decrease of 12% compared to 2019 and shows the impact of COVID-19 on the number of cases brought before the courts. Compared to previous years, the 2020 data reverses the trend that was experienced; for example, in 2019 compared to 2018. As previously stated, the number of cases received by judicial bodies throughout Spain rose by 4.8% in 2019 compared to 2018.[5]

By jurisdiction, the activity of judicial bodies in Spain during the whole of 2020 yielded the following data: in the Civil Court, 2,212,084 new cases were registered, representing a decrease of 7.3% compared to 2019; in the Social Jurisdiction there were 400,056 new cases, which represents a decrease of 7.5% compared to 2019; 2,720,219 new cases were registered in the criminal jurisdiction, which represents a decrease of 15.3% compared to 2019. 194,223 new cases were registered in the Litigation and Administrative Jurisdiction, which represents a decrease of 22.1% compared to 2019.[6]

Figure 6.1 shows the number of cases that have registered judicial bodies in recent years. The change in trend in 2020 is very evident. The new cases registered in 2020 was notably lower than in previous years. However, this variation

5   General Council of the Judiciary, 'The Entry of Cases in the Judicial Bodies in 2020 Suffered the Consequences of the Health Crisis and Fell by 12% Throughout Spain' (*Communication Judiciary*) <www.poderjudicial.es/cgpj/es/Poder-Judicial/En-Portada/El-ingreso-de-asuntos-en-los-organos-judiciales-en-2020-sufrio-las-consecuencias-de-la-crisis-sanitaria-y-descendio-un-12-por-ciento-en-toda-Espana> accessed 2 April 2021.
6   ibid.

does not represent a change in trend as can be seen in the graph (the line discontinuous represents the trend).[7]

Therefore, the figures for 2020 reverse the trend that existed in 2019, and these figures cannot be read in isolation. In reality this change in trend is due to the impact of the suspension of judicial activity, and once the judicial activity was reactivated, the number of new cases was very high as was the impact of the conflict arising from the health crisis.

Finally, it is important to note that even before the pandemic Spain was classified as a very litigious country; and the situation in which the courts find themselves today reflects this reality. In this regard, it should be noted that the increase in the litigation rate is linked to a number of factors that influence the task of dealing with a scenario such as the pandemic. According to Mora-Sanguinetti, these factors can be divided into two categories. On the one hand, "internal" factors of the actors acting in the judicial system, such as the system of incentives available to lawyers. On the other hand, "external" factors relating to general characteristics of the country's economy or to cultural features common to all actors. The latter includes, for example, the fact that the number of disputes brought before the courts in a country is a result of the frequency of conflicts between citizens and companies of the country. This in turn is a function of the volume and complexity of transactions in the economy, the quality of social relations, and/or the efficiency and integrity of the Public Administration.[8] These factors will now be analysed to determine the impact of the pandemic on the litigation rate.

Developments in the congestion of judicial bodies and the length of court proceedings

The congestion rate of judicial bodies in Spain (a ratio where the numerator is the sum of the cases pending at the beginning of the period and those registered during that period, and where the denominator is the cases settled during that period) has increased in the last five years, and many feel that measures need to be taken to prevent judicial collapse. In 2018, Lesmes, president of the Supreme Court and of the General Council of the Judiciary, stated that more than 60% of the courts were clearly overloaded and if this situation were prolonged over time, this could have the consequence that the justice system is weakened.[9] In this sense, as Barona Vilar points out, the pre-coronavirus justice model is not prepared to 'respond in an agile, flexible, fast, accessible and economically adequate way to all people in post-coronavirus society.'[10]

7   Source: Authors' own compilation based on data from the General Council of the Judiciary.
8   Juan S Mora-Sanguinetti, 'The Functioning of the Judicial System: New Comparative Evidence' (2013)11 *Economic Bulletin – Bank of Spain* 66.
9   General Council of Spanish Lawyers, 'The President of the CGPJ Urges a Major Organizational Reform of the Justice Before the Collapse of Many Judicial Bodies' (*General Council of Spanish Lawyers*, 20 June 2018) <www.abogacia.es/actualidad/noticias/el-presidente-del-cgpj-urge-una-gran-reforma-organizativa-de-la-justicia-ante-la-situacion-de-colapso-de-muchos-organos-judiciales/> accessed 2 April 2021.
10   Silvia Barona Vilar, 'Post-coronavirus Civil Justice, from the Crisis to Some of the Reforms EUnvisaged' (2020)12 *Iberoamerican Legal Current Journal* 777.

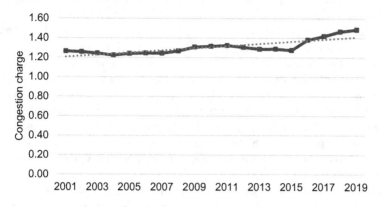

Figure 6.2 Congestion rate of judicial bodies in Spain

Source: Authors' own compilation based on data from the General Council of the Judiciary.

According to data published by the General Council of the Judiciary, in 2019 the number of cases decided by the courts and tribunals increased by 5.1%, to 6,079,137. At the end of the year, a total of 2,835,149 cases were pending, representing an increase of 8.6% over the previous year.[11] The impact of COVID-19 was also reflected in the congestion rate, as the number of cases resolved by the courts in 2020 was 5,224,742, representing a decrease of 14.1% compared to 2019. In addition, 3,156,877 cases were processed, representing an increase of 11.3% compared to 2019.[12]

The activity of the judiciary closed in 2020 with the following figures: In the Civil Court, 2,040,640 cases were resolved, 9.2% less than in 2019. However, 1,736,425 were processed, 10.9% more than at the end of the previous year. In the Social Court, 335,499 cases were settled, a 15 % drop compared to the previous year, and 376,335 cases were pending, an 18.3% increase compared to the end of the previous year. The Administrative Court resolved 191,948 new cases, 15.3% less than in 2019, and those that remained pending at the end of the year amounted to 215,973 cases, 2.1% compared to the end of the previous year. In the criminal courts, 2,656,519 cases were resolved, a 17.3% drop. However, 828,030 cases remained pending, 11.7% more than at the end of the previous year.[13]

This data, as well as their historical evolution, shows the great problems we face with regard to the effectiveness of the resolution of disputes in the judicial system; and the pandemic has made the situation worse. Figure 6.2 shows the congestion rate of judicial bodies in Spain,[14] which illustrate the development of the congestion rate since 2001. Although there have been years when the rate

11 General Council of the Judiciary (n 3).
12 General Council of the Judiciary (n 5).
13 ibid.
14 Source: Authors' own compilation based on data from the General Council of the Judiciary.

appeared to be decreasing, the upward trend in the statistical data (discontinuous line) is worrying.

The current congestion of the courts, as well as its possible gradual increase, has a significant impact on the length of court proceedings and thus on the effectiveness of the ordinary courts in resolving disputes. In this respect, the estimate of the average length of court proceedings is high.[15] By way of example, according to data published by the General Council of the Judiciary in 2019, proceedings in the first instance civil courts in Spain lasted about 7.4 months, and in the commercial courts the duration was 12.2 months. Excessive length of court proceedings also occurs at higher levels. In the Provincial Hearings, the average length of civil cases was 8.9 months, and in the Supreme Court it lasted up to 14.8 months.[16]

Figure 6.3 shows the congestion rate and the average estimated length of court proceedings.[17] It shows that in the years when the congestion rate has decreased, the average estimate of the length of court proceedings has also decreased.

These figures, together with the litigation rate, reflect a reality which poses a major challenge, on the one hand, to reduce congestion and length of court proceedings and, on the other hand, to reduce litigation. This challenge must be faced from the conviction that a change in the justice system is both important and necessary. Thus, is not only a question of figures that impact on the effectiveness of the system, but also of the unsatisfactory results achieved through it.

COVID-19 has reinforced the view that it is desirable to promote dialogue between the parties in conflict and to focus on an effective, efficient, and sustainable justice system. In this sense, it is necessary to promote a paradigm shift in the way any conflict is faced, and to determine the most effective way to resolve it. This is because the judicial process is 'the implementation of the respective roles of the parties' counsel and the judge, rather than the scenario in which the protagonists of the conflict play the main role'.[18] Thus, as Arastey Sahún points out,

---

15   The Explanatory Memorandum of the Act 5/2012, of 6th July, on Mediation in Civil and Commercial Matters, begins by stating that 'One of the essential functions of the Rule of Law is to secure effective judicial remedy of citizens' rights. That function implies the challenge of implementing a quality justice able to resolve the diverse conflicts that arise in a modern and, at the same time, complex society.' The current congestion rate of the courts limits the effectiveness of the ordinary courts in resolving disputes. In this context, mediation has gradually taken on a growing importance as a complementary instrument. Its ability to provide practical, effective, economical solutions to certain conflicts between the parties must be emphasised and as that this makes it an alternative to judicial o of administration of Justice. Cf Spanish Constitution of 1978, s 24.

16   General Council of the Judiciary, 'Estimation of the Average Duration of Judicial Proceedings' (*Transparency Portal*) <www.poderjudicial.es/portal/site/cgpj/menuitem.87fc234e64fd592b3305d5a7dc432ea0/?vgnextoid=4980cbcce569f510VgnVCM1000006f48ac0aRCRD&vgnextlocale=en&vgnextfmt=default&lang_choosen=en> accessed 2 April 2021.

17   Source: Authors' own compilation based on data from the General Council of the Judiciary.

18   ML Arastey Sahún, 'Mediation: A Paradigm Shift Necessary for the Improvement of the Relationship from the Individual Point of View' (2020)11 *Galician Journal of Social Law* 9.

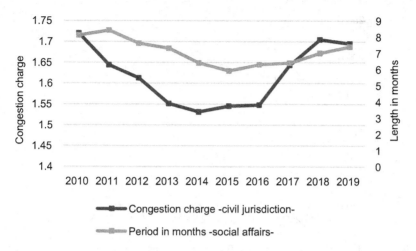

Figure 6.3 Congestion rate and average estimated length of court proceedings
Source: Authors' own compilation based on data from the General Council of the Judiciary.

judicial proceedings constitute the farthest scenario from the culture of dialogue, because in trials people do not listen in order to understand the conflict; they only act on the basis of a strategy designed to win and make the other side lose. The reality is, therefore, that judicial decision that resolve the conflict will meet the needs of the parties. Litigation transforms the conflict into a procedural reality that further separates the parties, causing relations to be broken and, therefore, the protagonists of the conflict to become irreconcilable. In this sense, as Ortuño Muñoz points out, 'the judges themselves know that their sentences rarely truly resolve conflicts'.[19] Thus:

> the emergence of ADRs implies a new paradigm of shaping the interrelation-ships of the parties to a contract and, consequently, an opening up of the concept of the content of judicial protection. The broadening of the scope of this fundamental right requires the incorporation of methods of dispute resolution in which the parties themselves can find the formula best suited to their interests.[20]

Thus, it is necessary to give back to the parties the responsibility of resolving their own conflict because it belongs to them, and they must be the protagonists in resolving it.

19   Pascual Ortuño Muñoz, *Justice Without Judges* (1st edn, Barcelona, Ariel 2018) 88.
20   Arastey Sahún (n 18) 12.

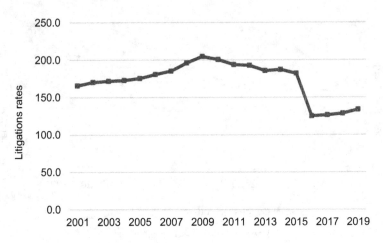

Figure 6.4 Litigation rate in Spain | Total jurisdictions

Source: Authors' own compilation based on data from the General Council of the Judiciary.

The impact of COVID-19 on the resolution of disputes through the ordinary courts

The extraordinary situation that has arisen as a result of the pandemic has given rise to numerous contractual breaches, resulting from the present impossibility to fulfil the obligations assumed previously under COVID-19, and therefore in a situation completely different from the one we are now facing. These breaches have increased the level of conflict, especially in the areas of work, business, family, neighbourhood, and real estate. This increase will impact on the litigation rate in 2021; since although this rate decreased in 2020 due to the suspension of judicial activity for a few months, the current scenario of COVID-19 will be reflected in the litigation rate if the option chosen to resolve disputes is to rely exclusively on the ordinary courts.

Figure 6.4 shows the evolution of the litigation rate in Spain from 2001 to 2019 (series available in the database of the General Council of the Judiciary).[21] From 2011 to 2018, there had been a decrease in the litigation rate. However, as noted earlier, 2019 represents an increase over the previous years.

Currently, the question that needs to be resolved is what impact COVID-19 will have on the litigation rate in 2021. As already mentioned, it is expected that this will increase due to the rise in conflicts due, among other reasons, to contractual breaches. The next step, however, is to determine whether this conflict will result in a proportionate increase in the litigation rate. To this end, it is appropriate to draw attention to the study carried out by Mora-Sanguinetti, and published

21   Source: Authors' own compilation based on data from the General Council of the Judiciary.

by the Bank of Spain, on the functioning of the judicial system in different countries of the Organisation for Economic Cooperation and Development (OECD). This study by the Directorate-General of the Research Service is based on an OECD project with the Bank of Spain and the Bank of Italy to obtain statistical information on this subject.[22] The study posits several factors that influence the litigation rate that each country has suffered and, therefore, allows us to both understand and anticipate the effect that the pandemic will have on litigation.[23]

Firstly, the sectoral composition of the economy influences the volume and complexity of economic transactions, this significantly affect litigation fees. In this respect, it is argued that a greater weight towards agriculture and services in relation to industry is linked to higher litigation rates. This relationship is explained by the fact that contracts in the service sector tend to be less complete than in the industrial sector, or that agricultural output is subject to a greater number of unforeseeable or contractually controlled circumstances, such as climatology, when compared with other sectors.[24] In this respect, if one considers that in Spain the share of GDP of the services sector is by far the most significant, and that this sector has been particularly affected by COVID-19, the result is an increase in the litigation rate.

Secondly, the cyclical position of the economy affects litigation fees. In periods of economic crisis, economic operators face complex situations that make it difficult to fulfil contracts. Therefore, if the pandemic is the source of a new economic crisis, litigation will increase as it did in the previous crisis, and it will not be a one-off problem for Spain. However, depending on the current state of the justice system in each country, the litigation rate in each legal system will be different.

Thirdly, litigation is influenced by the quantity and quality of the legislation. In Spain, regulatory output is high, and the complexity of the regulatory framework has increased. Thus, while before the 1978 Constitution the volume of "regulatory production" was less than 3,000 provisions per year, in 2018 this figure amounted to 11,737 (four times as many). Not only have there been changes in terms of "volume", but the structure and fragmentation of the regulatory framework have also been transformed.[25] Thus, the previously mentioned increase in regulation was almost entirely due to the development of the Autonomous State and with greater regulation at the local level. Autonomies account for 70% of all

---

22 V Giuliana Palumbo and others, 'The Economics of Civil Justice: New Cross-country Data and Empirics' (2013) *OECD Economics Department Working Papers* 1060 <https://doi.org/10.1787/5k41w04ds6kf-en> accessed 18 May 2021. See also Giuliana Palumbo and others, 'Judicial Performance and Its Determinants: A Cross-Country Perspective' (2013) *OECD Economic Policy Paper* 5 <www.oecd.org/economy/growth/FINAL%20Civil%20Justice%20Policy%20Paper.pdf> accessed 18 May 2021.
23 Mora-Sanguinetti (n 8) 66.
24 ibid 67.
25 Juan S Mora-Sanguinetti, 'The "Complexity" of Spanish Regulation. How to Measure It? What Economic Impact Does It Have?' (2019)907 *ICE: Journal of Economics* 152.

provisions, while the General Administration of the State approves 15%.[26] Mora-Sanguinetti points out that 'the volume of new regulations approved in Spain by both autonomous and local administrations is positively related to the number of civil and administrative disputes: the more regulation, the more litigation'.[27] Therefore, it is predictable that this factor will also influence litigation in Spain in the current scenario, the current pandemic and economic crisis.

Fourthly, litigation rates may also depend on the availability of alternative dispute resolution mechanisms. On this factor, Mora-Sanguinetti points out that there is no conclusive evidence on the impact of these mechanisms on litigation, because, among other reasons, these mechanisms are administered by private institutions for which no data is available.[28] However, if alternative mechanisms are to have a positive impact on the litigation rate by reducing it, the availability of such mechanisms must go hand in hand with a culture of collaborative conflict management. In this regard, it is essential for lawyers to inform clients of the various options available to reach a solution in each case.

This being the case, everything points to the fact that COVID-19 will have a major impact on the litigation rate and, as a result, there will be more congestion and more litigation. These factors allow us to analyse the situation in which each country finds itself and to be able to know what impact that COVID-19 will have on the litigation rate.

Mediation as alternative system of conflict resolution: the conflict as an opportunity to improve what is not working

Mediation has the ability to adapt to different expressions that conflicts have and allows them to be resolved in a way that better satisfies the interests of the parties. Mediation promotes a dialogue scenario, and this dialogue allows the parties to take advantage of this conflictive situation to assess everything that does not work well and seek formulas to improve the situation.

Approach

The classic ways of resolving disputes arising from contractual breaches are, on the one hand, the will of the parties expressed in an agreement they have reached themselves, and, on the other, through the intervention of the courts when an out-of-court settlement between the parties proves impossible. The first option is the most desirable yet the most complex, since when there is a conflict the ability to reach areas of understanding and generate agreements to resolve that conflict

26   ibid 153.
27   Juan S Mora-Sanguinetti, 'Normative Production, the Law Market and Litigation in Spain' (*Thomson Reuters*, 2019) <https://participa.gencat.cat/uploads/decidim/attachment/file/1543/_ES-dossier-produccion-normativa-espana.pdf> accessed 18 May 2021.
28   Mora-Sanguinetti (n 8) 67.

is significantly reduced. The second option corresponds to an adversarial (confrontational) model in which the decision on how to resolve this conflict rests with a third party; and the solution does not always fully meet the interests and needs of the parties.

Given that one of the essential functions of the rule of law is to ensure that citizens' rights are protected by the courts, the question arises as to whether a higher quality of justice can be achieved to effectively resolve the various conflicts that arise in modern society. In this sense, as Arastey Sahún rightly argues, it is a matter of considering on a case-by-case basis whether the claim for protection is actually satisfied. Consequently, it is necessary to consider whether the courts should continue to offer the only answer to adversarial proceedings, which result in a winner and a loser. Alternatively, it is necessary to change the focus and emphasise the search for conflict resolution from the perspective of the reality underlying the process and thus delve into the needs of the parties. In this sense, it is time to affirm that 'mediation is part of effective legal protection and of the right to access the process and obtain a quality response, while being as light as possible'.[29]

The General Council of the Judiciary in Spain maintains that mediation is justice and represents a new aspect of the right of access to justice. From his perspective, 'it is not a question of justice without judges, but a tool of judges at the service of justice.'[30] In this sense, mediation should be understood as 'a response that improves the quality of solutions and justice through the recognition of legal protection and the citizens' right of access to justice, as well as an instrument for citizen participation and involvement in justice'.[31]

Mediation can provide practical, effective and cost-effective solutions to certain conflicts between parties and thus constitutes an alternative to the judicial process. The resolution of disputes through mediation represents a change in the scheme, since in court proceedings it is not the parties who express themselves and try to reach an agreement, but rather the 'legal side of the real dispute', which in many cases does not address or respond to the real interests and needs of the parties.[32] For example, in mediation the relationship and emotions are worked.[33]

Thus, the need and desirability of promoting mediation before the pandemic was already a reality. In a situation such as the present, however, it is even more essential to provide a definitive impetus to out-of-court settlement of disputes and to ensure that ordinary jurisdiction is reserved as a last resort in cases where

29 Arastey Sahún (n 18)11.
30 General Council of the Judiciary, Statement of the General Council of the Judiciary on the European Mediation Day (*Judiciary*, 2021) <www.poderjudicial.es/cgpj/es/Poder-Judicial/En-Portada/Comunicado-del-CGPJ-en-el-Dia-Europeo-de-la-Mediacion> accessed 18 May 2021.
31 ibid.
32 Arastey Sahún (n 18) 12.
33 V William Wilmot and Joyce Hocker, *Interpersonal Conflict* (8th edn, New York, McGraw-Hill 2011) 71–99; Santiago Madrid Liras, *Motivational Mediation: Towards an Accompanying Relationship in Conflicts* (Madrid, Reus 2017) 153–71.

non-court settlement is impossible and not effective. To that end, however, it is vital that the vast number of parties to a conflict should see mediation as the most appropriate method of resolving their conflicts, and that the courts should no longer be the first option.

Mediation as a non-adversarial process: the current regulatory situation

Mediation is an alternative method of dispute resolution in which the parties voluntarily try to reach an agreement by themselves to end their dispute with the help of the mediator.[34] Mediation makes it possible to resolve conflicts without confrontation through an agreement compatible with mutual interests, renouncing individual victory with the alternative aim of reaching a collaborative solution in which victory is for both parties. Mediation as a self-composing system of conflict resolution is an effective tool for the resolution of disputes when the legal conflict affects subjective rights of an available nature.

In Spain, mediation is regulated by Law 5/2012 of 6 July on mediation in civil and commercial matters. This law transposes into Spanish law Directive 2008/52/EC of the European Parliament and of the Council of 21 May 2008 on certain aspects of mediation in civil and commercial matters. The preamble to the rule makes it clear that mediation, as an institution is designed to bring about legal peace, helps to conceive of the courts of justice in this area of the legal system being a last resort, unless it is not possible to resolve the situation by the mere will of the parties.

Before the declaration of emergency resulting from COVID-19, in March 2019 the plenary of the General Council of the Judiciary approved a report on the 'Preliminary Draft Law on Impetus to Mediation'.[35] This preliminary draft, presented before the pandemic, had been the subject of intense debate in order to determine whether it really contained everything required to provide a definitive impetus to mediation in Spain. However, in the past year, since the issuance of Royal Decree 463/2020 of 14 March declaring a state of alert for the management of

34   Silvia Barona Vilar, 'Non-Judicial or Procedural Means of Conflict Resolution: From Negotiation to Mediation' in Gómez Colomer JL and Barona Vilar S (eds), *Introduction to Procedural Law: Procedural Law I* (Madrid, Dykinson 2009) 345–64. See also Christopher Moore, *The Mediation Process: Practical Strategies for Resolving Conflict* (3rd edn, San Francisco, Jossey-Bass 2003) 43; Susan Blake and others, *A Practical Approach to Alternative Dispute Resolution* (2nd edn, Oxford, OUP 2012) 200.

35   The Council of Ministers, at the proposal of the Minister of Justice, approved on 11 January 2019 a Draft Law for the Promotion of Mediation. This regulation is intended to promote the definitive implementation of mediation, a complementary figure of the Administration of Justice for the extrajudicial resolution of conflicts in civil and commercial areas in a more agile way and with a lower economic and personal cost for the parties. Unfortunately, the Draft Law was not approved and in 2021 the debate centres on the Draft Law on Procedural Efficiency Measures which, among other conflict resolution mechanisms, includes mediation.

the health crisis caused by COVID-19 to date, there have been constant legislative changes and agreements on mediation by the Standing Committee of the General Council of the Judiciary. Thus, after the state of alarm, the first document of the so-called 'Shock Plan for the Administration of Justice after the State of Alarm' was published. Here it was expressly stated that it is necessary to take measures to promote the extrajudicial solution of conflicts and hence improve the judicial response to the difficulties arising from the COVID-19 health crisis.[36]

Further, during the state of alarm the Legal and Institutional Response to COVID-19, prepared by the General Council of the Spanish Bar, reference is made to mediation as 'an instrument to be applied appropriately in the current situation'. This was 'to promote the reduction of litigation in these times of alarm and to resolve possible conflicts that may arise' in order to 'build on relations between parties affected by this crisis, and to achieve practical, effective and cost-effective solutions'.[37]

At the end of 2020, the Council of Ministers approved the Draft Law on the Procedural Efficiency of the Public Justice Service, one of the main pillars of which is the Appropriate Means of Dispute Resolution (MASC). The Preliminary Project is part of the Justice 2030 Strategy, framed and linked to the Recovery, Transformation and Resilience Plan and the European Union's Next Generation Plan. In addition, it aims to respond to the challenges arising from the COVID-19 pandemic. In this regard, the Explanatory Memorandum of the Draft Law indicates that there is currently a 'conjunctural need to introduce efficient mechanisms that are essential to accommodate the foreseeable increase in litigation in the near future, and to regain the pulse of judicial activity upon the resumption of the procedural terms after the termination of the first state of alarm declared as a consequence of the COVID-19 pandemic. This is without prejudice to the reforms in the procedural laws that are introduced in this legal text as measures to streamline the procedures in the different jurisdictional orders, linked on some occasions to the correlative and necessary modifications in substantive laws.'

Following the approval of the preliminary draft, the Ministry of Justice opened the public consultation process to provide input into the draft law and to seek the views of citizens, organisations, and associations prior to the preparation of the draft law. In this regard, the European Judges Group for Mediation of Spain (GEMME Spain) believes that the Preliminary Draft Law represents an

---

36 General Council of the Judiciary, 'Shock Plan for the Administration of Justice after the State of Alarm, Block 2: Measures on Extrajudicial Conflict Resolution' (*General Council of the Judiciary*, 16 June 2020) <www.poderjudicial.es/cgpj/es/Poder-Judicial/En-Portada/El-Pleno-del-organo-de-gobierno-de-los-jueces-aprueba-el-plan-de-choque-del-CGPJ-para-la-reactivacion-tras-el-estado-de-alarma> accessed 18 May 2021.

37 General Council of Spanish Lawyers, 'Legal and Institutional Response to COVID-19, Block 7: Particular Analysis of Conflict Resolution Methods in this Situation National Arbitration – International Arbitration. Mediation' (*General Council of Spanish Lawyers*, 29 June 2020) <www.abogacia.es/wp-content/uploads/2020/03/2020-06-29-MANUAL-COVID19-ABOGADOS.pdf> accessed 18 May 2021.

important impetus. However, GEMME states that 'in order to achieve effective, efficient and sustainable justice, different methods of dispute resolution must be combined without confusing concepts and purpose. The text of the Preliminary Draft could be improved by clearly regulating intra-court/intra-court mediation'.[38]

In any event, as recognised by the General Council of the Judiciary, the development of appropriate means for the settlement of disputes is an unavoidable step towards modernizing and streamlining procedures and improving the quality of justice. However, no reform should be detrimental to the procedural guarantees of the parties to the conflict, nor should it undermine the quality of the judicial service, the right of access to justice and effective judicial protection.[39]

Finally, if mediation is to be consolidated as an alternative dispute resolution mechanism, it is not enough to publish a good law; it must also be accompanied by financial support.

The benefits of mediation

The acceptance and consolidation of mediation and other alternative dispute resolution systems in different legal systems is due to them offering a number of benefits both for the administration of justice and for the users of the justice system. That is why institutions, organisations and legal operators have tried to promote mediation in Spain.

The European Parliament and the Commission of the European Union have pointed out in various reports that there is a general lack of awareness and a weak and minimal culture, practice and use of mediation and the various means of dispute settlement within the member countries of the European Union. This is despite there being an implicit demand for quality legal instruments and institutions and for self-contained intra- or extra-judicial solutions.[40] In this context, the Parliament points out that under the 'Justice for Growth' programme and the Europe 2020 strategy, mediation could be seen as a means of increasing the efficiency of the justice system and reducing the obstacles that long and costly legal proceedings create for citizens and businesses; it can therefore contribute to economic growth.[41] Mediation can also help to

---

38 European Judges Group for Mediation (GEMME Spain), GEMME Spain Proposals <https://mediacionesjusticia.com/wp-content/uploads/2021/02/AportesGEMME. ALEP_.pdf> accessed 18 May 2021.

39 Cf Spanish Constitution of 1978, s 24, and European Convention on Human Rights, s 6.

40 Report from the Commission to the European Parliament, the Council and the European Economic and Social Committee on the application of Directive 2008/52, of August 26, 2016 and Resolution of the European Parliament of September 12, 2017 on the application of the Directive 2008/52.

41 Report on the implementation of Directive 2008/52/EC of the European Parliament and of the Council of 21 May 2008 on certain aspects of mediation in civil and commercial matters (2016/2066(INI)).

maintain good relations between the parties since, unlike court proceedings, there are no "winners" or "losers", which is particularly important, for example in family law matters.

The benefits of mediation are set out next and are applicable to the process regardless of the setting in which it takes place; for example, in the case at hand in both pandemic and post-pandemic times.

Mediation is applicable to all types of disputes

Many disputes can be channelled and resolved through mediation, civil mediation (e.g. civil liability claims, disputes between co-heirs and/or co-owners, insurance contracts, contracts for the sale of a home), commercial mediation (e.g. disputes between partners, disputes between companies and clients, disputes between companies and suppliers, disputes between companies and employees, disputes over intellectual property). It can also be used in family mediation (e.g. family disputes over inheritance, matrimonial disputes, disputes over parental rights and guardianship).

Mediation makes it possible to resolve disputes in less time than a court procedure

Mediation saves time, as the average duration of a mediation process is a few weeks, compared to much longer court time. The duration of the mediation procedure will depend on the nature, complexity and conflict of the issues under discussion.[42] For instance, Act 5/2012, of 6 July, on Mediation in Civil and Commercial Matters expressly states that the duration of the mediation procedure shall be as short as possible and that its proceedings shall be concentrated into the minimum number of sessions.[43] Thus, in view of the high level of court congestion, mediation represents a faster way of resolving disputes.

The first part of this chapter presented the latest data on the congestion rate for courts and the average estimated length of court proceedings. In this regard, it was stated that a greater number of disputes, representing a greater number of cases to be resolved, resulted in greater congestion of the judicial system, therefore prolonging the resolution periods. The difference between the time of resolution through the court procedure and the mediation process is very considerable. According to the comparative analysis carried out in the Report of the European Parliament on the implementation of mediation for civil and commercial matters of 2014, a dispute in Spain took an average of

---

42 Julia Ruiz-Rico Ruiz Morón, 'Family Mediation' in Guillermo Orozco Pardo and José Luis
     Monereo Pérez (eds), *Treaty of Mediation in Conflict Resolution* (Madrid, Tecnos 2015) 170.
43 Act 5/2012, of 6th July, on Mediation in Civil and Commercial Matters, s 20.

510 days to resolve at that time, while a mediation process lasted an average of 50 days.[44]

Although there is no up-to-date comparison, according to the latest data from the General Council of the Judiciary published between 2014 – the year of publication of the previously mentioned report – and 2019, the average estimate of the duration of court proceedings has not changed significantly and the duration of a mediation remains unchanged.[45] Therefore, the results highlighted in the European Parliament's report at the time continue to be a reality today. Predictably at this time, due to the crisis caused by the pandemic and the impact that this will have on the litigation rate, this increases the time difference between the two procedures.

Thus, while court proceedings often take months, even more than a year, the mediation process may take several weeks or a few months, depending on the complexity of the matter.

Mediation is less expensive than court proceedings

Mediation involves a reduction of costs, since as Murciano Álvarez points out:

> the legal process for most of the society presupposes that it must be accompanied by technical advice to be able to defend ourselves properly and that our rights are not diminished, this means that we had to go to a lawyer, often to a solicitor and in many other cases to experts. And all this is not free, a well-built defence by a good professional justifies price, and that multiplied by three. In addition, being accompanied by a good lawyer does not always guarantee winning, as it may be the case that the client insists and tries to defend the indefensible and ends up being ordered to pay costs. And, in any case, you have to keep in mind that there is always a loser.[46]

With respect to the lower cost of the process and the consequent savings of mediation, the European Parliament's report on the implementation of mediation in civil and commercial matters reveals that mediation reduces costs for both litigants and the administration. In this regard, the report points out that the average total cost of legal proceedings in Spain amounts to 8,015 euros, while

---

44   Giuseppe De Palo and others, '"Rebooting" the Mediation Directive: Assessing the Limited Impact of its Implementation and Proposing Measures to Increase the Number of Mediations in the EU' (2014) *European Parliament* 124.

45   General Council of the Judiciary, 'Estimation of the Average Duration of Judicial Proceedings' (*Transparency Portal*) <www.poderjudicial.es/portal/site/cgpj/menuitem.87fc234e 64fd592b3305d5a7dc432ea0/?vgnextoid=4980cbcce569f510VgnVCM1000006f48ac0a RCRD&vgnextlocale=en&vgnextfmt=default&lang_choosen=en> accessed 2 April 2021.

46   Gema Murciano Álvarez, 'Mediation Is Not "Mediation"' (*Sepin*, 21 January 2014) <https://blog.sepin.es/2014/01/mediacion-no-es-mediacion/> accessed 2 May 2021.

the average cost of a mediation process is 1,833 euros.[47] These figures include the average cost of a lawyer in court proceedings (5,918€) and in mediation proceedings (1,133€), as well as the cost of the court (2,097€) and the cost of the mediator (700€). The report states that there is an average cost saving of around 60% in favour of mediation.[48]

This data is from 2014 and can therefore only be taken as a guide. However, based on that data, as well as the assertion of authoritative voices on the subject, it can be asserted that mediation is less costly than court proceedings.

Mediation facilitates the generation of creative solutions that address the real interests and needs of the parties to the conflict

The mediation procedure is simple and flexible, as it is up to the parties involved in the mediation to determine their fundamental stages. In this respect, the rules merely lay down those essential requirements for the validity of the agreement that the parties may reach. In this sense, the preamble of Law 5/2012, of 6 July on mediation in civil and commercial matters, stresses flexibility as an incentive to favour the use of mediation. This is because it does not have an impact on subsequent procedural costs or allow its approach as a strategy to delay the fulfilment of the contractual obligations of the parties.

The aim is that each mediation is tailored to the circumstances of the particular case and to the parties involved. It is precisely in this respect that the principle of free disposal, with the help of the mediator, allows the parties to determine the best way to conduct the mediation.

The role of the mediator is fundamental because, thanks to the flexibility of mediation and the handling of tools by parties of the mediator, it is possible to reach agreements with creative solutions that truly respond to the needs of the parties. It is important to note that reaching an agreement is not mandatory, and that often mediation is simply aimed at improving relations, without the intention of reaching a concrete agreement.

Effective: the success rates of mediation

Mediation favours the creation of agreements that meet the interests of both parties. As agreements are the result of joint work during the mediation process, they are usually implemented voluntarily. This is for two reasons: firstly, because the parties have proposed the content of the agreement and have committed themselves to fulfilling it because they perceive that their needs are being met; and, secondly, because mediation helps to understand the conflict and the position of the other, thereby reducing the tension between the parties. There is also a greater willingness to collaborate because mediation helps to understand the

---

47   De Palo and others (n 44) 126.
48   ibid.

conflict and the position of the other. According to studies carried out by countries with a long tradition of mediation, such as the United States, 'the rate of
compliance with mediation agreements is higher than the rate of compliance with
court decisions, with a difference of 15%'.[49]

The following observations should be made about the outcome of the mediation process. Firstly, it is important to note that the goal of mediation does not
always have to be reaching an agreement, as mediation may simply be aimed
at improving relations without the intention of reaching a specific settlement.
Therefore, it is not correct to measure the success of a mediation solely by reference to whether or not an agreement is reached between the parties. In practice, it is possible to find scenarios where mediation leads to an understanding
between the parties and the parties feel able to agree privately on how to meet
each other's needs.

Secondly, the options for reaching agreements vary depending on whether the
mediation arises before litigation or after litigation begins. Thus, extrajudicial
mediation that takes place outside the judicial sphere has a very high success rate.
This success rate is due to the fact that the parties that have conflict have a better ability to reach an agreement before litigation begins, since the initiation of a
judicial proceeding generates mistrust in the other party and distances positions
regarding the conflict.

On the other hand, intrajudicial mediation, which takes place within the judicial sphere and is therefore carried out as a result of judicial referral, achieves a
lower success rate, according to data published by the General Council of the
Judiciary.[50] The difference between one assumption and another makes sense if
one takes into account that, on the one hand, in the first assumption, mediation
is voluntarily attended, and, therefore, a genuine interest in resolving the conflict
collaboratively is shown. On the other hand, in the second case, mediation is used
because the judge understands that this conflict is capable of being resolved in a
mediation procedure, and the parties attempt mediation after having initiated a
dispute before the courts.

Thirdly, it is important to note that practically everything that is done in mediation has legal consequences, and therefore the role of the lawyer is of great
significance.[51] However, it is important to bear in mind that in court proceedings,

---

49 Ramón Herrera de las Heras, 'Mandatory Mediation for Certain Civil and Commercial
    Matters' (2017)1 *InDret: Journal for the Analysis of Law* 10.
50 General Council of the Judiciary, 'Intrajudicial Mediation' (*Judicial Statistics*) <www.
    poderjudicial.es/cgpj/es/Temas/Estadistica-Judicial/Plan-Nacional-de-Estadistica-Judi-
    cial/Mediacion/Mediacion-Intrajudicial-> accessed 2 April 2021.
51 Arturo Almansa, 'Practically Everything That Is Done in Mediation Has Legal Conse-
    quences, and the Role of the Lawyer Has and Will Have a Great Importance' (*General
    Council of Spanish Lawyers*, 16 January 2021) <www.abogacia.es/ro/actualidad/noticias/
    arturo-almansa-practicamente-todo-lo-que-se-hace-en-mediacion-tiene-consecuencias-
    juridicas-y-el-papel-del-abogado-tiene-y-tendra-una-gran-transcendencia/> accessed 20
    May 2021.

the real interests of the parties are often not given weight, whereas in mediation, the search for those interests is fundamental and the search for solutions that satisfy both parties must not be limited to the options provided for by law. Thus, creativity in reaching effective agreements that meet the needs of the parties is very important and, to the extent that everything has legal implications, counsel is a key player in the mediation process; although this must be for the sake of the settlement and not for the win-win mentality of a dispute.

Reducing emotional costs and promoting the preservation of relationships

In addition to the economic cost, conflicts and their resolution through the ordinary courts also have an emotional cost. Conflicts have a negative impact on relationships, as getting what you want ("being right" and "winning") are confrontational and cause the relationship to deteriorate. In this regard, there is a clear consensus, especially in some types of conflict, that, it is very important to preserve the relationship and, therefore, a court resolution will never be a complete victory for either side.

As discussed previously, the mediator facilitates dialogue between the parties and helps them to understand that the conflict is not one-sided and that there are multiple perspectives. Further, an efficient approach to the conflict requires an understanding of the conflict in its entirety. The mediation process makes this approach to the conflict possible, and it is possible to go further. Thus, as Quintana states, in 'mediation we work with the conflict, the relationship, the emotions and those issues that are relevant to the mediators'.[52] Therefore, mediation not only favours the preservation of relations between the parties, but can also help them to overcome situations that may adversely affect them. Thus, as Ortuño Muñoz explains, mediation is a 'collaborative solution, external to the emotional and economic wear and tear that judicial processes involve',[53] and is alien to the antagonistic position of winner-loser.

Electronic and online mediation: an opportunity for resolving effective conflicts in pandemic times

Information and communication technologies are present in all areas and spheres of society. The justice system is not alien to this reality and its future depends inexorably on its digitalisation. This reality is already present in alternative dispute resolution

52 Amparo Quintana, 'Mediation Works with Conflict, Relationships, Emotions and Those Issues That are Relevant to the Media' (General Council of Spanish Lawyers, 18 January 2021) <https://www.abogacia.es/actualidad/noticias/amparo-quintana-en-mediacion-se-trabaja-con-el-conflicto-la-relacion-las-emociones-y-aquellas-cuestiones-que-resulten-relevantes-para-los-mediados/> accessed 20 May 2021.
53 Pascual Ortuño Muñoz, *Justice Without Judges* (1st edn, Barcelona, Ariel 2018) 88.

(Online Dispute Resolution – ODR) systems, including e-mediation. These essentially telematic solutions will be a reference point in post-COVID-19 justice.[54]

In a context of restrictions and limitations due to the crisis of COVID-19, the flexibility of mediation allows this procedure to be configured as one of the most effective for resolving conflicts at the present time. It is precisely this flexibility that allows the mediation process to be carried out online.[55] Recital 9 of Directive 2008/52/EC of the European Parliament and of the Council of 21 May 2008 on certain aspects of mediation in civil matters, states that it 'should not in any way prevent the use of new communications technologies in mediation proceedings.' The Act 5/2012, of 6 July, on Mediation in Civil and Commercial Matters, which transposes that Directive into the Spanish legal system, expressly states that all or some of the mediation proceedings, including the constitutive session and any subsequent proceedings deemed appropriate, may be carried out by electronic means. This includes videoconferencing or other similar means of transmission of voice or image, provided that the identity of the parties involved and respect for the principles of mediation provided for in the Act are guaranteed.[56] This system is also recommended for claims up to 600 euros.[57]

In April 2020, the British Institute of International Comparative Law produced a paper entitled *Breathing Space*, which addresses the effects of the pandemic on commercial contracts.[58] Among other issues, this document proposes as an alternative the use of mediation and negotiation through technological means to resolve conflicts arising from the COVID-19 crisis. Thus, ODR systems in general, and e-mediation in particular, are needed more than ever, and the present moment should be seen as an opportunity to push mediation, both face-to-face and online.

Finally, it should be mentioned that the pandemic has accelerated the development of technological tools and the advancement of technology, telecommunications and computing will, thus, be unstoppable. In this context, as Martín Diz points out, the combination of artificial forensic intelligence and out-of-court means of online dispute resolution has great potential for future development.[59]

---

54   Fernando Martín Diz, 'Post-covid19 Digital Justice: The Challenge of ODR Solutions and Artificial Intelligence' (2020) 2 *Journal of Legal and Criminological Studies* 62.

55   Esther Pérez Marcos, 'Alternative Methods of Conflict Resolution in Times of COVID-19: The Great Opportunity of Mediation' (ELDERECHO.COM, 5 May 2020) <https://elderecho.com/metodos-alternativos-de-resolucion-de-conflictos-en-tiempos-de-covid-19-la-gran-oportunidad-de-la-mediacion> accessed 15 May 2021.

56   Act 5/2012, of 6 July, on Mediation in Civil and Commercial Matters, s 24 (1).

57   ibid, s 24 (2).

58   Eva Lein, 'Concept Note 2 on the Effect of the 2020 Pandemic on Commercial Contracts' (*British Institute of International and Comparative Law*, 28 September 2020) <www.biicl.org/publications/concept-note-2-on-the-effect-of-the-2020-pandemic-on-commercial-contracts-september-2020-update?cookiesset=1&ts=1620309166> accessed 15 May 2021.

59   Fernando Martín Diz, 'Artificial Intelligence and ADR: Evolution in Arbitration and Mediation' (2020)2 *The Law: Mediation and Arbitration* 1.

Conclusion

The study and analysis carried out led to the following conclusions:

First, the modernisation and streamlining of procedures and improving the quality of justice require the promotion of alternative dispute resolution systems, including mediation. In this regard, a paradigm shift is required, since the best way to resolve a conflict is not in a "winner" and "loser" scenario. In a judicial process, even the "winner" is not entirely satisfied with the judgment, much less does the judgment take into account and serve the real interests of the parties.

Secondly, Spain is a highly litigious country with a limited culture of dialogue and collaborative conflict resolution. The figures before COVID-19 already showed the need to rethink the justice system to make it effective, efficient, and sustainable. Mediation should not be seen merely as a way of reducing the litigation rate, but as offering citizens the best option for resolving each dispute; since ordinary courts are not the most effective way of dealing with all types of disputes.

Furthermore, COVID-19 and the measures taken to deal with the health crisis resulted in the suspension of proceedings, hearings, and complaints for some months in 2020. Following the reactivation of the judiciary, the workload of the courts has increased significantly and, therefore, whilst before the pandemic there was already a high level of congestion and the average estimated length of court proceedings was correspondingly high, the current scenario is even more complex, and action is needed to address this situation. Moreover, mediation is an effective tool for responding to the increase in litigation resulting from COVID-19, as it facilitates the resolution of disputes in an expeditious, realistic and timely manner. In this sense, it is important to note that mediation has already been useful in responding to the conflicts that have arisen and has done so in a short space of time.

Further, mediation cannot be conceived as a one-off solution to the current growth of litigation that has arisen as a result of the pandemic. On the contrary, it is an opportune moment to give definitive impetus to mediation and to ensure that ordinary courts are the last resort in those cases where it is possible to resolve conflicts through mediation. In addition, E-mediation has gained importance at this time. The flexibility of mediation and the availability of technological tools makes it possible to resolve conflicts without the need for face-to-face presence, an issue of particular importance at the present time given the current constraints.

Finally, alternative conflict resolution systems, especially face-to-face mediation and online mediation, contribute to achieving an effective, efficient and sustainable justice system in any country. The culture of dialogue and collaborative conflict resolution is useful and beneficial for the parties, and positive for the legal system since it helps the parties to solve the real problems that arise in a conflict.

Bibliography

Almansa A, 'Practically Everything That Is Done in Mediation Has Legal Consequences, and the Role of the Lawyer Has and Will Have a Great Importance'
(*General Council of Spanish Lawyers*, 16 January 2021) <www.abogacia.es/ro/
actualidad/noticias/arturo-almansa-practicamente-todo-lo-que-se-hace-en-
mediacion-tiene-consecuencias-juridicas-y-el-papel-del-abogado-tiene-y-tendra-
una-gran-transcendencia/> accessed 20 May 2021.

Arastey Sahún ML, 'Mediation: A Paradigm Shift Necessary for the Improvement of
the Relationship from the Individual Point of View' (2020)11 *Galician Journal of
Social Law* 9.

Barona Vilar S, 'Non-Judicial or Procedural Means of Conflict Resolution: From
Negotiation to Mediation' in Gómez Colomer JL and Barona Vilar S (eds), *Introduction to Procedural Law: Procedural Law I* (Madrid, Dykinson 2009) 345–64.

Barona Vilar S, 'Post-Coronavirus Civil Justice, from the Crisis to Some of the
Reforms EUnvisaged' (2020)12 *Iberoamerican Legal Current Journal* 777.

Blake S and others, *A Practical Approach to Alternative Dispute Resolution* (2nd edn,
Oxford, OUP 2012).

De Palo G and others, ' "Rebooting" the Mediation Directive: Assessing the Limited
Impact of Its Implementation and Proposing Measures to Increase the Number of
Mediations in the EU' (2014) *European Parliament* 124.

Fernández R, 'Mediation Can Be a Very Timely Response to the Increase in Litigation
After the Covid' (*General Council of Spanish Lawyers*, 16 June 2020) <www.abogacia.
es/actualidad/entrevistas/10-preguntas-a/rosalia-fernandez-alayamagistrada-de-
la-audiencia-provincial-de-las-palmas-y-presidenta-de-gemme-la-mediacion-puede-
ser-una-respuesta-muy-oportuna-al-aumento-de-litigiosidad-tras-el-covid/>
accessed 20 May 2021.

Herrera de las Heras R, 'Mandatory Mediation for Certain Civil and Commercial
Matters' (2017)1 *InDret: Journal for the Analysis of Law* 10.

Lein E, 'Concept Note 2 on the Effect of the 2020 Pandemic on Commercial
Contracts' (*British Institute of International and Comparative Law*, 28 September 2020) <www.biicl.org/publications/concept-note-2-on-the-effect-of-the-
2020-pandemic-on-commercial-contracts-september-2020-update?cookiesset=1
&ts=1620309166> accessed 15 May 2021.

Macho Gómez C, 'Origin and Evolution of Mediation: The Birth of the "ADR Movement" in the United States and Its Expansion to Europe' (2014) *LXVII Civil Law
Yearbook* 931–96.

Madrid Liras S, *Motivational Mediation: Towards an Accompanying Relationship in
Conflicts* (Madrid, Reus 2017) 153–71.

Martín Diz F, 'Artificial Intelligence and ADR: Evolution in Arbitration and Mediation' (2020)2 *The Law: Mediation and Arbitration* 1.

Martín Diz F, 'Post-Covid19 Digital Justice: The Challenge of ODR Solutions and
Artificial Intelligence' (2020) 2 *Journal of Legal and Criminological Studies* 62.

Moore C, *The Mediation Process: Practical Strategies for Resolving Conflict* (3rd edn,
San Francisco, Jossey-Bass 2003).

Mora-Sanguinetti JS, 'The Functioning of the Judicial System: New Comparative
Evidence' (2013)11 *Economic Bulletin – Bank of Spain* 66.

Mora-Sanguinetti JS, 'The "Complexity" of Spanish Regulation. How to Measure It?
What Economic Impact Does It Have?' (2019) 907 *ICE: Journal of Economics* 152.

Mora-Sanguinetti JS, 'Normative Production, the Law Market and Litigation in Spain' (*Thomson Reuters*, 2019) <https://participa.gencat.cat/uploads/decidim/attachment/file/1543/_ES-dossier-produccion-normativa-espana.pdf> accessed 18 May 2021.

Murciano Álvarez G, 'Mediation Is Not "Mediation"' (*Sepin*, 21 January 2014) <https://blog.sepin.es/2014/01/mediacion-no-es-mediacion/> accessed 2 May 2021.

Ortuño Muñoz P, *Justice Without Judges* (1st edn, Barcelona, Ariel 2018).

Palumbo G and others, 'The Economics of Civil Justice: New Cross-Country Data and Empirics' (2013) *OECD Economics Department Working Papers* 1060 <https://doi.org/10.1787/5k41w04ds6kf-en> accessed 18 May 2021.

Palumbo G and others, 'Judicial Performance and Its Determinants: A Cross-Country Perspective' (2013) *OECD Economic Policy Paper* 5 <www.oecd.org/economy/growth/FINAL%20Civil%20Justice%20Policy%20Paper.pdf> accessed 18 May 2021.

Pérez Marcos E, 'Alternative Methods of Conflict Resolution in Times of COVID-19: The Great Opportunity of Mediation' (*Elderecho.com*, 5 May 2020) <https://elderecho.com/metodos-alternativos-de-resolucion-de-conflictos-en-tiempos-de-covid-19-la-gran-oportunidad-de-la-mediacion> accessed 15 May 2021.

Pilia C, *Aspects of Mediation in the European Level* (Madrid, Reus 2019).

Quintana A, 'Mediation Works with Conflict, Relationships, Emotions and Those Issues That Are Relevant to the Media' (*General Council of Spanish Lawyers*, 18 January 2021) <www.abogacia.es/actualidad/noticias/amparo-quintana-en-mediacion-se-trabaja-con-el-conflicto-la-relacion-las-emociones-y-aquellas-cuestiones-que-resulten-relevantes-para-los-mediados/> accessed 20 May 2021.

Ruiz-Rico Ruiz Morón J, 'Family Mediation' in Pardo GO and Monereo Pérez JL (eds), *Treaty of Mediation in Conflict Resolution* (Madrid, Tecnos 2015).

Vallejo Pérez G, *Alternative Methods of Conflict Resolution in Roman Law: Special Reference to Mediation* (Madrid, Dykinson 2018).

Wilmot W and Hocker J, *Interpersonal Conflict* (8th edn, New York, McGraw-Hill 2011).

Part III

Corporate governance and employment rights

7 Increased employees' engagement power at the time of crisis

Neshat Safari

Introduction

The outbreak of COVID-19 has put businesses all over the world under strain. While governments are trying to save companies from failure by implementing emergency measures, these measures will not prevent the long-term sever economic consequences of the pandemic for businesses. Therefore, the main responsibility for the survival of the company in this unprecedented time falls on the board of directors, who are responsible to make correct business decisions and take appropriate actions, often at speed and in response to rapidly-evolving circumstances. Corporate boards have faced a string of difficult tasks. They should navigate the COVID-19 crisis necessitates with careful consideration of a variety of issues. They should report to shareholders on how well the business is prepared to react to the pandemic challenges and what risk management strategies are in place for dealing with hardships that the business is confronted with. They should decide on payment or non-payment of dividends in light of the company's cash position and strategic plans. Also, they should deal with human resource issues, including redundancies, health and safety, corporate social responsibility and insolvency. In fact, the pandemic, more than any time, has heightened the importance of the role of the board of directors and the need for professional and ethical boardroom conduct. The reality is that boards are faced with a new set of complex challenges for which they have no precedent.[1] At the same time, they are exposed to increased demands and expectations from various groups of stakeholders and society. Therefore, the new environment has put directors' responsibility to the test: whether they can perform their duties adequately at the time the pandemic continues to impact businesses in various ways. The important question is what guarantees directors consider the interests of the company above all the other things? Who should monitor that they are well-versed and well

---

1 Saleh FA Khatib and Abdul Naser Ibrahim Nour, 'The Impact of Corporate Governance on Firm Performance During the COVID-19 Pandemic: Evidence from Malaysia' (2021)8(2) *Journal of Asian Finance Economics and Business* 943–52 <https://papers.ssrn.com/sol3/papers.cfm?abstract_id=3762393> accessed 5 May 2021.

DOI: 10.4324/9781003176848-11

trained in their obligations; whether are they transparent and have they engaged with all stakeholders; more importantly have appropriate risk management policies been put in place to mitigate both the short- and long-term consequences of the pandemic?[2]

Under section 170 of the Companies Act 2006, directors owe their fiduciary duties to the company itself and shareholders are the only group of stakeholders who can question whether their decisions and actions have been taken in a properly informed manner. The shareholders are also able to sue them if they fall short of performing their duties. On the other hand, directors report exclusively to shareholders on how they discharge their duties. In the UK, like most other common law systems, the main purpose of the company is to maximise profit for its shareholders. Therefore, directors should seek profit for shareholders in the short-term and should leave the other stakeholders rights to be protected outside the company law. In the author's view, this has proved to be a problematical approach.

In the current situation, survival of companies demands directors to take the interest of all stakeholders into account when they are making short- or long-term business decisions. All the parties in the company should work as a team and should equally share the burden in the firm's crisis. For instance, there should be a balance between a wage cut for employees or employees' dismissal and a dividend cut for shareholders. By accommodating the rights and interests of other stakeholders, the company might sacrifice some profits in the short term but will survive in the longer term. The pandemic has clearly highlighted that companies cannot meet the basic needs of the society solely by maximising returns for shareholders. Boards should be concerned not just with returns to shareholders, but with the full range of factors that enable the company to create value for all stakeholders over time.[3]

The concern is that shareholders do not always have a long-term orientation in the company. They may not be concerned if directors lack sufficient knowledge and information in making decisions, provided they receive substantial short-term returns on their investments. They may not even care when directors' opportunistic behaviour, negligence or risky business decisions put the faith of the company in jeopardy. Moreover, shareholders' desire for short-term high return are often the main reason for the company's high-risk business tactics and short-term business objectives, which could even sacrifice the long-term stability of a company.[4] Accordingly, this chapter argues that relying on shareholders to scrutinise

2   James Whitaker, 'UK: Directors Duties During the Pandemic' (*Ceomonthly*, 20 October 2020) <www.ceo-review.com/discharging-directors-duties-in-a-pandemic-world/> accessed 5 May 2021.
3   Lynn S Paine, 'COVID-19 Is Rewriting the Rules of Corporate Governance' (*Harvard Business Review*, 6 October 2020) <https://hbr.org/2020/10/covid-19-is-rewriting-the-rules-of-corporate-governance> accessed 20 May 2021.
4   House of Commons Business, Energy and Industrial Strategy Committee, 'Corporate Governance, Fourth Report of Session 2016–17' (30 March 2017) 23 <https://publications.

the directors' conducts could narrow down the company protection, because shareholders may seek short-term profit maximisation over long term protection of the company in the current situation. To that end, such an approach is not well suited to mitigate the current pandemic impact.

At least since 1970 the UK Government has taken some uncertain steps to incorporate other stakeholders' interests, including employees' interests, into the UK's corporate legal framework. In all these attempts, however, the other stakeholders' interests have been considered partially and only as instrumental to long-term shareholder wealth maximisation.[5] The latest attempt in this regard is under the UK revised corporate governance code. The new code was published in July 2018, following a comprehensive review by the UK Department for Business, Energy & Industrial Strategy (BEIS), with the aim of strengthening workers' and other stakeholders' voices on the board, reforming executive pay, and improving the corporate governance framework for large, privately held companies. The new code places emphasis on relationships between companies, shareholders and stakeholders, as well as establishing greater accountability and transparency in the company, thus ensuring appropriation of remuneration and the eradication of irresponsible corporate behaviour. Whilst the new corporate governance code presents an overall positive picture, particularly in terms of workforce engagement,[6] this chapter illustrates how these reforms have little impact in practice. The new corporate governance code still prioritises shareholders' interests over other stakeholders in the company. Fervently, shareholders remain the only executive arm of corporate governance. Even in terms of implementing the mechanisms of engagement for employees, shareholders play a greater role than workers themselves in determining which of the three methods for workforce engagement should be implemented in any company.

This chapter considers that the current reforms to the corporate governance code to be insignificant in terms of monitoring director's conduct in the post-COVID era. The lessons from the pandemic imply the need for an active role for other stakeholders to monitor boards' conduct. Thus, this chapter proposes that to enhance the long-term survival of businesses, the power for scrutinising the board of directors' conduct, and the right to pursue their actions, should be extended to employees. To that end it should be mandatory, not optional, for the companies to establish at least one of the mechanisms of engagement with

---

parliament.uk/pa/cm201617/cmselect/cmbeis/702/702.pdf> accessed 21 April 2020.

5　Companies Act 2006, s 172; Charles Wynn-Evans, 'The Companies Act 2006 and the Interests of Employees' (2007)36 *Industrial Law Journal* 188, 191.

6　One of the most eye-catching changes under the code is using the term 'workforce' which is broader than 'employees', as used in Section 172 CA 2006. Therefore, apart from people who have formal contracts of employment (permanent, fixed-term and zero-hours) companies should also consider the interest of other members of workforce who are affected by the decisions of the board such as individuals engaged under contracts of service and agency workers. Companies should be able to explain who they have included within the definition of workforce and why.

employees proposed by the new corporate governance code. Employees should be informed of directors' business decisions via these mechanisms. Moreover, they should have the right to report the directors' breach of duties that put company stability and their interests in danger to an independent inspectorate with powers of enforcement.

This proposal focuses exclusively on employees' empowerment because different stakeholders have different types of interests in the company, and not all of them have strong incentives and engagement with the company. Employees, however, remain important stakeholders in any company, as they play a vital role in its long-term success and stability. They invest in the company with their skills, and their economic fortune is tied to the company's well-being. Consequently, they have strong motivation to protect the company from any negligent or opportunistic behaviour that harms the company and puts their jobs at risk. This chapter, therefore, advocates that mandatory mechanisms of engagement for employees would increase company protection in situations when shareholders are absent or are reluctant to be involved in corporate governance matters. Accordingly, it discusses whether, when employees via any of these mechanisms of engagement notice directors breach of duty, they should be able to report to an independent inspectorate with enforcement powers. Upon employees' report, the inspectorate should investigate whether directors have met the requirements of section 172 of the CA 2006 and the new corporate governance code, particularly in considering employees' interests and taking enforcement action if it identifies any breach. In this regard, this chapter asserts that the role of the independent inspectorate could be delegated to the UK government's proposed Single Enforcement Body (SEB).

Employee voice and workforce engagement under the corporate governance code 2018

Although the UK neo-liberal corporate governance orientation seems to be clearly recognised, it still covers up a long history of debate as for whose benefit the company should be run. As mentioned earlier, at least since 1970 the UK Government has taken some attempts to consider other stakeholders, particularly employees' interests, under corporate law.[7] The latest attempt in this regard is under the UK 2018 corporate governance code. In fact, the need to amend the corporate governance code was highlighted following catastrophic corporate failures, such as BHS and Carillion, which highlighted the need for more serious mechanisms against director and controlling shareholders which

---

7 Historically there are two formative periods in which corporate law has attempted to diverge from its strict shareholder primacy orientation. The first period was flared up in 1977 during the Labour Government's attempt to pursue employees' board representation based on Bullock Report recommendation and the second period started in 1998 when the UK Labour government initiated the company object review and resulted in consideration of employees' interest under s 172 Companies Act 2006.

by their negligence and opportunistic behaviour put the companies' stability in jeopardy and damaged employees' and other stakeholders' interests in the company. Hence, in the aftermath of these corporate failures, in November 2016 the UK's Department for BEIS once again set out a comprehensive review of the corporate governance code to enhance transparency in companies, as well as discovering mechanisms that could strengthen the connection between boards of directors and stakeholders who have interests in the company, such as employees. The outcome of the Government review was a revised corporate governance code published in July 2018.

The new corporate governance code focuses on three areas: standardizing executive pay, strengthening workforce engagement and improving the governance of large private companies.[8] For large private companies, the FRC, through six principles known as the Wates Principles, tries to encourage large private companies to inform and develop their corporate governance practices and adopt them on an *"apply and explain"* basis.[9] In terms of strengthening employees' engagement in particular (the focus of this chapter), the Code proposes one or a combination of the following methods for premium-listed companies: a director appointed from the workforce, a formal workforce advisory panel, and a designated non-executive director.[10] In addition to these suggested mechanisms, directors should explain to shareholders in their strategic report how they had regard to the interest of employees under section 172 of CA 2006 when taking decisions during the financial year. Moreover, remuneration committees must review workforce pay, and related policies should explain how executive pay aligns with the wider company pay policy.[11]

The UK Government asserts that these reforms are in line with the UK's approach of strengthening corporate governance through non-legislative means, with the aim of improving corporate governance and giving workers and investors a stronger voice.[12] The Government's assumption is that these reforms will drive change in how large companies engage with their employees by putting higher expectations on such companies.

---

8 Federico More, 'Corporate Governance Reform' (*House of Commons Library*, 27 May 2020) <https://researchbriefings.parliament.uk/ResearchBriefing/Summary/CBP-8143> accessed 14 April 2021.

9 Financial Report Council, 'The Wates Corporate Governance Principles for Large Private Companies' (December 2018) <www.frc.org.uk/getattachment/31dfb844-6d4b-4093-9bfe-19cee2c29cda/Wates-Corporate-Governance-Principles-for-LPC-Dec-2018.pdf> accessed 12 January 2021.

10 Financial Report Council, 'The UK Corporate Governance Code' (July 2018) 5 <www.frc.org.uk/getattachment/88bd8c45-50ea-4841-95b0-d2f4f48069a2/2018-UK-Corporate-Governance-Code-FINAL.PDF> accessed 12 January 2021.

11 ibid prov 33.

12 Department for Business, Energy & Industrial Strategy, 'Corporate Governance Reform: The Government Response to the Green Paper Consultation' (August 2017) 33 <https://assets.publishing.service.gov.uk/government/uploads/system/uploads/attachment_data/file/640470/corporate-governance-reform-government-response.pdf> accessed 3 April 2021.

In this author's view, however, although the changes to the corporate governance are, rhetorically, promising, they are unlikely to have any practical impact. There are several reasons for this argument. For instance, there exists some general debate about the implementation of the Code's provisions based on the "*comply or explain*" principle. The code compliance requirements apply broadly to UK large-listed companies, so small or medium-sized companies are exempt from the Code requirement. Further, larger unlisted companies, including large private companies, are required to disclose their corporate governance arrangements in their directors' report and on their website, but only on a voluntary basis. If such companies decide to ignore some provisions of the code, they are at liberty to do so. Thus, based on these reasons, it is difficult to assess the level of monitoring companies' compliance and the quality of their explanations for non-compliance. Further, there is little chance that the proposed *Wates Corporate Governance Principles* for large private companies will prevent scandals comparable to BHS, because of the lack of scrutiny by markets and regulators and the absence of mandatory mechanisms to prevent wrongdoers' conduct. The transparency requested by the new corporate governance code is unlikely to affect internal management of these companies.

A more important concern is that the corporate governance code still assumes that shareholders are the main important group of stakeholders in the company, and yet relies on the stewardship of institutional shareholders to protect the employees and other stakeholders' interests and avoid corporate failure.[13] Therefore, under the new code, only shareholders receive a report on executive pay, and only shareholders will have a binding vote on it. Also, there is no detailed guidance on implementing employees' engagement mechanisms. Thus, it is likely that shareholders will play a greater role in forming the proposed workforce advisory council and choosing the workforce' director than the workers themselves. In fact, the new corporate governance code keeps the company power in the hands of shareholders, and this raises some serious concerns.

Some problems of keeping shareholders in power

As discussed in the previous section, the new corporate governance code remains fundamentally loyal to shareholder value primacy, and in the view of this chapter this is a problematic approach, particularly in the post-COVID era. In the life of a company, the interest of different stakeholders receive priority from time to time. There might be times when employees' interests come first, where at other time customer interests should take priority, or the public need is paramount.[14] Thus,

---

13 Department for Business, Energy & Industrial Strategy, 'Insolvency and Corporate Governance' (20 March 2018). <https://assets.publishing.service.gov.uk/government/uploads/system/uploads/attachment_data/file/691857/Condoc_-Insolvency_and_Corporate_Governance_FINAL_.pdf> accessed 2 January 2021.

14 Paine (n 3).

directors should have sufficient and ongoing engagement with all stakeholders and ensure their interests are considered in their decision-making. They should expand the company's business in a way that benefit shareholders and other stakeholders simultaneously. The pandemic crisis has demonstrated more than ever that prioritising the interests of shareholders is not an appropriate approach at the time that the interests of other stakeholders are at even greater risk than shareholders. During the pandemic, many workers have lost not only their jobs, but their lives. They have been at the frontline of retail, food and many other industries and many of them have risked their lives to stay at work and serve society. Further, in addition to workers, company insolvency is far more dangerous for creditors and suppliers than shareholders.[15] However, the problem is that the concept of a company as a separate legal personality has not been fully implemented into UK corporate law and corporate governance. Shareholders are still the only stakeholder group in the company who have the ultimate controlling power.[16] Under the shareholder primacy theory, still the predominant approach in UK corporate law, the main purpose of the company is to maximise profit for its shareholders. Therefore, directors should seek profit for shareholders in the short term and should leave the other stakeholders' interests to be protected outside company law.[17] However, such assumption narrows down the company protection because seeking shareholder short-term profit maximisation increases high risk, short-term decisions by directors. Shareholders have the right to remove directors by simple majority under section 168 of the CA 2006 and thus influence and control directors and their decision-making. Such ultimate controlling power force directors to prioritise shareholders' interest and curtails their power to consider other stakeholders rights in the company. By prioritising shareholders' interest, directors will be cautious about taking long-term business decisions, because shareholders make short-term investment and want short-term profit in return.[18] Hence, they usually avoid companies with long-term business plans. Shareholders, especially institutional shareholders who can diversify away a particular company's risk, are willing for the company to be aggressive in taking risky business decisions that bring them short-term profit return, even if it will result in company failure in the longer run. Also, despite shareholders' significant controlling power, they are only exposed to the insolvency of the company to the extent of their contribution. Therefore, in situations that directors' bad business decisions damage the long-term stability and productivity of the company, the risk shifts onto other stakeholders, particularly employees who are far

15 John Plender, 'Stakeholder Capitalism Must Find Ways to Hold Management to Account' (*The Financial Times*, 4 April 2021) <www.ft.com/content/4eeaa803-511c-4227-962e-018ea1dc2883> accessed 3 June 2021.
16 Andrew Johnston and Lorraine Talbot, 'Why Is Modern Capitalism Irresponsible and What Would Make It More Responsible? A Company Law Perspective' (2018)29(1) *King's Law Journal* 111–41.
17 Milton Friedman, *Capitalism and Freedom* (Chicago, Chicago UP 1962) 133.
18 Johnston and Talbot (n 16) 126.

less able to bear these harms and insure themselves against it.[19] Shareholders could be indifferent toward harms to the company and may not sue directors for their negligent, mismanagement and their exploitative behaviour at the time of economic stress, as long as they extract short-term benefit from the company.[20] They could, therefore, be passive towards their duty to monitor whether risk management strategies and contingency procedures and protocols are in place in the company, and reviewed regularly by the board at the time of crisis, and if the regulatory policies and precautionary measures issues by government in response to COVID-19 crisis have been implemented properly.

Institutional shareholders who are the "Stewards" of the company usually put no real effort into being engaged or evaluating company disclosures; instead considering the financial performance of the company as a sign that directors are complying with their duties.[21] However, the fact is that good performance by the company is not always a sign that the company is protected from directors' opportunistic behaviour. Directors could be involved in fraudulent activities or

19 Jeffrey Gordon, 'Addressing Economic Insecurity: Why Social Insurance Is Better Than Corporate Governance Reform' (*Columbia Law School Blog on Corporations and the Capital Market*, 21 August 2019) <http://clsbluesky.law.columbia.edu/2019/08/21/addressing-economic-insecurity-why-social-insurance-is-better-than-corporate-governance-reform/> accessed 10 December 2020.

20 Emeka Duruigbo, 'Tackling Shareholder Short-Termism and Managerial Myopia' (2011–12)100 *Kentucky Law Journal* 531; David Millon, 'Shareholder Social Responsibility' (2012)36 *Seattle University Law Review* 911; Marc Moore and Edward Walker-Arnott, 'A Fresh Look at Stock Market Short Termism' (2014)41 *Journal of Law and Society* 416; Department for Business, Energy & Industrial Strategy, 'The Kay Review of UK Equity Markets and Long-Term Decision Making' (*Final Report*, 23 July 2012) <www.ecgi.org/conferences/eu_actionplan2013/documents/kay_review_final_report.pdf> accessed 10 December 2020; Lorraine Talbot, 'Why Shareholders Shouldn't Vote: A Marxist-Progressive Critique of Shareholder Empowerment' (2013)76(5) *Modern Law Review* 791–816; Lynn Stout, *The Shareholder Value Myth: How Putting Shareholders First Harms Investors, Corporations, and the Public* (San Francisco, Berrett-Koehler Publishers 2013) 63.

21 Aidan O'Dwyer, 'Corporate Governance After the Financial Crisis: The Role of Shareholders in Monitoring the Activities of the Board' (2014)5 *Aberdeen Student Law Review* 112, 115; George Hadjikyprianou, 'The Principle of "Comply-or-Explain" Underpinning the UK Corporate Governance Regulation: Is There a Need for a Change?' (2015)7 *Corporate Governance Law Journal* 20; Sarah Kiarie, 'Crossroads: Shareholder Value, Stakeholder Value and Enlightened Shareholder Value: Which Road Should the United Kingdom Take?' (2006)17 *International Company and Commercial Law Review* 329, 338–40; Andrew Keay, 'Tackling the Issue of the Corporate Objective: An Analysis of the United Kingdom's Enlightened Shareholder Value Approach' (2007)29 *Sydney Law Review* 108–9; Lorraine Talbot, 'Polanyi's Embeddedness and Shareholder Stewardship: A Contextual Analysis of Current Anglo-American Perspectives on Corporate Governance' (2011)62 *Northern Ireland Legal Quarterly* 451; Leo Strine, 'One Fundamental Corporate Governance Question We Face: Can Corporations Be Managed for the Long Term Unless Their Powerful Electorates Also Act and Think Long Term?' (2010)66 *Business Lawyer* 1, 17 (suggesting that institutional investors have pushed US corporations toward more short-term orientation); Mark Roe, 'Corporate Short-Termism – In the Boardroom and in the Courtroom' (2013)68 *Business Lawyer* 977, 1005–6 (suggesting that the short-termism problem in the US is insufficiently proven).

other opportunistic conduct, yet the company may still do financially well, at least in the short-term.[22]

This concern for shareholder passivity was reinforced by the UK Parliament's BEIS Committee, which, in response to the Government Green Paper for Corporate Governance Reform,[23] referred to the considerable concerns about the quality of shareholder engagement in the evidence received by them.[24] In addition, an increasing proportion of institutional shareholders of UK-listed companies are now represented by non-UK interests, such as foreign sovereign wealth funds, which may not be so interested in the welfare of UK companies, let alone that of UK-listed companies, many of which are non-UK companies.[25] Given this, the new corporate governance code fails to address deep-rooted problems of shareholder short-termism. The concern still is that the consideration of employee and other stakeholder interests will not be a priority of shareholders because, as mentioned earlier, shareholders will likely only be concerned about directors' conduct to the extent that it is relevant to their own interests. Therefore, it is unlikely that the new code increases directors and controlling shareholders' accountability toward the company, unless the UK government adopts more pragmatic solutions to empower employees and preserve company stability in post-COVID period.

Why businesses should be more concerned about employees?

Corporatist short-termism not only harms non-shareholder constituencies' interest in the company but can produce detrimental consequences for society. The corona virus pandemic already has left many negative impacts on society: it has resulted in economic crisis. Many businesses have not been able to operate in the usual way; many people have lost their jobs or part of their income and customers have faced difficulties in buying their favourite products or services. The pandemic has demonstrated that society depends on well-functioning companies to meet its most basic needs, such as consumer products, communication, transportation and these demands will not be addressed if businesses only focus on maximising profit return for shareholders or merely rely on shareholders to monitor and check the board conducts.[26]

Directors' opportunistic behaviour or their negligence and mismanagement could result in the company's insolvency and employee job losses. Employees are often dependent on the company for their livelihood and their pension benefits, and in situations where they lose their job because of directors' failure to protect the company, not only do employees suffer personal harm, but it could also

22 ibid.
23 House of Commons Business, Energy and Industrial Strategy Committee (n 4).
24 ibid.
25 Chizu Nakajima, 'Corporate Failures and Governance – The UK Government's Response' (2018)4 *The Company Lawyer* 1.
26 Paine (n 3).

have a harmful social effect. Loss of jobs often leads to unpayable debts, loss of homes, break up of families, mental and physical illnesses and other detrimental social consequences. Even if not resulting in job losses, directors' deliberation in delivering shareholder value could still result in low company's productivity, which then impacts on wages and the standard of living for employees.[27] Whilst the traditional agency theory assumes employees' interests to be fully protected outside company law and by their contractual rights,[28] in reality contractual protections are limited. In fact, contract theory suggests that real life contracts are incomplete because payoff and the distribution of rights among parties cannot always be foreseen.[29]

Employees are often deeply invested in a company by virtue of their human capital and by playing a key role in the productivity and profitability of the company. They have stronger incentives – even more than shareholders – to protect the company from any mismanagement or negligent and opportunistic behaviour that could harm the company and damage their jobs and interests. They have more incentives to want directors on check in post-COVID difficult times and scrutinise whether they are fully performing their obligations and having regard to the interests of all stakeholders in the business, including the impact their decisions have on them when making short- or long-term business decisions. Enhancing employees' power would therefore support long-term protection of the company that benefit the minority shareholders and other stakeholders as well as society.

Time for increasing employees' engagement with the company

The COVID-19 pandemic has amplified the importance of the boards' decisions in survival of the company when they are exploring different options, weighing competing considerations and dealing with novel issues and matters for them where they have no precedent or policy.[30]In the current situation shareholders are the only group of stakeholders who are responsible to act as a watchdog for directors' conduct and check their decision-making processes and the reasons underlying key decisions. The concern is that due to shareholders' passivity and their lack of long-term orientation in the company, the board's ability

---

27   Johnston and Talbot (n 16) 128.
28   Frank Easterbrook and Danial Fischel, *The Economic Structure of Corporate Law* (Cambridge, MA, Harvard UP 1991) 17.
29   Martin Gelter, 'Tilting the Balance Between Capital and Labour? The Effects of Regulatory Arbitrage in European Corporate Law on Employees' (2010)33 *Fordham International Law Journal* 796; Alan Schwartz, 'Incomplete Contracts' in Newman P (ed), *The New Palgrave Dictionary of Economics and the Law* (London, Palgrave Macmillan 1999) 277; Margaret Blair and Lynn Stout, 'A Team Production Theory of Corporate Law' (1999)85 *Virginia Law Review* 247, 249–50.
30   Paine (n 3).

to deliberate thoughtful decisions and expose possible breaches of duty would remain unchecked.

Employees on the other hand are an integral part of the company and have sufficient reasons to save the company because they typically have only one job; hence the company's well-being and stability are significantly more important for their continued ability to earn a livelihood.[31] In fact, they have far more concern for long-term prosperity survival and development of the company than diversified shareholders with liquid portfolios. The current "comply or explain" model of employees' engagement mechanisms under corporate governance code will not give employees a strong voice. This is not only because of their non-mandatory nature, but also because it is not clear how they are going to be implemented. Therefore, in order to increase the accountability of directors toward the company and to enhance companies' long-term stability, employees should have mechanisms of engagement of a mandatory nature (either an employees' advisory panel or having a representative on board) and they should be able to receive reports from the directors via these mechanisms. They should also be able to report their concerns over directors' business decisions to an independent inspectorate with enforcement powers. Upon employees' reports, the inspectorate could investigate whether directors have met the requirements of both section 172 of the CA 2006 and the new corporate governance, and take enforcement action if it identifies any breach.

Without establishing such an enforcement mechanism for employees, it is unlikely that the existing mechanisms work effectively in preventing harm to the company. What would be the advantage of employees being aware of director mismanagement when there was no enforcement power to stop it? Accordingly, it is suggested that investigation and enforcement rights should be granted to the UK government's proposed Single Enforcement Body (SEB).

An independent enforcement inspectorate as an enforcement mechanism

Given the concerns surrounding the current-non-mandatory mechanisms of engagement for employees, it is proposed that employees should have at least one mandatory mechanism of engagement (preferably an employees' advisory panel or having a representative on board) that would enable them to receive report on directors' business decisions. Moreover, they should have the right to report their concerns over directors' breach of duty to an independent inspectorate with powers of enforcement.

In this regard, it is argued that the role of the independent inspectorate could be delegated to the UK government's proposed Single Enforcement Body

---

31 Neshat Safari and Martin Gelter, 'British Home Stores Collapse: The Case for an Employee Derivative Claim' (2018)19(1) *Journal of Corporate Law Studies* 51; Kent Greenfield, 'The Place of Workers in Corporate Law' (1998)39 *Boston College Law Review* 283, 302.

(SEB).[32] Under the government's proposal, the SEB would hold responsibility for those areas that sit under employment law as well as the additional areas that government has committed to state enforcement. This chapter argues the SEB power could be expanded to cover employees' interests under s. 172 of the CA 2006 and the corporate governance code. Such a proposal would strengthen the employees' engagement mechanisms and reduce opportunities for employees to be exploited by the company. In fact, as part of the consultation, the government has proposed the Single Enforcement Body could have a role in any other area or sector relevant to employees.[33] Such a proposal potentially opens the ground for the expansion of SEB power to consider employees' rights and interests under company law.

Extending a labour inspectorate power to enforce employees' rights under other areas of law is not an invention. In New Zealand, the labour inspectorate not only has the right to monitor and enforce employer compliance with employment law, it also has the power to investigate other duties they have toward employees under other legislation.[34] Such power would alert directors that if shareholders are absent or not concerned, there are still another group of stakeholders who are observing their conduct, reviewing their skill matrices and scrutinising their decisions.

Similar to the New Zealand's labour inspectorates, the proposed inspectorate could have a range of tools to deal with directors' deliberate breaches of duty: from issuing warrants in bringing civil proceeding in court, to publicising the case, or issuing an infringement notice for less serious breaches. Notably, and for more serious breaches, such as wrongdoer directors' negligence or mismanagement that takes the company on the verge of insolvency, the inspectorate could apply to the court for a declaration of breach. Depending on the severity, facts, evidence and the circumstances, following the declaration of breach the inspectorate could, on behalf of employees apply to the court for compensation or injunction orders, against the directors and those involved in the breach.

Investigating and enforcing directors' breach of duties through such an inspectorate would have several advantages. One is that such inspectors would investigate potential breaches impartially before making a decision. Also, making a claim through an independent inspectorate entails no cost for employees. Furthermore, employees could report directors' breach of duty to the inspectorate anonymously or could request that their identities be undisclosed. In this way, the complaint employees would not be victimised for reporting illegal practices that harm the company and their respective interests.

32 Department for Business, Energy & Industrial Strategy, 'Good Work Plan: Establishing a New Single Enforcement Body for Employment Rights' (*Department for Business, Energy& Industrial Strategy Website*, 6 October 2019) <www.gov.uk/government/consultations/good-work-plan-establishing-a-new-single-enforcement-body-for-employment-rights> accessed 14 November 2019.

33 ibid 22, 42.

34 New Zealand Ministry of Business, Innovation and Employment, 'Labour Inspectorates' (*Employment New Zealand*, 9 October 2020) <www.employment.govt.nz/resolving-problems/steps-to-resolve/labour-inspectorate/> accessed 4 June 2021.

Conclusions

Although the COVID-19 pandemic cannot be categorised under a financial crisis, its impact on the global economy has led to financial crisis. The current situation has increased the demand on boards of directors to protect the long-term health and growth of the corporation by overseeing an expanded set of risks, making decisions in a properly informed manner and considering the impact of their decisions on all stakeholders and the society.

Under the current situation, shareholders are the only executive arm of the company. Nevertheless, they may not care when directors fall short of performing their duties and put the survival of the company and the interest of other stakeholders in jeopardy, as long as they are benefiting from short-term developments in the company. Employees often have better incentives than shareholders to protect the company in the long run. Hence, this chapter posits that the government needs more pragmatic solutions to increase employees' power and strengthen the overall protection of the company. Employees play a significant role in the company's ability to function, thrive and succeed over time. Unless equipped with a mandatory mechanism of engagement with the board and are granted the power to report directors' breach of duty to an independent inspectorate, the reforms would be insufficient to protect them in practice. In this regard, this chapter proposes that employees should have at least one mandatory mechanism of engagement with the board of directors. They should also be able to report directors' negligence or opportunistic behaviour, that harms their interest in the company to an inspectorate with an enforcement power which could investigate these claims under section 172(1)(b) of the CA 2006. In the UK context, this inspectorate could be the Single Enforcement Body, which has already been proposed by the UK's Department for BEIS.

In conclusion, such a proposal would enhance the survival of businesses at a time that the COVID-19 pandemic has resulted in financial and economic crisis and has had sever impacts on businesses activities. By empowering employees to scrutinise boards' conduct, directors would be aware that their misconduct can be challenged by a larger group of applicants, and they will be more likely to be deterred from acting without care and due diligence. Further, such a new regime would ensure that directors are less likely to run the company in a way conducive to their personal benefit, whilst harming the company itself and its other stakeholders.

Bibliography

Blair M and Stout L, 'A Team Production Theory of Corporate Law' (1999)85 *Virginia Law Review* 247, 249–50.

Department for Business, Energy & Industrial Strategy, 'The Kay Review of UK Equity Markets and Long-Term Decision Making' (*Final Report*, 23 July 2012) <www.ecgi.org/conferences/eu_actionplan2013/documents/kay_review_final_report.pdf> accessed 10 December 2020.

Department for Business, Energy & Industrial Strategy, 'Corporate Governance Reform: The Government Response to the Green Paper Consultation' (August 2017) 33 <https://assets.publishing.service.gov.uk/government/uploads/system/uploads/attachment_data/file/640470/corporate-governance-reform-government-response.pdf> accessed 3 April 2021.

Department for Business, Energy & Industrial Strategy, 'Insolvency and Corporate Governance' (20 March 2018) <https://assets.publishing.service.gov.uk/government/uploads/system/uploads/attachment_data/file/691857/Condoc_-Insolvency_and_Corporate_Governance_FINAL_.pdf> accessed 2 January 2021.

Department for Business, Energy & Industrial Strategy, 'Good Work Plan: Establishing a New Single Enforcement Body for Employment Rights' (*Department for Business, Energy& Industrial Strategy Website*, 6 October 2019) <www.gov.uk/government/consultations/good-work-plan-establishing-a-new-single-enforcement-body-for-employment-rights> accessed 14 November 2019.

Duruigbo E, 'Tackling Shareholder Short-Termism and Managerial Myopia' (2011–12)100 *Kentucky Law Journal* 531.

Easterbrook F and Fischel D, *The Economic Structure of Corporate Law* (Cambridge, MA, Harvard UP 1991).

Financial Report Council, 'The UK Corporate Governance Code' (July 2018) 5 <www.frc.org.uk/getattachment/88bd8c45-50ea-4841-95b0-d2f4f48069a2/2018-UK-Corporate-Governance-Code-FINAL.PDF> accessed 12 January 2021.

Financial Report Council, 'The Wates Corporate Governance Principles for Large Private Companies' (December 2018) <www.frc.org.uk/getattachment/31dfb844-6d4b-4093-9bfe-19cee2c29cda/Wates-Corporate-Governance-Principles-for-LPC-Dec-2018.pdf> accessed 12 January 2021.

Friedman M, *Capitalism and Freedom* (Chicago, Chicago UP 1962).

Gelter M, 'Tilting the Balance Between Capital and Labour? The Effects of Regulatory Arbitrage in European Corporate Law on Employees' (2010)33 *Fordham International Law Journal* 796.

Gordon J, 'Addressing Economic Insecurity: Why Social Insurance Is Better Than Corporate Governance Reform' (*Columbia law School Blog on Corporations and the Capital Market*, 21 August 2019) <http://clsbluesky.law.columbia.edu/2019/08/21/addressing-economic-insecurity-why-social-insurance-is-better-than-corporate-governance-reform> accessed 10 December 2020.

Greenfield K, 'The Place of Workers in Corporate Law' (1998)39 *Boston College Law Review* 283, 302.

Hadjikyprianou G, 'The Principle of "Comply-or-Explain" Underpinning the UK Corporate Governance Regulation: Is There a Need for a Change?' (2015)7 *Corporate Governance Law Journal* 20.

House of Commons Business, Energy and Industrial Strategy Committee, 'Corporate Governance, Fourth Report of Session 2016–17' (30 March 2017) 23 <https://publications.parliament.uk/pa/cm201617/cmselect/cmbeis/702/702.pdf> accessed 21April 2020.

Johnsto A and Talbot L, 'Why Is Modern Capitalism Irresponsible and What Would Make It More Responsible? A Company Law Perspective' (2018)29(1) *King's Law Journal* 111–41.

Keay A, 'Tackling the Issue of the Corporate Objective: An Analysis of the United Kingdom's Enlightened Shareholder Value Approach' (2007)29 *Sydney Law Review* 108–9.

Khatib S and Ibrahim Nour A, 'The Impact of Corporate Governance on Firm Performance During the COVID-19 Pandemic: Evidence from Malaysia' (2021)8(2) *Journal of Asian Finance Economics and Business* 943–52 <https://papers.ssrn.com/sol3/papers.cfm?abstract_id=3762393> accessed 5 May 2021.

Kiarie S, 'Crossroads: Shareholder Value, Stakeholder Value and Enlightened Shareholder Value: Which Road Should the United Kingdom Take?' (2006)17 *International Company and Commercial Law Review* 329, 338–40.

Millon D, 'Shareholder Social Responsibility' (2012)36 *Seattle University Law Review* 911.

Moore M and Walker-Arnott E, 'A Fresh Look at Stock Market Short Termism' (2014)41 *Journal of Law and Society* 416.

More F, 'Corporate Governance Reform' (*House of Commons Library*, 27 May 2020) <https://researchbriefings.parliament.uk/ResearchBriefing/Summary/CBP-8143> accessed 14 April 2021.

Nakajima C, 'Corporate Failures and Governance – The UK Government's Response' (2018)4 *The Company Lawyer* 1.

New Zealand Ministry of Business, Innovation and Employment, 'Labour Inspectorates' (*Employment New Zealand*, 9 October 2020) <www.employment.govt.nz/resolving-problems/steps-to-resolve/labour-inspectorate> accessed 4 June 2021.

O'Dwyer A, 'Corporate Governance After the Financial Crisis: The Role of Shareholders in Monitoring the Activities of the Board' (2014)5 *Aberdeen Student Law Review* 112, 115.

Paine L, 'COVID-19 Is Rewriting the Rules of Corporate Governance' (*Harvard Business Review*, 6 October 2020) <https://hbr.org/2020/10/covid-19-is-rewriting-the-rules-of-corporate-governance> accessed 20 May 2021.

Plender J, 'Stakeholder Capitalism Must Find Ways to Hold Management to Account' (*The Financial Times*, 4 April 2021) <www.ft.com/content/4eeaa803-511c-4227-962e-018ea1dc2883> accessed 3 June 2021.

Roe M, 'Corporate Short-Termism – In the Boardroom and in the Courtroom' (2013)68 *Business Lawyer* 977, 1005–6.

Safari N and Gelter M, 'British Home Stores Collapse: The Case for an Employee Derivative Claim' (2018)19(1) *Journal of Corporate Law Studies* 51.

Schwartz A, 'Incomplete Contracts' in Newman P (ed), *The New Palgrave Dictionary of Economics and the Law* (London, Palgrave Macmillan 1999) 277.

Stout L, *The Shareholder Value Myth: How Putting Shareholders First Harms Investors, Corporations, and the Public* (San Francisco, Berrett-Koehler Publishers 2013).

Strine L, 'One Fundamental Corporate Governance Question We Face: Can Corporations Be Managed for the Long Term Unless Their Powerful Electorates also Act and Think Long Term?' (2010)66 *Business Lawyer* 1, 17.

Talbot L, 'Polanyi's Embeddedness and Shareholder Stewardship: A Contextual Analysis of Current Anglo-American Perspectives on Corporate Governance' (2011)62 *Northern Ireland Legal Quarterly* 451.

Talbot L, 'Why Shareholders Shouldn't Vote: A Marxist-Progressive Critique of Shareholder Empowerment' (2013)76(5) *Modern Law Review* 791–816.

Whitaker J, 'UK: Directors Duties During the Pandemic' (*Ceomonthly*, 20 October 2020) <www.ceo-review.com/discharging-directors-duties-in-a-pandemic-world/> accessed 5 May 2021.

Wynn-Evans C, 'The Companies Act 2006 and the Interests of Employees' (2007)36 *Industrial Law Journal* 188, 191.

8 Dangerous circumstances, discipline and dismissal

Some employment law impacts of COVID-19

Alex Simmonds[1]

Introduction

This chapter will examine how the right of employees to refuse to work in dangerous circumstances and their right to be heard at disciplinary and investigatory hearings have been enjoyed during the era of COVID-19. A comparative law approach will then seek to determine the existence of similar rules globally and endeavour to ascertain their effectiveness. Firstly, "Dangerous Circumstances" will outline and examine the existing UK rules and protections for workers in this regard and seek to investigate whether these rules have been effective in the age of COVID-19. This will be followed by a comparative review of a number of jurisdictions along with available evidence on the perceived effectiveness of such rules prior to a discussion of enforcement measures. "Discipline and Dismissal" will firstly provide an overview of the main rules relating to the administration of disciplinary proceedings in the UK before assessing the potential impact that COVID-19 has had on these before making some suggestions as to how this impact can be mitigated. There will also be some comparative assessment before the drawing of some overall conclusions.

Collective dismissals/redundancies will not be examined in the chapter and nor will issues relating to employment status or specific duties relating to the supply of adequate personal protective equipment (PPE) insofar as this can be regarded as independent of the idea of "dangerous circumstances", e.g. where a failure to provide PPE amounts to creating a dangerous circumstance. Comparisons will only be made to other jurisdictions insofar as they can be said to offer a meaningful degree of insight and, given the novelty of the overall situation, will often be limited to opportunistic sampling of news reports.

It is apparent that the employment legislation of most jurisdictions was not framed with a global pandemic in mind. The events of the past year or so can be viewed as a useful "stress test" of existing provisions, highlighting any inadequacies or shortcomings. Regarding "Dangerous Circumstances" the author

1 Lecturer in Law, Coventry University. With special thanks to Robin Sisson and Maxine Eliot.

DOI: 10.4324/9781003176848-12

ultimately found that existing provisions in the law of England and Wales had, to an extent, proven effective, with documented incidents of employees asserting their rights in this regard and refusing to work in unsafe conditions. However, it is likely that many other individuals either did not personally know of such rights – "walkouts" or refusals to work tended to be reported mainly from unionised workplaces – or if they did know of such rights were too afraid to assert them for fear of losing their job in what is undoubtedly a very uncertain economic climate, severely exasperated by COVID-19. Stronger criticism was reserved for the practice of enforcement of COVID-19 rules by the police and Health and Safety Executive (HSE).

Regarding "Discipline and Dismissal" the existing law on disciplinary procedures appears sufficiently flexible to cope with the large shift towards remote working and the problems associated with lockdown. Uncertainties still abound, however, in respect of delay, which could potentially impact upon the fairness of any dismissal. Other peripheral, but important, aspects are identified as the difficulties associated with conducting "virtual" disciplinary, investigatory and dismissal hearings.

Dangerous circumstances

In the United Kingdom (UK) statute law, the most important provisions defining "dangerous circumstances" and proscribing certain acts on behalf of employers in such circumstances are contained in section 100(1) and (2) of the Employment Rights Act 1996 (ERA):

(1) An employee who is dismissed shall be regarded for the purposes of this Part as unfairly dismissed if the reason (or, if more than one, the principal reason) for the dismissal is that –

    (. . .) (d) in circumstances of danger which the employee reasonably believed to be serious and imminent and which he could not reasonably have been expected to avert, he left (or proposed to leave) or (while the danger persisted) refused to return to his place of work or any dangerous part of his place of work, or

    (e) in circumstances of danger which the employee reasonably believed to be serious and imminent, he took (or proposed to take) appropriate steps to protect himself or other persons from the danger.

(2) For the purposes of subsection (1)(e) whether steps which an employee took (or proposed to take) were appropriate is to be judged by reference to all the circumstances including, in particular, his knowledge and the facilities and advice available to him at the time.[2]

---

2   ERA 1996.

Section 100 (3) further provides that:

> Where the reason (or, if more than one, the principal reason) for the dis-
> missal of an employee is that specified in subsection (1)(e), he shall not be
> regarded as unfairly dismissed if the employer shows that it was (or would
> have been) so negligent for the employee to take the steps which he took (or
> proposed to take) that a reasonable employer might have dismissed him for
> taking (or proposing to take) them.[3]

Section 44 is similar except the focus is on ensuring that such employees are not?
subject to a "detriment" as a result of having refused to work in such dangerous circumstances. Examples of detriment include deductions from wages under
section 13 of the ERA,[4] but, surprisingly, they have not been held to go as far as
refusing to provide a reference.[5]

The UK's Statutory provisions owe their existence to Directive 89/391/
EEC[6] (also known as the Framework Health and Safety Directive). Other interesting points within the Directive include article 8(3)(c),[7] article 8(4),[8] article
8(5),[9] and article 13(2)(d),[10] which, respectively, require an employer not to
resume work in dangerous circumstances save in exceptional cases, stipulate that
workers should be protected against detriment/harmful and unjustified consequences for any such refusal to work, empower workers to take action avoiding
such danger, and place a duty on workers to inform the employer of circumstances they reasonably believe to represent serious and imminent danger.

3   ibid.
4   *Edwards & Others v the Secretary of State for Justice*, Appeal No UKEAT/0123/14/DM
     (2014); [2014] ALL ER (D) 83.
5   *Fadipe v Reed Nursing Personnel* [2005] ICR 1760 at para 25.
6   Council Directive 89/391/EEC of 12 June 1989 on the introduction of measures to
     encourage improvements in the safety and health of workers at work OJ L 183.
7   Council Directive 89/391/EEC of 12 June 1989 on the introduction of measures to
     encourage improvements in the safety and health of workers at work art 8(3)(c): The
     employer shall: . . . save in exceptional cases for reasons duly substantiated, refrain from
     asking workers to resume work in a working situation where there is still a serious and
     imminent danger.
8   ibid art 8(4): Workers who, in the event of serious, imminent and unavoidable danger, leave
     their workstation and/or a dangerous area may not be placed at any disadvantage because
     of their action and must be protected against any harmful and unjustified consequences, in
     accordance with national laws and/or practices.
9   ibid art 8(5): The employer shall ensure that all workers are able, in the event of serious and
     imminent danger to their own safety and/or that of other persons, and where the immediate
     superior responsible cannot be contacted, to take the appropriate steps in the light of their
     knowledge and the technical means at their disposal, to avoid the consequences of such danger.
10   ibid art 13 (2) (d): (the worker shall. . .) immediately inform the employer and/or the
     workers with specific responsibility for the safety and health of workers of any work situ-
     ation they have reasonable grounds for considering represents a serious and immediate
     danger to safety and health and of any shortcomings in the protection arrangements;

The case of *Balfour Kilpatrick Ltd v Acheson*[11] concerned the latter provision as the words 'or to communicate these circumstances by any appropriate means to the employer' were read into section100(1)(e) of the ERA in line with the directive.[12] This case concerned a number of electricians who had refused to work in wet and potentially dangerous conditions. The employers' argument was that the correct way to raise concerns regarding health and safety matters was through designated Health and Safety Representatives, but the Employment Appeals Tribunal took the view that this was only in cases where it was reasonably practicable to do so.

Further, the case of *Oudahar v Esporta Group Ltd*[13] concerned an employee who was dismissed, in part, owing to his refusal to use a mop near exposed wires on the grounds that this was dangerous. The Employment Appeal Tribunal proposed a two-stage test on the interpretation of section 100(1)(e):

> Firstly, the tribunal should consider whether the criteria set out in that provision have been met, as a matter of fact. Were there circumstances of danger which the employee reasonably believed to be serious and imminent? Did he take or propose to take appropriate steps to protect himself or other persons from the danger? Or . . . did he take appropriate steps to communicate these circumstances to his employer by appropriate means? If these criteria are not satisfied, section 100(1)(e) is not engaged.
>
> Secondly, if the criteria are made out, the tribunal should then ask whether the employer's sole or principal reason for dismissal was that the employee took or proposed to take such steps. If it was, then the dismissal must be regarded as unfair.[14]

The Employment Appeal Tribunal held that the employer had erred in law by not following this test.

What, then is the position of an employee asked to work in the absence of an offer of reasonable/adequate personal protective equipment and/or a workplace which could be regarded as "non-covid secure"? It would appear that an employer has no right to dismiss an employee for such a refusal, nor subject them to any detriment (short of a refusal to provide a reference) where they refuse to work on the basis of reasonably held fears of workplace safety in the COVID age, where infection with the disease would be likely. Given the paramount levels of danger to society at large by the virus including the significant risk of death and serious illness for a significant number of people, by extension this danger must extend to most workplaces and, given the significant death toll, extensive government guidance and news coverage, most beliefs in such danger are surely 'reasonably held'.

---

11 [2003] IRLR 683 (EAT).
12 ibid para 54.
13 [2011] IRLR 730 (EAT).
14 ibid paras 25–26.

The existing case law in this area is instructive. In *Edwards & Others v The Secretary of State for Justice*,[15] the Employment Appeal Tribunal held that knowledge of the treacherous conditions on Devonshire roads that had been the subject of closure was a reasonably held belief of serious and imminent danger by Prison Officers who needed to use them to reach HMP Dartmoor. The fact that other officers had made the same journey without incident was held to be irrelevant. It has also been held that dangerous circumstances can arise from the actions of fellow employees. In *Harvest Press Ltd v McCaffrey*,[16] an employee's colleague, half the age of the claimant, who had been making threats and acting aggressively was found by the tribunal to constitute a serious and imminent danger for the purposes of the Employment Rights Act 1996:

> . . . As to the submission that the circumstances of danger referred to in section 100(1)(d) means the circumstances of danger generated by the workplace itself, it seems to us that that is too narrow a view of works which are quite general. It seems to us clear that premises or the place of work may become dangerous as a result of the presence or absence of an employee. For example, premises might become unsafe as a result of the presence of an unskilled and untrained employee working on dangerous processes in the workplace where the danger of a mistake is not just to that employee, but to the colleagues who are working with him. It seems to us that the circumstances of danger contemplated by section 100(1)(d) would be apt to cover such a situation and it seems to us that had a fellow employee walked out because of the presence of an unskilled and untrained operative in those circumstances, he would be entitled to the protection of the legislation.[17]

Further at paragraph 16:

> Another example might be where there was a foolhardy employee who, not through lack of training, but through determination to indulge in horseplay, persisted in adopting dangerous practices in the place of work so as to render the place at work dangerous. It seems to us that that might again be a situation in which fellow employees would be entitled to say to their employer; "so long as this person is at the workplace, my workplace is dangerous and I will not be willing to stay there during this time". Again, it seems to us that that falls within the words "in the circumstances of danger" and there is nothing in the statute to indicate that these examples would be out with the protection granted by section 100.[18]

---

15   *Edwards* (n 4).
16   [1999] IRLR 778 (EAT).
17   ibid.
18   ibid.

Should an employee's co-workers not use PPE or take other precautions as reasonably instructed a similar line of reasoning could be followed. Yet other questions arise. What if an employee were to observe a co-worker breaching COVID restrictions through social media posts, for example, refusing to observe social distancing evidenced through the publication of photographs? Would the employee be able to refuse to work with this person on the basis that they may present a serious and imminent danger?

The provisions themselves can be viewed as highly subjective. As shown by the case of *Edwards*,[19] one person's conception of what is to be regarded as "dangerous" may differ – in some cases, drastically from that of another person. This could lead to significant disagreements in the workplace over what is and is not a reasonable request in such circumstances and, moreover, difficult questions for a tribunal to resolve as to whether or not a dismissal was fair in the circumstances. As stated in *Oudahar*,[20] 'If an employee was liable to dismissal merely because an employer disagreed with his account of the facts or his opinion as to the action required, the statutory provisions would give the employee little protection.'[21]

It is strongly arguable that the fact of COVID-19 (or, importantly, any other disease at the core of a pandemic), in the early days at least, renders every workplace a "dangerous" one. Commuting to work in crowded conditions could also be regarded as dangerous – for example, the London underground at rush hour.

The Health and Safety at Work Act 1974 is the main Act of Parliament in respect of general workplace safety is. It is clearly stated within section 2(1) that 'It shall be the duty of every employer to ensure, so far as is reasonably practicable, the health, safety and welfare at work of all his employees.'[22] This section is used, not infrequently, against employers deemed to have created – or allowed to exist – unsafe working conditions and can result in criminal sanctions.[23] The Health and Safety at Work Act also created the HSE under section 10, and under section 11(2) it is empowered to give advice and information to both employers and employees regarding matters of health and safety.

It is also responsible for issuing notices to employers failing to adhere to Health and Safety rules and guidance. According to one source, however, there have been no such notices issued in respect of COVID-19 in the workplace.[24] Indeed, there have been a disparaging number of improvement or prohibition

19   *Edwards* (n 4).
20   *Oudahar* (n 13).
21   ibid para 30 per Richardson, J.
22   Act of Parliament year, s 2(1).
23   See, for example, *R v Palmer & Harvey McLane Ltd* [2012] EWCA Crim 993 – non provision of adequate PPE resulted in fine of £50,000.
24   Tom Wall, 'Firms Accused of Putting Workers Lives at Risk by Bending Lockdown Trading Rules' (*The Observer*, 16 January 2021) <https://www.theguardian.com/politics/2021/jan/16/bosses-accused-putting-workers-lives-risk-bending-lockdown-trading-rules?CMP=Share_iOSApp_Other> accessed 26 March 2021.

notices issued – apparently just 0.1% of nearly 97,000 safety cases referred to the agency.[25] Moreover, according to the HSE website there have been no prosecutions relating to breaches of COVID-19 rules.[26] This is in stark contrast to the number of private individuals who have been fined or prosecuted for breaches of such rules which regularly make the headlines – apparently 6,500 offences prosecuted in the first six months of the crisis,[27] as compared to 306 fixed penalty notices issued to employers for breaches of the Health Protection Regulations 2020 as of September 2020.[28] Curiously, COVID-19 was also apparently regarded as a "significant" rather than a "serious" workplace risk by the agency.[29]

One such mandatory rule that employers must follow is that of producing a COVID-19 Risk Assessment.[30] The impact of this is difficult to measure because of the dearth of available statistics and/or inspections. The author also questions whether every single employer in the country would be able to undertake such an assessment in the absence of training or qualification. Given the nature of COVID-19, it is virtually impossible to prove whether any given individual contracted the disease at their workplace or elsewhere. However, an examination of the statistics shows that those in certain occupational groups were more susceptible to dying from the disease, suggesting at least some causal connection between workplaces and contraction of the disease.[31] Indeed, the "statistician's quote" on the ONS website goes so far as to state that 'Today's analysis shows that jobs with regular exposure to COVID-19 and those working in

25 ibid.
26 The Health and Safety Executive, 'Management Information: Coronavirus (COVID-19) Disease Reports' (*Health and Safety Executive*) <https://www.hse.gov.uk/statistics/coronavirus/index.htm> accessed 26 March 2021.
27 According to the Crown Prosecution Service website there were almost 6,500 Coronavirus offences prosecuted in the first six months of the pandemic, see Crown Prosecution Service, '6,500 Coronavirus-related Prosecutions in First Six Months of Pandemic' (Crown Prosecution Service, 21 January 2021) <www.cps.gov.uk/cps/news/6500-coronavirus-related-prosecutions-first-six-months-pandemic> accessed 26 March 2021.
28 National Police Chiefs' Council, 'Update on national Crime Trends, and Fixed Penalty Notices issued under Covid Regulations' (*National Police Chiefs' Council*, 8 January 2021) <https://news.npcc.police.uk/releases/update-on-national-crime-trends-and-fixed-penalty-notices-issued-under-covid-regulations> accessed 26 March 2021.
29 Hazards Campaign, 'People's Court Verdict: Government Guilty! HSE Guilty! Employers Guilty!' (*Hazards Campaign*, 9 April 2021) <http://www.hazardscampaign.org.uk/> accessed 26 March 2021.
30 The Health and Safety Executive, 'Risk Assessment During the Coronavirus (COVID-19) Pandemic' (*Health and Safety Executive*) <www.hse.gov.uk/coronavirus/working-safely/risk-assessment.htm> accessed 26 March 2021.
31 Office for National Statistics, 'Coronavirus (COVID-19) Related Deaths by Occupation, England and Wales: Deaths Registered Between 9 March And 28 December 2020' (*ONS*) <www.ons.gov.uk/peoplepopulationandcommunity/healthandsocialcare/causesofdeath/bulletins/coronaviruscovid19relateddeathsbyoccupationenglandandwales/deathsregisteredbetween9marchand28december2020> accessed 26 March 2021.

close proximity to others continue to have higher COVID-19 death rates when compared with the rest of the working age population'.[32] Moreover, there have been a significant amount of reports detailing employers insisting that staff work in demonstrably dangerous conditions. One such high-profile report centred around the offices of the Driver and Vehicle Licensing Agency, where it was alleged that staff were requested to come in to work in spite of there being over 500 cases registered there since September 2020.[33] Other reports also detail similar circumstances.[34]

There have also been numerous reports of employees refusing to work in COVID unsafe environments or staging "walkouts" regarding the failure of employers to provide safe working conditions in light of the virus. Examples of reported incidences include architectural employees,[35] food operatives at multiple sites in Northern Ireland,[36] in addition to a number of Royal Mail workers in Belfast.[37] Amazon workers in Darlington,[38] workers at the ASOS warehouse

---

32 ibid.

33 Tom Wall, 'Grant Shapps Faces Fury Over Mass Covid Outbreak at DVLA' (*The Guardian*, 23 January 2021) <www.theguardian.com/world/2021/jan/23/minister-faces-fury-over-mass-covid-outbreak-at-top-government-agency?CMP=Share_iOSApp_Other> accessed 26 March 2021.

34 For example, Tom Banner, 'Covid Breaches at Worcester Supermarket's Warehouse, Says Worker' (*Worcester News*, 20 January 2021) <www.worcesternews.co.uk/news/19023095. covid-breaches-worcester-supermarkets-warehouse-says-worker/> accessed 26 March 2021.

35 United Voices of the World, 'Breaking: Architectural Workers Are Walking Out Over COVID-19 Safety Concerns' (*UVWN Union*, 8 January 2021) <www.uvwunion.org. uk/en/news/2021/01/architectural-workers-are-walking-out-over-covid-19-safety-concerns/> accessed 26 March 2021.

36 1 APB Meats in Lurgan: ITV News, 'Workers Walk Out at Food Plants Over Coronavirus Safety Fears' (*ITV News*, 25 March 2020) <www.itv.com/news/utv/2020-03-25/workers-walk-out-at-factories-over-coronavirus-safety-fears> accessed 26 March 2021; Linden Foods in Dungannon: BBC News, 'Coronavirus: Workers Walk Out Over "Lack of Social Distancing"' (*BBC News*, 27 March 2020) <www.bbc.co.uk/news/uk-northern-ireland-52058613> accessed 26 March 2021; Moy Park in Portadown, Rory Sullivan, 'Workers Walk Out at Major Poultry Plant Over Coronavirus Fears' (*The Independent*, 25 March 2020) <www.independent.co.uk/news/uk/home-news/northern-ireland-corona virus-worker-walk-out-poultry-plant-a9425161.html> accessed 26 March 2021. Section 44 and section 100 of the Employment Rights Act 1996 are implemented in Northern Ireland by the Order in Council under sections 68 and 132 respectively of the Employment Rights (Northern Ireland) Order 1996).

37 Shaun Keenan, 'Coronavirus Northern Ireland: Royal Mail Staff Walk Out Over Covid-19 Fears' (*BelfastLive*, 20 October 2020) <www.belfastlive.co.uk/news/coronavirus-northern-ireland-royal-mail-19133570> accessed 26 March 2021.

38 The Independent, 'Amazon Contract Workers "Walk Out" of UK Warehouse Over Safety Fears' (*The Independent*, 15 April 2020) <www.independent.co.uk/news/business/news/amazon-workers-protest-coronavirus-walkout-safety-fears-ppe-a9466881.html> accessed 26 March 2021.

near Barnsley in South Yorkshire,[39] postal workers in Didcot,[40] and a number of workers at a Marks and Spencer's warehouse operated by DHL International GmBh in Swindon.[41] These findings are significant as they demonstrate that, in some sectors at least, employees have the confidence to avail themselves of their statutory rights in such circumstances. It is notable, however, that the reported instances all seem to be from unionised workplaces and that data on whether any such employees were subjected to detriment or dismissal following such actions has yet not been forthcoming.

In terms of the right to refuse to work in dangerous circumstances, the seemingly low reliance on such rights could be explained with reference to a number of factors, the most likely being the fear of losing one's job. Moreover, the precarious nature of employment for many means that refusing to work may not be an option for financial reasons. As far as the paltry level of enforcement action taken in respect of workplaces is concerned, along with alarming reports of rules being flaunted, this shows that the HSE must either be given more power or use its existing powers more extensively in order to enforce the law more effectively.

Some comparative evidence

As the great Otto Kahn-Freund wrote upon comparatists, 'the gods have bestowed the most dangerous of all their gifts, the gift of freedom'.[42] In undertaking this study, it was felt that the choice of jurisdictions needed to be accessible, manageable and relevant. Moreover, the question of "why" must be addressed. Why choose these jurisdictions and why undertake a comparative approach at all? The second question can be answered instantly – this is arguably the first time that modern Labour Law has been tested by a global pandemic – an examination of the approaches of the various jurisdictions to certain problems arising – and, whether they are effective – is, thus, important.

Not every jurisdiction has published the full text of the legal instruments promulgated since the outbreak, and the pre-dating existing legislation remains obscure; whilst the language barrier inevitably put some beyond comprehension. Information on how the rules have been enforced in practice has been easier to find from some jurisdictions than others. For various – mostly

---

39   Alex Grove, 'ASOS Staff at Yorkshire Warehouse Walk Out of Shifts Over Coronavirus Fears' (*Examiner Live*, 26 March 2021) <www.examinerlive.co.uk/news/local-news/asos-staff-yorkshire-warehouse-walk-18006054> accessed 26 March 2021.

40   David Lynch, 'Didcot Postmen Walk Out on Strike due to Coronavirus Safety Worries' (*Oxford Mail*, 8 April) <www.oxfordmail.co.uk/news/18366677.didcot-postmen-walk-strike-due-coronavirus-safety-worries/> accessed 26 March 2021.

41   GMB Union, 'M&S Workers Stage Walkout Over Coronavirus Safety Fears' (*GMB Union*, 1 April 2020) <www.gmb.org.uk/news/mands-workers-stage-walkout> accessed 26 March 2021.

42   Otto Kahn-Freund, 'Comparative Law as an Academic Subject' (1966)82 *Law Quarterly Review* 40–41.

political – reasons, news about, for example, the enforced closure of unsafe workplaces is easier to obtain from the United States than it is from, say, the People's Republic of China.

It appears that the majority of states recognise similar legal principles to section 100 and section 44 of the Employment Rights Act 1996.[43] From the 133 countries available to examine on the website of the International Labour Organisation (ILO),[44] 46 had no data available but the others all embodied their laws in ways that were more similar than different to the UK position.[45]

For example, in France, employees have the legal right to withdraw their labour when facing danger or a potential danger under article L4131–3 of the French Labour Code which, translated, states: 'No sanction or deduction of wages may be taken against a worker or a group of workers who have withdrawn from a work situation which they had reasonable grounds to believe presented a danger, serious and imminent, for the life or health of each of them'.[46] Similarly, article 26 of South Korea's Occupational Safety and Health Act 1981 provides protection in respect of an "industrial accident":

(2) Where any employee suspends work and evacuates due to any urgent risk of an industrial accident, he or she shall promptly report it immediately to the superior officer, who shall take appropriate measures to address the situation.
(3) Where reasonable grounds exist to believe that any imminent danger of an industrial accident exists, a business owner shall not dismiss or otherwise disadvantage employees by reason of their suspending work and evacuating pursuant to paragraph.

In the United States section 11(c)(1) of the Occupational Safety and Health Act of 1970 prohibits employers from dismissing or discriminating against an employee who avails themselves of "any right afforded by" the Act – in this case the right to refuse to work in dangerous circumstances. This position was clarified in the US Supreme Court case of *Whirlpool Corp. v Marshall*,[47] a case involving two workers refusing to perform 'a cleaning operation because of a genuine fear

---

43 International Labour Organisation, 'LEGOSH Compare Results' (*International Labour Organisation*) <www.ilo.org/dyn/legosh/en/f?p=14100:2100:0::NO::P2100_COUNTRYLIST,P2100_NODELIST:AF;AM;AR;AS;EU;GBR,104392> accessed 26 March 2021.
44 ibid.
45 Botswana seemed to refer specifically to mines/work equipment-Mines, Quarries, Works and Machinery Regulations 1978. No 127. (section 70 and section 548) and the Sierra Leone Factories Act 1974 [No. 3 of 1974]. (article 37) – referred more to faults with machinery rather. Libya's code stated that a right to leave employment without notice would arise in such circumstances-Law No. 12 of 1378 [2010] on Labour Relations. (pt 3, ch 1, s 75, paras 1 and 5).
46 Republique Francaise, Legifrance, 'Code du travail' <www.legifrance.gouv.fr/codes/article_lc/LEGIARTI000006903157/> accessed 26 March 2021.
47 445 US 1 (1980).

of death or serious bodily harm'.[48] Here it was held that employees have a general right under this provision to refuse to work in dangerous conditions. If they did not have such measures before, he states of the European Union, are likely to have similar measures now, following the Framework Health and Safety Directive which prompted the UK legislation.[49]

As in the UK, there have been reports of workers staging walkouts and strikes over what they perceive to be unsafe working conditions or a failure to provide adequate COVID-related safety measures in other parts of the world. For example, in the United States, this has included Amazon workers in New York,[50] bus drivers in Detroit and Birmingham, along with sanitation workers in Pittsburgh and warehouse workers in Memphis.[51] Across Europe, this has included (again) Amazon workers[52] and workers at a Fiat plant in Italy.[53]

Regarding individual assertion of the right to refuse to work in dangerous conditions, it is possible that variations in domestic legislation account for at least some of the reasons why there are not more widespread reports of such cases. In a recent article,[54] it was reported that whilst there were many incidents of strike action and protests regarding COVID-related unsafe working conditions in the United States, there were very few – if any – in Canada against similar companies. It was reported that most of these actions were against large employers such as Amazon and McDonalds, and were mostly by non-unionised workers.[55] Under section 7 of the National Labour Relations Act, the most important legislation in employee protection in the United States, collective – though not necessarily unionised – actions over what is honestly believed to be unsafe working conditions are protected provided they are carried out in

48   ibid.
49   For a list of the Member States and the measures adopted by each under the directive see <https://eur-lex.europa.eu/legal-content/EN/NIM/?uri=CELEX:31989L0391> accessed 26 March 2021.
50   Kari Paul, 'Hundreds of Amazon Warehouse Workers to Call in Sick in Coronavirus Protest' (*The Guardian*, 21 April 2020) <www.theguardian.com/technology/2020/apr/20/amazon-warehouse-workers-sickout-coronavirus> accessed 26 March 2021.
51   Steven Greenhouse, 'Is Your Grocery Delivery Worth a Worker's Life?' (*The New York Times*, 30 March 2020) <www.nytimes.com/2020/03/30/opinion/coronavirus-worker-strike.html> accessed 26 March 2021.
52   Paola Tamma, 'Coronavirus Sparks Nationwide Strikes in Italy' (*Politico*, 13 March 2020) <www.politico.eu/article/coronavirus-sparks-nationwide-strikes-in-italy/> accessed 26 March 2021.
53   isNews, 'Coronavirus, Trade Unions Proclaim Strike at Fiat: We Do Not Jeopardise the Health of Workers' (*isNews*, 11 March 2020) <www.isnews.it/politica/67413-coronavirus-i-sindacati-proclamano-lo-sciopero-alla-fiat-non-mettiamo-a-rischio-la-salute-dei-lavoratori.html> accessed 26 March 2021.
54   Sara J Slinn, 'Protected Concerted Activity and Non-Unionized Employee Strikes: Worker Rights in Canada in the Time of COVID-19' (2021)57(3) *Osgoode Hall Law Journal* 605–35 <https://digitalcommons.osgoode.yorku.ca/ohlj/vol57/iss3/4>accessed 26 March 2021.
55   ibid 606.

good faith.[56] In certain cases, such "concerted" activity can be activity by an individual.

Under United States Federal Law, there is more emphasis on the protection of "individual" rights, whereas in Canada, Labour Law is more geared towards preserving industrial peace.[57] There is further no statutory "right to strike" in Canadian Labour Law, which contrasts with the NLRA.[58] Furthermore, section 502 of the Labour Management Relations Act in the United States gives the right to individual workers to stop work in the face of danger. However, the Canadian Labour Code of 1985 gives a similar right to many other employees across the world. Section128(1) states 'Subject to this section, an employee may refuse to use or operate a machine or thing, to work in a place or to perform an activity with reasonable cause'.[59]

It is sometimes difficult to decipher exactly which of the aforementioned "walkouts" was effectively a refusal to work in dangerous circumstances, analogous to sections 44 and 100 in the Employment Rights Act. A strike can be regarded as a technical point of law to be distinct from such a right, although it is entirely likely that in the minds of many striking workers that the two are conflated. In jurisdictions where the law purports to prevent those who refuse to work in dangerous conditions from suffering any detriment – including deductions from wages – it could be argued that such strikes are a symptom of failure in the law; why do workers need to strike – and earn no wages – when, alternatively, they could refuse to work in dangerous conditions and suffer no such detriment? Although strikes are an invaluable and important aspect of industrial democracy, perhaps in some instances there would have been no need to undertake them if there was confidence and/or awareness that under the law they should suffer no detriment for refusing to work in dangerous circumstances.

Similar to the UK, most of the jurisdictions examined promulgated emergency legislative and soft-law measures designed to mitigate the impact of COVID-19, all with a reasonably uniform flavour. For example, Brazil put forward SEPRT/MS Joint Ordinance No20 requiring employers to introduce COVID-specific safety measures,[60] covering areas such as the wearing of face-coverings, social distancing and hygiene. Similar provisions were put forward in a number of other states.[61] In Asia, Indonesia promulgated Health Decree No HK.01.07/MENKES/328/2020 concerning Guidelines for Prevention and Control of COVID-19 in Office and Industrial Workplaces in Supporting Business

---

56 ibid 616.
57 ibid 622.
58 ibid 623.
59 Canadian Labour Code of 1985, s128(1).
60 Brazil National School of Labour Inspection, 'Coronavirus Guidelines' <https://enit.trabalho.gov.br/portal/index.php/covid-19-coronavirus/> accessed 26 March 2021.
61 See Germany's SARS-CoV-2 Occupational Safety Standard for a further example.

Sustainability in Pandemic Situations.[62] Further, the Republic of Ireland's National Standards Authority published a COVID-19 Guide to assist employers,[63] and Belgium's Ministerial Decree of 30 April 2020 obliges employers to ensure a 'sufficient level of protection'[64] for employees unable to work from home.[65] Many jurisdictions such as Finland, Mexico and South Africa also issued industry specific guidance.[66] Notably, it was reported that the Netherlands did not bring any specific health and safety measures to bear to specifically cater for COVID-19,[67] although a number of sector-specific protocols were issued,[68] as was found to be the case in Luxembourg.[69]

Enforcement

As outlined previously, in the UK enforcement measures undertaken by the HSE and police appear to have been minimal. This has been labelled as "state failure" by Keith Ewing and John Hendy.[70] These authors attribute the lack of enforcement – in part at least – to the cuts in state funding that have prevailed since 2010. This, the author's assert, has coincided with significant falls in workplace inspections generally, service of improvement notices and prosecutions and convictions for breaches of health and safety law.[71]

62 Rizaldy Anggriawan, 'Responding to COVID-10: Indonesian Occupational Health and Safety Policy for Corporate Compliance' (2020)5(1) *Journal of Industrial Hygiene and Occupational Health* 51.

63 David Mangan, 'Covid-19 and Labour Law in Ireland' (2020)11(3) *European Labour Law Journal* 298–305.

64 ibid 281.

65 Frank Hendrickx, Simon Taes and Mathias Wouters, 'Covid-19 and Labour Law in Belgium' (2020)11(3) *European Labour Law Journal* 276–85.

66 Finnish Government, 'Guidelines for Workplaces' (*Finish Institute of Occupational Health*, 16 March 2020) <www.ttl.fi/en/fioh-coronavirus-instructions/> accessed 15 April 2021; Government of Mexico, 'Agreement Establishing Extraordinary Actions to Address the Health Emergency Generated by the SARS-CoV2 Virus' <www.dof.gob.mx/nota_detalle.php?codigo=5590914&fecha=31/03/2020> accessed 19 April 2021; South African Department of Employment and Labour, 'Direction by the Minister of Employment and Labour In Terms of Regulation 4(10) of the Regulations r480 of 29 April 2020 Issued by the Minister of Cooperative Governance And Traditional Affairs in Terms of Section 27(2) of the Disaster Management Act, 2002 (Act No. 57 of 2002)' (4 June 2021) <www.gov.za/sites/default/files/gcis_document/202006/43400rg11128gon639.pdf> accessed 4 June 2021.

67 Hanneke Bennaars, 'Covid-19 and Labour Law in the Netherlands' (2020)11(3) *European Labour Law Journal* 324–31, 330.

68 ibid.

69 Luca Ratti, 'Covid-19 and Labour Law in Luxembourg' (2020)11(3) *European Labour Law Journal* 314–18, 317.

70 Keith D Ewing and Lord Hendy, 'Covid-19 and the Failure of Labour Law: Part I' (2020)49(4) *Industry Law Journal* 497–538, 522.

71 ibid.

Elsewhere, it was reported in Canada that in British Columbia alone there were more than 21,000 workplace inspections, which found more than 1,600 violations of COVID rules,[72] with more than 392 violations being detected in December 2020 alone.[73] Ewing and Hendy report that there were only 727 workplace inspections by the HSE between 1 March and 20 May 2020.[74] In Singapore it was reported that "Stop Work" orders were made in respect of 13 construction sites who were observed to have been allowing COVID-19 positive workers to continue working.[75]

Regarding court-based enforcement in the United States, court documents reveal that the Attorney General of New York and others are suing e-commerce giant Amazon for, amongst other things, failing to provide adequate personal protective equipment and failing to ensure COVID-specific workplace safety.[76] Other litigation includes the estate of a deceased Walmart employee bringing an action against his employer for negligence.[77] However, it has also been reported that 'most' of the firms that have been fined for breaches of COVID health and safety measures have refused to pay them.[78] This action against Amazon was also mirrored in France where the company was forced to cease operations there for not having carried out thorough risk assessments with employee

72 CBC News, 'WorkSafeBC Finds More Than 1,600 Violations of COVID-19 Safety Plans' (*CBC*, 31 January 2021) <www.cbc.ca/news/canada/british-columbia/covid-19-worksafe-bc-violations-health-safety-compliance-numbers-worksites-1.5893893> accessed 26 March 2021.

73 ibid.

74 ibid.

75 Yip Wai Yee, 'Stop Work Orders Issued to 13 Worksites After Dorm Cluster' (*The Straits Times*, 25 August 2020) <www.straitstimes.com/singapore/stop-work-orders-issued-to-13-worksites-after-dorm-cluster> accessed 26 March 2021.

76 Papers filed by the New York County Clerk, online at <https://iapps.courts.state.ny.us/nyscef/ViewDocument?docIndex=muvelgaOEvSt6Yc1gGqzAg==> accessed 26 March 2021.

77 Thomson-Reuters, 'Health and Safety at Work – Testing the Limits' (2002) *IDS Employment Law Brief* 2, 1124 <https://uk.westlaw.com/Document/I763EE160874F-11EA97EDCE672EBCA316/View/FullText.html?navigationPath=Search%2Fv1%2Fresults%2Fnavigation%2Fi0ad604ac00000179b2726ee874199a37%3Fppcid%3D347b79f3f7a44f84af478c97d265ab08%26Nav%3DRESEARCH_COMBINED_WLUK%26fragmentIdentifier%3DI763EE160874F11EA97EDCE672EBCA316%26parentRank%3D0%26startIndex%3D1%26contextData%3D%2528sc.Search%2529%26transitionType%3DSearchItem&listSource=Search&listPageSource=b9549a128a0b70fccfb2db0c901ae955&list=RESEARCH_COMBINED_WLUK&rank=1&sessionScopeId=4a4f68e1b57fc9bc06abbddbc80f6570d602f369d490b49534c6864dd487f57c&ppcid=347b79f3f7a44f84af478c97d265ab08&originationContext=Search%20Result&transitionType=SearchItem&contextData=(sc.Search)&comp=wluk> accessed 28 May 2021.

78 Chris Kirkham, 'Exclusive: Most US Firms Hit with COVID-19 Safety Fines Aren't Paying Up' (*Reuters*, 18 February 2021) <www.reuters.com/article/us-health-coronavirus-workplace-fines-ex-idUSKBN2AI1JT> accessed 26 March 2021.

representatives, and having not assessed the psychological risks.[79] From the research undertaken there is yet to be a comparable legal action taken against an employer in the UK.

Discipline and dismissal

This section examines the potential impact of the Coronavirus on Disciplinary proceedings and dismissals which could arise out of the unique circumstances of the virus.

On the 23 of March 2020 the United Kingdom went into what has come to be known as a state of "lockdown".[80] Anybody who could work from home was ordered to do so by the government and any travel was limited to essential purposes. At the beginning of June, the lockdown was eased, but two further "lockdowns" of a similar nature were subsequently imposed. Whilst the unavoidable disruption caused by such measures cannot be understated, it is recognised that certain workplace processes and procedures will have been running in the background regardless, including payroll functions, human resources processes and disciplinary and investigation procedures.

As a result of these regular lockdowns, periods of delay impact on disciplinary and investigative processes. This may have initially been compounded and complicated by the furloughing of employees. Although the Advisory Conciliation and Arbitration Service (ACAS) has stated that furloughed employees can still raise grievances or be involved in a disciplinary matter,[81] the legal status of this is questionable insofar as ACAS does not have the power to issue strictly binding proclamations. Where disciplinary and investigatory processes have been carried out remotely, this too could bring problems.

Whilst there is no statutory guidance on what an "unreasonable delay" might be, paragraph 4 of the non-binding ACAS Code of Practice stipulates that workplace disciplinary incidents should be investigated 'promptly or without delay'.[82] The updated guidance, however, states that employers should consider whether 'minor' allegations can wait to be heard at a later date.[83] In terms of case law in

79 Tatiana Sachs, 'Covid-19 and Labour Law in France' (2020)11(3) *European Labour Law Journal* 286–91, 289.
80 Press Association Reporters, 'Coronavirus Timeline of Key Events Since UK Was Put into Lockdown Six Months Ago' (*The Independent*, 23 September 2020) <www.independent.co.uk/news/uk/home-news/coronavirus-uk-timeline-lockdown-boris-johnson-pubs-test-and-trace-vaccine-b547630.html> accessed 26 March 2021.
81 ACAS, 'Disciplinary and Grievance Procedures During the Coronavirus Pandemic' (*ACAS*, 6 May 2020) <www.acas.org.uk/disciplinary-grievance-procedures-during-coronavirus> accessed 26 March 2021.
82 ACAS, 'Acas Code of Practice on Disciplinary and Grievance Procedures' <https://acas.org.uk/media/1047/Acas-Code-of-Practice-on-Discipline-and-Grievance/pdf/11287_CoP1_Disciplinary_Procedures_v1__Accessible.pdf> accessed 26 March 2021.
83 N81.

this area, in *Marley Homecare Ltd v Dutton*,[84] an employee was investigated about an incident which had occurred seven days prior. This was held to be an unreasonable delay – the tribunal recognising that people's memories of an incident can fade within a short period of time. Since there is no concrete guidance on what "delay" actually looks like, employers would be well-advised to ensure there is as little delay as possible.

In cases of action falling short of dismissal there is generally, unless contractually agreed between the parties, no ground to claim damages for breach of a disciplinary procedure. In respect of actions resulting in dismissal the method of dismissal will fall outside the *Johnson* exclusion zone, for example the way in which the dismissal was handled.[85] However, an application for an equitable grant of injunctive relief prohibiting an employer from continuing a disciplinary procedure following a long period of delay (once some form of normality has resumed), is theoretically possible. Moreover, employers, taking their lead from the updated ACAS guidance, should still try to ensure that investigations into even minor matters are carried out without undue delay as a matter of best practice. After all, what may seem like a minor issue to one person may not be so trivial to the accused individual. Nobody likes to be kept in suspense and it is perfectly foreseeable that what is perceived as an unnecessary delay to proceedings could, in and of itself, form the basis of an independent grievance.

To avoid any such delay, an employer may wish to carry out investigatory and disciplinary proceedings remotely, for which there is a sound legal basis. The line taken in *Pirelli General Cable Works Ltd v Murray*[86] was that 'The concept of natural justice does not include the right to be personally present throughout'.[87] In many respects, "virtual" disciplinary proceedings should be legally unproblematic as long as the principles of *audi alteram partem* and natural justice are accommodated as much as reasonably possible in the circumstances.

As was stated by Slynn J in the case of *Bentley Engineering Co Ltd v Mistry*:[88]

> We do not say that in every case any particular form of procedure has to be followed . . . On the other hand it is clear that in a matter of this kind, natural justice does require not merely that a man shall have a chance to state his own case in detail; he must know in one way or another sufficiently what is being said against him. If he does not know sufficiently what is being said against him, he cannot properly put forward his own case. It may be, according to the facts, that what is said against him can be communicated to him in writing, or it may be that it is sufficient if he hears what the other protagonist is saying, or it may be that, in an appropriate case, for matters which

84   [1981] IRLR 380 (EAT).
85   *Johnson v Unisys Ltd* [2001] UKHL 13.
86   [1979] IRLR 190 (EAT).
87   ibid 192 per Bristow J.
88   [1979] ICR 47.

have been said by others to be put orally in sufficient detail is an adequate satisfaction of the requirements of natural justice. As Bristow J. said, it is all a question of degree.[89]

What this quote shows us is that rules of procedural fairness can be flexible and that a rigid standard need not be followed, it all being 'a question of degree', which may thus legitimise 'virtual disciplinaries'. In the case of *Fountaine v Chesterton*,[90] the so-called 'rules of natural justice' were summarised as: 'the right to be heard by an unbiased tribunal; the right to have notice of charged misconduct; and the right to be heard in answer to those charges'.[91] Regardless of whether the forum is a virtual or physical one, such rights should be guaranteed as far as reasonably possible. With respect to giving notice of the allegations against an employee, this must extend to sending the required documentation by post or email a reasonable time ahead of the actual hearing itself. If sent by post, then any associated delays should be factored in to the overall timeframe with an employee being afforded sufficient time to prepare a response. The right to be accompanied by a Trade Union representative or colleague under section 10 of the Employment Relations Act 1999 would also need to be facilitated virtually.

In cases of digital poverty or where internet connections may not be strong enough to facilitate a full hearing, it should be permissible to deal with such matters in writing should the employee provide consent to this and has been offered adequate resource to advice and consultation with their Trade Union representative or a colleague. However, if an investigation or hearing is likely to result in dismissal this is not an ideal situation. In any case, it is recommended that, at the very least a telephone conference should be arranged where possible.

It must be stressed that should any questions be asked in clarification of any of the employee's written evidence, these should be asked in the presence of the Trade Union, colleague or employee representative, Alternatively, if requested in writing, it would be diligent to include a statement advising the employee that they have the right to take advice from their Trade Union, colleague or employee representative.

Whilst it may be legally permissible to hold such hearings remotely, consideration should be given to the potential for interference with privacy. A commonly encountered trope of the lockdown age is the (often unwitting) encroachment of family members, partners and children upon meetings held on digital platforms. If all concerned parties are working from home, including the investigating officer, the decision-maker, the accused employee, in addition to Trade Union representatives/other colleagues/human resources staff, the potential for sensitive information to be overheard whilst being broadcast simultaneously into

---

89   ibid 51 per Slynn J.
90   (1968) 112 Sol Jo 690.
91   ibid per Megarry J.

three or more homes cannot be understated. Whilst it is beyond the scope of this chapter, consideration of this point in light of the General Data Protection Regulations[92] may be an interesting avenue to investigate. Relatedly, the potential impact on privacy could persist even if such matters are dealt with at the workplace. With increased priority given to ventilation within confined office-spaces it may well be that the privacy of an investigatory or disciplinary hearing is compromised; perhaps to the extent that an accused party is unwilling to engage in a full and frank discussion for fear of being overheard.

Procedural matters in respect of discipline aside, substantive matters such as those relating to the employee's capability could arise regarding hearings under sickness-absence management procedures and the requirements of self-isolation. Employees with a good attendance record are likely to be unaffected by the implications of such, but where employers operate a "strike" system as regards incidents of absence there could potentially be problems for employees with a less than perfect attendance. In *International Sports Ltd v Thomson*,[93] an employee with a record of persistent absenteeism for a variety of reasons over an 18-month period was dismissed following a final warning. There was no examination by the company doctor as there was apparently no underlying condition or link between the illnesses suffered. The dismissal was held to be fair. If the absenteeism in this case were related to the need to self-isolate or, otherwise COVID-19 related, would the result have been the same? The fairness of a dismissal for persistent absenteeism could potentially fall to be decided as a matter of conduct – as in this case – or capability more generally, and such a dismissal could be contested by the employee as potentially unfair. Section 98(2) of the Employment Rights Act 1996 states that fairness

> (a) depends on whether in the circumstances (including the size and administrative resources of the employer's undertaking) the employer acted reasonably or unreasonably in treating it as a sufficient reason for dismissing the employee, and (b) shall be determined in accordance with equity and the substantial merits of the case.

However, In *Davis v Tibbett and Britten Group plc*,[94] it was stated as a long-established rule that in cases of frequent and persistent absenteeism the question of whether the reason for the absence is genuine is inconsequential.[95] The question of "reasonableness" on the employer's part turns on the question of whether the employer should have to tolerate and pay the cost of persistent absenteeism on the employee's behalf. It is at least possible that COVID-19 related absence in

92 Regulation (EU) 2016/679 (General Data Protection Regulation).
93 [1980] IRLR 340.
94 (2000) EAT 460/99.
95 As reported in 'Dealing with persistent short-term absences, IDS Emp. L. Brief 2018, 1095, 11–18 at p 4.

such circumstances may not receive any special treatment in respect of those on a final warning for absenteeism, which is concerning.

In response to the COVID-19 outbreak, many of the jurisdictions observed made provisions for remote working or "tele-working". Some of the pitfalls highlighted earlier have been heeded by law firms in Canada,[96] and it has been recognised that delays to any proceedings resulting from COVID in Australia may be frowned upon by the Courts.[97] Hard data on these matters is very difficult to source and, other than the consistent promulgations on "tele-working" established by most states examined as part of this study, there do not appear to have been any legislative changes made specifically to cope with these matters. One matter that is worth noting, however, is that some jurisdictions have much tighter rules on matters such as timeframes than others, which would provide more certainty regarding what is and is not an acceptable delay. Examples of such systems embodying such rules include the majority of former Eastern Bloc countries.[98] Providing an answer to charges in writing is common practice in a number of jurisdictions.[99]

Conclusions

It goes without saying that the events of the past year have been, in modern times at least, without parallel. From the perspective of England and Wales – and in a number of comparable jurisdictions – the law in respect of dangerous circumstances appears to be functional. The law gives rights to workers to refuse to work in dangerous circumstances and it appears that at least some of them have availed themselves of these rights. The law seemingly allows individual dismissals and disciplinary proceedings to be conducted remotely, albeit with inevitable – but not unsurmountable – difficulties. It is likely that the human cost of COVID-19 across the working population may be in spite of these rules, rather than owing to a lack of them. Lack of enforcement, precarious employment,[100] and the overall novelty of the situation may be more to blame for the high death toll.

96 Jennifer Costin, 'Conducting Workplace Investigations COVID-Style' (*Siskinds LLP*, 23 November 2020) <www.mondaq.com/canada/operational-impacts-and-strategy/1009242/conducting-workplace-investigations-covid-style> accessed 26 March 2021.
97 Adriana Orifici, 'Under the Cloak of COVID-19: How the Pandemic Affects Workplace Investigations' (*Monash University*, 24 June 2020) <https://www2.monash.edu/impact/articles/labour-market/under-the-cloak-of-covid-19-how-the-pandemic-affects-workplace-investigations/> accessed 26 March 2021.
98 See, for example, the Azerbaijani Labour Code s187(1), the Kazakh Labour Code Art 73(2), the Lithuanian Labour Code art 240(1), the Moldovan Labour Code art 208 (1) and the Tajikistan Labour Code s124.
99 See the Labour Codes of Azerbaijan, Bulgaria, Kazakhstan, Lithuania, Moldova and Tajikistan.
100 For an interesting discussion of employment status in the context of COVID-19 see the case of *Regina (Independent Workers' Union of Great Britain) v Secretary of State for Work and Pensions and Another* [2020] EWHC 3050 (Admin).

In a general sense however, observing the attitude of the United Kingdom to international rules may be instructive. It was reported that the United Kingdom has ratified less than one in five of the most recent ILO health and safety instruments, putting it behind the majority of EU states and on a similar level to Mozambique and Saudi Arabia.[101] Regarding the ratification status of the ILO's 1981 Occupational Safety and Health Convention,[102] the United States, Colombia, India, Italy, Germany, France and the United Kingdom have not ratified this instrument,[103] and all of these countries have experienced exceptionally high COVID-19 rates.[104] At the time of writing, all fall within the top ten countries for incidences of cases.[105] Whilst this is just as likely to be a pure coincidence rather than a consequence of these jurisdictions' cultural alignment with notions of health and safety, it is submitted that, all the same, a new international convention on pandemic workplace health and safety should be put forward and framed on the basis of good practice.

Domestically, whilst it is certainly true that some jurisdictions appear to have been more successful at prosecuting breaches of COVID safety by employers than others, it is clear that reform should be considered in order to lessen the blows of future pandemics. If the exercise of rights such as the right to refuse to work in dangerous circumstances are only exercisable by those without precarious employment situations, it may be that the fault does not lie with the law itself. If precarious employment is set to be a continuing feature of the modern economy other solutions must be sought, possibly in the form of a state emergency fund that workers could access without prejudice should they find themselves dismissed as a result of standing up for, or asserting, such rights. This dispute then be resolved by a tribunal in safer times, the outcome of whose decision could mean such a worker or employee may be required to pay any funds back should the employers' action be found to be justified.

Regarding disciplinary proceedings and dismissals, it is likely that working from home may become a concrete part of the employment landscape within England and Wales post-pandemic. It follows that more investigatory; disciplinary and dismissal procedures could be conducted remotely. Whilst this may have been the only way to deal with certain problems during the worst stages of the pandemic,

---

101 Rory O'Neil, 'The UK's Health and Safety Laws Deliberately Fall Below International Norms, and Workers Are Paying the Price' (*Institute for Employment Rights*, 28 April 2020) <www.ier.org.uk/comments/the-uks-health-and-safety-laws-deliberately-fall-below-international-norms-and-workers-are-paying-the-price/> accessed 29 March 2021.
102 Convention No 155 Convention concerning Occupational Safety and Health and the Working Environment 1981.
103 International Labour Organisation, 'Countries that Have Not Ratified This Convention' (*ILO Website*) <www.ilo.org/dyn/normlex/en/f?p=NORMLEXPUB:11310:0::NO:1131 0:P11310_INSTRUMENT_ID:312300:NO> accessed 30 March 2021.
104 Johns Hopkins University and Medicine, 'COVID-19 Dashboard by the Center for Systems Science and Engineering (CSSE) at Johns Hopkins University' (29 March 2020) <https://coronavirus.jhu.edu/map.html> accessed 19 May 2021.
105 ibid.

it is not desirable that this way of conducting disciplinaries should persist. For the reasons previously stated, it is more desirable for such hearings to be carried out in the traditional way. However, if an employee expresses a preference for this option, for whatever reason, perhaps it would be unreasonable to refuse unless there are other compelling reasons not to.

The last year has been unparalleled and, as tragic as it has doubtlessly been, it has been interesting to observe the effects on employment practices from a legal perspective. The best way forward legally is to learn from this collective experience and to try our upmost to formulate a more effective strategy ahead of the next sadly inevitable pandemic.

Bibliography

ACAS, 'Acas Code of Practice on Disciplinary and Grievance Procedures' <https://acas.org.uk/media/1047/Acas-Code-of-Practice-on-Discipline-and-Grievance/pdf/11287_CoP1_Disciplinary_Procedures_v1__Accessible.pdf> accessed 26 March 2021.

ACAS, 'Disciplinary and Grievance Procedures During the Coronavirus Pandemic' (*ACAS*) <www.acas.org.uk/disciplinary-grievance-procedures-during-coronavirus> accessed 26 March 2021.

Balfour Kilpatrick Ltd v Acheson [2003] IRLR 683 (EAT).

Banner T, 'Covid Breaches at Worcester Supermarket's Warehouse, Says Worker' (*Worcester News*, 20 January 2021) <www.worcesternews.co.uk/news/19023095.covid-breaches-worcester-supermarkets-warehouse-says-worker/> accessed 26 March 2021.

BBC News, 'Coronavirus: Workers Walk Out Over "Lack of Social Distancing" ' (*BBC News*, 27 March 2020) <www.bbc.co.uk/news/uk-northern-ireland-52058613> accessed 26 March 2021.

Bennaars H, 'Covid-19 and Labour Law in the Netherlands' (2020)11(3) *European Labour Law Journal* 324–31.

Bentley Engineering Co Ltd v Mistry [1979] ICR 47.

Brazil National School of Labour Inspection, 'Coronavirus Guidelines' <https://enit.trabalho.gov.br/portal/index.php/covid-19-coronavirus/> accessed 26 March 2021.

Bulgarian Labour Code 1986.

CBC News, 'WorkSafeBC Finds More Than 1,600 Violations of COVID-19 Safety Plans' (*CBC*, 31 January 2021) <www.cbc.ca/news/canada/british-columbia/covid-19-worksafe-bc-violations-health-safety-compliance-numbers-work sites-1.5893893> accessed 26 March 2021.

Costin J, 'Conducting Workplace Investigations COVID-Style' (*Siskinds LLP*, 23 November 2020) <www.mondaq.com/canada/operational-impacts-and-strategy/1009242/conducting-workplace-investigations-covid-style> accessed 26 March 2021.

Council Directive 89/391/EEC of 12 June 1989 on the Introduction of Measures to Encourage Improvements in the Safety and Health of Workers at Work OJ L 183.

Crown Prosecution Service, '6,500 Coronavirus-related Prosecutions in First Six Months of Pandemic' (*Crown Prosecution Service*, 21 January 2021) <www.cps.gov.uk/cps/news/6500-coronavirus-related-prosecutions-first-six-months-pandemic> accessed 26 March 2021.

Davis v Tibbett and Britten Group plc EAT 460/99.

Edwards & Others v The Secretary of State for Justice, Appeal No UKEAT/0123/14/DM.

Employment Rights Act 1996.

Employment Rights (Northern Ireland) Order 1996 No 1919 (N I 16).

Ewing, DK and Hendy J, 'Covid-19 and the Failure of Labour Law: Part I' (2020)49(4) *Industry Law Journal* 497–538, 522.

Fadipe v Reed Nursing Personnel [2005] ICR 1760.

Finnish Government, 'Guidelines for Workplaces' (*Finish Institute of Occupational Health*, 16 March 2020) <www.ttl.fi/en/fioh-coronavirus-instructions/> accessed 15 April 2021

Fountaine v Chesterton (1968) 112 Sol Jo 690.

GMB Union, 'M&S Workers Stage Walkout Over Coronavirus Safety Fears' (*GMB Union*, 1 April 2020) <www.gmb.org.uk/news/mands-workers-stage-walkout> accessed 26 March 2021.

Government of Mexico, 'Agreement Establishing Extraordinary Actions to Address the Health Emergency Generated by the SARS-CoV2 Virus' <www.dof.gob.mx/nota_detalle.php?codigo=5590914&fecha=31/03/2020> accessed 19 April 2021.

Greenhouse S, 'Is Your Grocery Delivery Worth a Worker's Life?' (*The New York Times*, 30 March 2020) <www.nytimes.com/2020/03/30/opinion/coronavirus-worker-strike.html> accessed 26 March 2021.

Grove A, 'ASOS Staff at Yorkshire Warehouse Walk Out of Shifts Over Coronavirus Fears', (*Examiner Live*, 26 March 2021) <www.examinerlive.co.uk/news/local-news/asos-staff-yorkshire-warehouse-walk-18006054> accessed 26 March 2021.

Harvest Press Ltd v McCaffrey [1999] IRLR 778.

Hazards Campaign, 'People's Court Verdict: Government Guilty! HSE Guilty! Employers Guilty!' (*Hazards Campaign*, 9 April 2021) <www.hazardscampaign.org.uk/> accessed 26 March 2021.

Hendrickx F, Taes S and Wouters M, 'Covid-19 and Labour Law in Belgium' (2020)11(3) *European Labour Law Journal* 276–85.

Health and Safety at Work Act 1974.

The Health and Safety Executive, 'Management Information: Coronavirus (COVID-19) Disease Reports' (*Health and Safety Executive*) <www.hse.gov.uk/statistics/coronavirus/index.htm> accessed 26 March 2021.

The Health and Safety Executive, 'Risk Assessment During the Coronavirus (COVID-19) Pandemic' (*Health and Safety Executive*) <www.hse.gov.uk/coronavirus/working-safely/risk-assessment.htm> accessed 26 March 2021.

ILO Convention No. 155 Convention Concerning Occupational Safety and Health and the Working Environment 1981.

The Independent, 'Amazon Contract Workers "Walk Out" of UK Warehouse Over Safety Fears' (*The Independent*, 15 April 2020) <www.independent.co.uk/news/business/news/amazon-workers-protest-coronavirus-walkout-safety-fears-ppe-a9466881.html> accessed 26 March 2021.

Indonesia Health Decree No. HK.01.07/MENKES/328/2020 2020.

International Labour Organisation, 'LEGOSH Compare Results' (*International Labour Organisation*) <www.ilo.org/dyn/legosh/en/f?p=14100:2100:0::NO::P2100_COUNTRYLIST,P2100_NODELIST:AF;AM;AR;AS;EU;GBR,104392> accessed 26 March 2021.

International Labour Organisation, 'Countries That Have Not Ratified This Convention' (*ILO Website*) <www.ilo.org/dyn/normlex/en/f?p=NORMLEXPUB :11310:0::NO:11310:P11310_INSTRUMENT_ID:312300:NO> accessed 30 March 2021.

International Sports Ltd v Thomson [1980] IRLR 340.

isNews, 'Coronavirus, Trade Unions Proclaim Strike at Fiat: We Do Not Jeopardise the Health of Workers' (*isNews*, 11 March 2020) <www.isnews.it/politica/67413-coronavirus-i-sindacati-proclamano-lo-sciopero-alla-fiat-non-mettiamo-a-rischio-la-salute-dei-lavoratori.html> accessed 26 March 2021.

ITV News, 'Workers Walk Out at Food Plants Over Coronavirus Safety Fears' (*ITV News*, 25 March 2020) <www.itv.com/news/utv/2020-03-25/workers-walk-out-at-factories-over-coronavirus-safety-fears> accessed 26 March 2021.

Johns Hopkins University and Medicine, 'COVID-19 Dashboard by the Center for Systems Science and Engineering (CSSE) at Johns Hopkins University' (29 March 2020) <https://coronavirus.jhu.edu/map.html> accessed 30 March 2021.

Kahn-Freund O, 'Comparative Law as an Academic Subject' (1966)82 *Law Quarterly Review* 40–41.

Kazakh Labour Code 2007.

Keenan S, 'Coronavirus Northern Ireland: Royal Mail Staff Walk Out Over Covid-19 Fears' (*BelfastLive*, 20 October 2020) <www.belfastlive.co.uk/news/coronavirus-northern-ireland-royal-mail-19133570> accessed 26 March 2021.

Kirkham C, 'Exclusive: Most US Firms Hit with COVID-19 Safety Fines Aren't Paying Up' (*Reuters*, 18 February 2021) <www.reuters.com/article/us-health-coronavirus-workplace-fines-ex-idUSKBN2AI1JT> accessed 26 March 2021.

Lithuanian Labour Code 2002.

Lynch D, 'Didcot Postmen Walk Out on Strike Due to Coronavirus Safety Worries' (*Oxford Mail*, 8 April) <www.oxfordmail.co.uk/news/18366677.didcot-postmen-walk-strike-due-coronavirus-safety-worries/> accessed 26 March 2021.

Mangan D, 'Covid-19 and Labour Law in Ireland' (2020)11(3) *European Labour Law Journal* 298–305, 281.

Moldovan Labour Code 2003.

National Police Chiefs' Council, 'Update on national Crime Trends, and Fixed Penalty Notices Issued Under Covid Regulations' (*National Police Chiefs' Council*, 8 January 2021) <https://news.npcc.police.uk/releases/update-on-national-crime-trends-and-fixed-penalty-notices-issued-under-covid-regulations> accessed 26 March 2021.

Office for National Statistics, 'Coronavirus (COVID-19) Related Deaths by Occupation, England and Wales: Deaths Registered Between 9 March And 28 December 2020' (*ONS*) <www.ons.gov.uk/peoplepopulationandcommunity/healthandsocialcare/causesofdeath/bulletins/coronaviruscovid19relateddeathsbyoccupationenglandandwales/deathsregisteredbetween9marchand28december2020> accessed 26 March 2021.

O'Neil R, 'The UK's Health and Safety Laws Deliberately Fall Below International Norms, and Workers Are Paying the Price' (*Institute for Employment Rights*, 28 April 2020) <www.ier.org.uk/comments/the-uks-health-and-safety-laws-deliberately-fall-below-international-norms-and-workers-are-paying-the-price/> accessed 29 March 2021.

Orifici A, 'Under the Cloak of COVID-19: How the Pandemic Affects Workplace Investigations' (*Monash University*, 24 June 2020) <https://www2.monash.edu/

impact/articles/labour-market/under-the-cloak-of-covid-19-how-the-pandemic-affects-workplace-investigations/> accessed 26 March 2021.

Oudahar v Esporta Group Ltd [2011] IRLR 730.

Paul K, 'Hundreds of Amazon Warehouse Workers to Call in Sick in Coronavirus Protest' (*The Guardian*, 21 April 2020) <www.theguardian.com/technology/2020/apr/20/amazon-warehouse-workers-sickout-coronavirus> accessed 26 March 2021.

Pirelli General Cable Works Ltd v Murray [1979] IRLR 190.

Press Association Reporters, 'Coronavirus Timeline of Key Events Since UK Was Put into Lockdown Six Months Ago' (*The Independent*, 23 September 2020) <www.independent.co.uk/news/uk/home-news/coronavirus-uk-timeline-lockdown-boris-johnson-pubs-test-and-trace-vaccine-b547630.html> accessed 26 March 2021.

Ratti L, 'Covid-19 and Labour Law in Luxembourg' (2020)11(3) *European Labour Law Journal* 314–18, 317.

Regina (Independent Workers' Union of Great Britain) v Secretary of State for Work and Pensions and another [2020] EWHC 3050 (Admin).

Republique Francaise, 'Code du travail' 2017.

R v Palmer & Harvey McLane Ltd [2012] EWCA Crim 993.

Sachs T, 'Covid-19 and Labour Law in France' (2020)11(3) *European Labour Law Journal* 286–91, 289.

Slinn JS, 'Protected Concerted Activity and Non-Unionized Employee Strikes: Worker Rights in Canada in the Time of COVID-19' (2021)57(3) *Osgoode Hall Law Journal* 605–35. <https://digitalcommons.osgoode.yorku.ca/ohlj/vol57/iss3/4>accessed 26 March 2021.

South African Department of Employment and Labour, 'Direction by the Minister of Employment and Labour In Terms of Regulation 4(10) of the Regulations r480 of 29 April 2020 Issued by the Minister of Cooperative Governance and Traditional Affairs in Terms of Section 27(2) of the Disaster Management Act, 2002 (Act No. 57 of 2002)' (4 June 2021) <www.gov.za/sites/default/files/gcis_document/202006/43400rg11128gon639.pdf> accessed 4 June 2021.

Sullivan R, 'Workers Walk Out at Major Poultry Plant Over Coronavirus Fears' (*The Independent*, 25 March 2020) <www.independent.co.uk/news/uk/home-news/northern-ireland-coronavirus-worker-walk-out-poultry-plant-a9425161.html> accessed 26 March 2021.

Tajikistan Labour Code 1997.

Tamma P, 'Coronavirus Sparks Nationwide Strikes in Italy' (*Politico*, 13 March 2020) <www.politico.eu/article/coronavirus-sparks-nationwide-strikes-in-italy/> accessed 26 March 2021.

Thomson-Reuters, 'Health and Safety at Work – Testing the Limits' (2002) *IDS Employment Law Brief* 2, 1124. <https://uk.westlaw.com/Document/I763EE160874F11EA97EDCE672EBCA316/View/FullText.html?navigationPath=Search%2Fv1%2Fresults%2Fnavigation%2Fi0ad604ac00000179b2726ee874199a37%3Fppcid%3D347b79f3f7a44f84af478c97d265ab08%26Nav%3DRES-EARCH_COMBINED_WLUK%26fragmentIdentifier%3DI763EE160874F11EA97EDCE672EBCA316%26parentRank%3D0%26startIndex%3D1%26contextData%3D%2528sc.Search%2529%26transitionType%3DSearchItem&listSource=Search&listPageSource=b9549a128a0b70fccfb2db0c901ae955&list=RESEARCH_COMBINED_WLUK&rank=1&sessionScopeId=4a4f68e1b57fc9bc06abbddbc8

0f6570d602f369d490b49534c6864dd487f57c&ppcid=347b79f3f7a44f84af478c97d265ab08&originationContext=Search%20Result&transitionType=SearchItem&contextData=(sc.Search)&comp=wluk> accessed 28 May 2021.

United Voices of the World, 'Breaking: Architectural Workers Are Walking Out Over COVID-19 Safety Concerns' (*UVWN Union*, 8 January 2021) <www.uvwunion.org.uk/en/news/2021/01/architectural-workers-are-walking-out-over-covid-19-safety-concerns/> accessed 26 March 2021.

UK Government, 'Working Safely During Coronavirus (COVID-19)' (*Gov.UK*) <www.gov.uk/guidance/working-safely-during-coronavirus-covid-19> accessed 26 March 2021.

Wall T, 'Firms Accused of Putting Workers Lives at Risk by Bending Lockdown Trading Rules' (*The Observer*, 16 January 2021) <www.theguardian.com/politics/2021/jan/16/bosses-accused-putting-workers-lives-risk-bending-lockdown-trading-rules?CMP=Share_iOSApp_Other> accessed 26 March 2021.

Wall T, 'Grant Shapps Faces Fury Over Mass Covid Outbreak at DVLA' (*The Guardian*, 23 January 2021) <www.theguardian.com/world/2021/jan/23/minister-faces-fury-over-mass-covid-outbreak-at-top-government-agency?CMP=Share_iOSApp_Other> accessed 26 March 2021.

Whirlpool Corp v Marshall 445 US 1 (1980).

Wilson v Post Office [1980] IRLR 340.

Yee WY, 'Stop Work Orders Issued to 13 Worksites After Dorm Cluster' (*The Straits Times*, 25 August 2020) <www.straitstimes.com/singapore/stop-work-orders-issued-to-13-worksites-after-dorm-cluster> accessed 26 March 2021.

Zoe Zelman v Billboard Media [2020] FWC 5.

9 Labour force, suspended rights and entrepreneurs' disruption of activities

Andrés Jerónimo Arenas Falótico and Jessica Bayón Pérez

Introduction

As we have experienced, COVID-19 is a global virus that does not understand the concept of borders among nations nor laws or regulations, indiscriminately affecting every citizen worldwide (whether a wealthy person in the US or a labourer in India). COVID-19's transmission has been deeply accelerated due to globalisation: the interconnectedness of every country and the constant flow of goods and people between nations has played a key role. Not only has it caused thousands of deaths and millions of infections it has also forced countries, with or without any legal framework, to put their society into quarantine (even if this risks their business). These measures also created a state of alarm (including suppression of its citizens' rights), which has lasted in some cases for several months and has had a severe impact on the worldwide economy. However, as countries' wealth, laws, power and resources vary from one another, and the measures taken by their governors and Central Banks are different, the impact that COVID-19 is having in the economy is different (even within regions of the same country). Coronavirus can be seen as a completely unforeseen and extraordinary event; countries were not prepared for a global pandemic. Thus, as a contingency plan was not developed their response depends on the actions and the speed of implementing effective measures that can mitigate or limit the impact of the virus on its economies.

This pandemic is shaping the world drastically and the shift to a more digitalised economy is taking place at greater strides: as examples, fashion events and sports' games are broadcasted without physical public attendance, e-commerce webs such as Amazon have seen an increase in their benefits, Netflix has seen a rise in their profits. Those countries who have the latest technology, the resources, and the right skilled workforce have suffered less from the impact of the crisis and have in certain cases benefited. Nonetheless, those variables will deepen the inequality between developed and undeveloped countries. Moreover, even within developed nations the gap will be widened. The Spanish case can be considered, where tourism makes a 12.4% of its GDP and 12.9% of total employment,[1] where

1 Instituto Nacional de Estadística, 'Cuenta satélite de turismo en España 2019 (Satellite Tourism Account in Spain 2019)' (*INE*, 11 December 2020) <www.ine.es/dyngs/

DOI: 10.4324/9781003176848-13

temporary contracts compose a large part of their workforce and there are not so many high-tech firms in existence.

What is more, the largest concern for the economic landscape is small and medium enterprises (SME's). Due to this crisis, quarantines have obliged them to close their businesses for long periods of time. Further, the lack of the resources to continue their business is problematic; a large part of SMEs all around the world are expected to go bankrupt due to the quarantine and the upcoming economic crisis.[2]

The countries' responses to the pandemic

The COVID-19 pandemic has brought a health crisis that has affected virtually every country. The response of developed countries to the pandemic was based on stay-at-home policies that paralyzed their economic activity for several months, and probably years. Due to this economic paralysis, global growth is projected to moderate to 3.8% in 2022, weighed down by the pandemic's lasting damage to potential growth. In particular, the impact of the pandemic on investment and human capital is expected to erode growth prospects in emerging market and developing economies (EMDEs) and set back key development goals.[3]

The economic position for the future is quite pessimistic, as there is a consensus that COVID-19 is going to bring a global recession never seen before. It will be different from the Asian debt crisis of 1997, or the 2008 global crisis that occurred due to the fall of Lehman Brothers; a crisis that does not resemble any previous crisis and for which we were not prepared. In such uncertain times, countries need to implement effective measures, where the timing is crucial. However, a dilemma arises: what is more important – to save the people or the economy? As appeared logical and humane, countries decided to save their citizens and to put them into quarantine at the expense of paralyzing the economy.[4]

Most countries' quick response to the crisis involved the adoption of an Expansionary Monetary Policy where interest rates were lowered, money was injected

---

INEbase/es/operacion.htm?c=estadistica_C&cid=1254736169169&menu=ultiDatos&idp=1254735576863> accessed 10 May 2021.

2   Jonathan Dimson and others, 'COVID-19 and European Small and Medium-size Enterprises: How They Are Weathering the storm' (*McKinsey & Company*, 22 October 2020) <www.mckinsey.com/industries/public-and-social-sector/our-insights/covid-19-and-european-small-and-medium-size-enterprises-how-they-are-weathering-the-storm> accessed 12 December 2020.

3   World Bank Group, 'Global Economic Prospect, January 2021' (*World Bank*, January 2021) <https://openknowledge.worldbank.org/bitstream/handle/10986/34710/9781464816123.pdf> accessed 12 February 2021.

4   P Ozili and T Arun, 'Spillover of COVID-19: Impact on the Global Economy' (*Research Gate*, 2020) <www.researchgate.net/publication/340236487_Spillover_of_COVID-19_impact_on_the_Global_Economy> accessed 18 May 2020.

into the economy or to buy public debt from the European Central Bank whose emergency fund was created during the pandemic in the form of PEPP. This was a temporary asset purchase programme whose budget has been increased the initial €750 billion envelope for the PEPP by €600 billion on 4 June 2020 and by €500 billion on 10 December, for a new total of €1,850 billion.[5] This monetary policy tool has been relatively effective as investors have recovered some trust and European stock markets have been trading positively.

However, individuals and families have not responded in the same way as markets. There has been an increased number in unemployment, and families' incomes have been disrupted due to the economic paralysis. In Spain, around 99.8% of the companies is comprised of SMEs.[6] Because they could not open their businesses during quarantine, they had no income. Consumption has decreased since the worldwide spread of the pandemic; some countries have even adopted a bailout package without almost any answer.[7]

Impact of government policies in a global pandemic context: labour impact on employment

Lockdown quarantine and restriction of movement policies adopted by governments, for example in the United States of America (USA), have been thought to be inefficient,[8] and counter-productive by a large part of the population. Instead of carrying out substantial tests, detecting positive cases, tracking their social circles and putting those positive cases into isolation so that the spread can be controlled, countries such as the US or Spain have attempted to devalue the COVID-19 pandemic at its early stage. Moreover, some governments such as Spain have been accused of concealing and distorting the impact that the virus was having, including the numbers of infections and deaths.[9] In addition, instead of recognizing its government mismanagement of the pandemic, during the last administration the US attempted to divert North Americans' anxiety and dissatisfaction by condemning China. Trump's actions towards freeze US funding and its initiative of leaving the World Health Organization (WHO) have been

---

5 European Central Bank, 'Pandemic Emergency Purchase Programme' (*ECB*) <www.ecb. europa.eu/mopo/implement/pepp/html/index.en.html> accessed 10 December 2020.
6 Ministerio de Industria, Comercio y Turismo, 'Marco Estratégico en Política de Pyme 2030 (Strategic SME`s Political Framework 2030)' (*Ministry of Industry, Commerce and Tourism*, April 2019) <https://industria.gob.es/es-es/Servicios/MarcoEstrategicoPYME/Presentacion_Estrategia_PYME.pdf> accessed 23 May 2020.
7 Ozili and Arun (n 4).
8 Charles Silver and David A Hyman, 'COVID-19: A Case Study of Government Failure' (*CATO Institute*, 15 September 2020) <www.cato.org/pandemics-policy/covid-19-case-study-government-failure> accessed 15 December 2020.
9 Raphael Minder, 'Counting Bodies and Pointing Fingers as Spain Tallies Coronavirus Dead' (*The New York Times*, 16 April 2020, Updated 16 November 2020) <www.nytimes.com/2020/04/16/world/europe/coronavirus-spain-death-toll.html> accessed 10 December 2020.

possible under the COVID-19 spread pretext. The spread of the Coronavirus in the US was the fault of WHO, not his administration.[10]

In the case of the European Union, which has been deeply affected by COVID-19, the quarantine measures have increased, for example in March 2021, the euro area seasonally-adjusted unemployment rate was down 8.1%, from 8.2% in February 2021 and up from 7.1% in March 2020.[11] The EU unemployment rate was 7.3% in March 2021, also down from 7.4% in February 2021 and up from 6.4% in March 2020.[12] The economic status of the Eurozone countries has been damaged deeply and a large number of citizens have seen their economic status jeopardised. This volatile situation and economic paralysis have brought dissatisfaction among citizens, as witnessed for example with the "Caceroladas" in different regions of Spain.[13]

The European Central Bank has indeed designated 1.35 billion euros to mitigate the effects of the pandemic.[14] Nonetheless, it is important to point out that due to the quick and firm hand of the ECB's measures, volatility on the financial markets has calmed and has re-established the important role of the European Union as a global actor, whose objective is to act as a unique, conglomerated actor in the international scenario.

How different sectors have been affected – some brief explanations

The tourism and aviation sector and the workforce impact

The tourism sector has been one of the most affected, as travel bans and restrictions on non-essential trips became the norm. According to data from the World Travel and Tourism Council (WTTC), global tourist arrivals dropped by 73% in 2020, with a loss of nearly 62 million travel-and tourist-related jobs.[15]

10   Thomas J Bollyky and Jeremy Konyndyk, 'It's Not the WHO's Fault That Trump Didn't Prepare for the Coronavirus' (*The Washington Post*, 14 April 2020) <www.washington post.com/outlook/2020/04/14/trump-who-coronavirus-response/> accessed 31 March 2020.

11   Eurostat, 'Unemployment Statistics' (*Eurostat Statistics Explained*, March 2021) <https://ec.europa.eu/eurostat/statistics-explained/index.php?title=Unemployment_statistics#Unemployment_in_the_EU_and_the_euro_area> accessed 10 May 2021.

12   ibid.

13   El Independiente, 'Las "caceroladas" contra Sánchez se extienden desde Madrid a otras ciudades (The Caceroladas Against Sánchez Extent from Madrid to Other Cities)' (*El Independiente*, 18 May 2020) <www.elindependiente.com/politica/2020/05/18/las-caceroladas-contra-sanchez-se-extienden-desde-madrid-a-otras-ciudades/> accessed 23 July 2020.

14   European Central Bank, 'Monetary Policy Decisions' (*European Central Bank*, 4 June 2020) <www.ecb.europa.eu/press/pr/date/2020/html/ecb.mp200604~a307d3429c.en.html> accessed 30 August 2020.

15   Zhanjie Chen, 'Economic Watch: Europe Prepares to Reopen Tourism Sector, But Unlikely to Reach Pre-pandemic Level Soon' (*Xinhua*, 8 May 2021) <www.xinhuanet.com/english/2021–05/08/c_139932689.htm> accessed 10 May 2021.

In the aviation sector, massive cancellations of already booked flights and a sharp drop in the demand due to the strict travel measures imposed by the government have dealt a severe blow to the sector. A large share of the airlines first cancelled flights to Asia, and then it spread to the cancellation of more international destinations flights. Malaysia Airport reported a 96.4% passenger decline in November 2020,[16] USA airlines have reached 25 billion dollars in loans,[17] and UK airlines have urged a 7.5 billion pounds' emergency bailout.[18] The Netherlands are implementing strategies in order to ensure the continuation of Air France and KLM.[19]

In general terms, as most international destinations have not opened their borders to tourism, the government are trying to encourage their citizens to travel nationally so that the tourism sector can be revived.

The hotel industry and the workforce impact

This industry is one of the most affected sectors. Marriot Hotels has been obliged to put tens of thousands of workers into furlough. Hilton Hotels have asked for a 1.75 billion dollars' precautionary loan.[20] In China, occupancy rates fell by 89% in January 2020, causing several layoffs and reduced working hours.[21] In the US, hotel companies are asking for a 150 billion dollars' direct aid as their estimated losses have been of 1.5 billion dollars since February 2020,[22] one of the largest legislative rescue packages in more than a decade in that country. In Germany, hotel occupancy decreased over 36%.[23]

---

16 Wong Ee Lin, 'MAHB's November Passenger Traffic Down 30.8 % m-o-m on CMCO Extension' (*Theedgemarkets.com*, 15 December 2020) <www.theedgemarkets.com/article/mahbs-november-passenger-traffic-down-308-mom-cmco-extension> accessed 23 January 2021.

17 Alan Rappeport and Niraj Chokshi, 'Crippled Airline Industry to Get $25 Billion Bailout, Part of It as Loans' (*The New York Times*, 17 March 2021) <www.nytimes.com/2020/04/14/business/coronavirus-airlines-bailout-treasury-department.html> accessed 23 February 2021.

18 Maria Nicola and others, 'The COVID-19 Pandemic Has Resulted in Over 4.3 Million Confirmed Cases and Over 290' (2020)78 *IJS* 189 <https://reader.elsevier.com/reader/sd/pii/S1743919120303162?token=72AF42040776348CA53570BA50511A24CD08 6B1976C8F6044EA281969FF9F878D87FD8EE6F106444A5AD85D0D4D1AA49> accessed 13 July 2020.

19 ibid.

20 Gillian Tan, 'Hilton Draws Down $1.75 Billion Credit Line to Ease Virus Hit' (*Bloomberg*, 11 March 2020) <www.bloomberg.com/news/articles/2020-03-11/hilton-to-draw-down-part-of-1-75-billion-line-as-virus-spreads> accessed 12 June 2020.

21 Godwell Nhamo and others, *Counting the Cost of COVID-19 on the Global Tourism Industry* (Cham, Switzerland, Springer Nature 2020) 6.

22 Ted Mann and Alison Sider, 'Hotels Seek $150 Billion in Aid as Travel Plummets' (*The Wall Street Journal*, 17 March 2020) <www.wsj.com/articles/hotels-seek-150-billion-in-aid-as-travel-plummets-11584486738> accessed 23 June 2020.

23 ibid.

The healthcare industry and the workforce impact

This pandemic has provided an unprecedented challenge for worldwide health care systems. It has also highlighted the precarious conditions of the health system in some developed countries. This has included the lack of essential material such as surgical masks, testing equipment that put into risk the health of those workers (which saw hundreds of thousands of infected and tragic deaths of nurses and doctors who were infected while working due to the shortage of materials).

The pharmaceutical industry and the workforce impact

The paralysation of its supply chain caused severe supply problems, as this industry relies heavily on ingredients imported, mainly from Asia (about 60% or 70% of the world's active pharmaceutical ingredients were made in China).[24]Thus, when the COVID-19 outbreak took place, the worldwide supply chain of pharmaceutical companies was disrupted. On the other hand, this outbreak has seen an opportunity for the sector, as companies have invested in drug development and the research for the different vaccines that are now being distributed around the world. Further, products such as alcohol, hand sanitizers, protective face mask and similar products related to disinfection have been the big winners during this pandemic period. Jobs have increased steadily from May 2020 to April 2021.[25]

The finance industry and the workforce impact

This sector has been heavily affected due to its globalised context and the uncoordinated responses that the different governments have given to the COVID-19 crisis. Private sector banks had the highest exposure to credit risk as the pandemic was developing, as SME, airlines, hotels, restaurants and retail demanded loans. Due to quarantine, there has been a decrease in the volume of bank transactions and a fall in the use of ATMs worldwide, implying that banks collected fewer fees, a fact which affected their profits. The biggest example of the COVID-19 impact in the financial sector is the global stock market, as the market reflects the fear, volatility and conservatism of investors during the developing uncertain times. Europe's bond and the US ten-year bond dropped its price. In order to face the effects of the pandemic, Central Banks decided to buy public debt or to inject liquidity so that investment was motivated. Lagarde

---

24   Steven Lynn, 'China's Role in Global Generic Pharmaceutical Supply Chain' (*GLG*, 4 February 2020) <https://glginsights.com/articles/chinas-role-in-global-generic-pharmaceutical-supply-chain/> accessed 3 March 2020.

25   Pharmaceutical Technology, 'Pharma Jobs Index Vs Other Sectors (Last 12 Months)' (*Global Data Jobs Analytics Database*, May 2021) <www.pharmaceutical-technology.com/jobs-analytics/> accessed 12 May 2021.

(president of the European Central Bank – ECB) rescued Mario Draghi (ex-president of the ECB): a "whatever it takes" approach in order to save the Eurozone economy.[26]

Nonetheless, 'Banks have been gradually closing branches due to customers' preferences to use their mobile phone applications'.[27] COVID-19 has accelerated this process and has given banks the opportunity to change faster than expected, making them more profitable in that specific retail banking area. Naturally, jobs have been lost in the process without any legal or government protection for those affected.

Petroleum and oil industry and the workforce impact

Due to the oil price war between Saudi Arabia and Russia, prices fell at the beginning of 2020 and the COVID-19 worsened the situation. OPEP countries held a meeting in order to reduce the oil produced as demand fell sharply (as citizens were confined to their houses and travel restrictions were imposed). But that reduction in the production was not enough, as producers feared not having the capacity of holding so much stock caused by the drop of demand. This caused, for the first time in its history, the West Texas Intermediate to trade in the negative: on 18 April 2020 its price reached $-37.63.[28]

The fall in oil prices together with the reduction in demand has worsened the balance of payment of oil-dependent countries such as Venezuela, Angola and Nigeria.[29] This might trigger salary reduction, the non-renewal of temporary contracts; further, salary increases will be difficult in those countries. Also, this drop of demand has caused a domino effect in this industry. Gas stations cannot give employment to as many people as before, since people are not pumping gas at the same levels.

Education and the workforce impact

As confinement was declared in virtually every country, it affected all the educational fields: pre-school, high schools, universities were forced to close their doors in order to mitigate the spread of the virus between students. UNESCO reported that the COVID-19 outbreak disrupted the education of at least 290.5 million

---

26 Adam Tooze, 'The Eurozone's "Whatever It Takes" Mantra Has a Problem' *Financial Times* (London, 3 April 2020) 34.

27 Jessica Bayón Pérez and Andrés Jerónimo Arenas Falótico, 'Various Perspectives of Labor and Human Resources Challenges and Changes Due to Automation and Artificial Intelligence' (2019) *AISJ* (20) 112.

28 BBC news editor, 'Caída del precio del petróleo: El crudo estadounidense WTI se desploma y se cotiza en negativo por primera vez en la historia (Oil Price Drop: US WTI Crude Slumps and Trades Negative for the First Time in History)' (*BBC News*, 20 April 2020) <https://www.bbc.com/mundo/noticias-52362339> accessed 19 June 2020.

29 Ozili and Arun (n 4).

students.[30] Moreover, the imposition of online learning has not been possible in every institution, as some lacked the materials, resources and a contingency plan to face the pandemic. It also increased the gap between low-income families whose children are not able to access the online materials so that their education is disrupted and high-income ones who can afford the online materials for their children to continue their education. Some universities have laid off professors and have asked them to record videos.[31]

The leisure sector and the workforce impact

Since the "stay at home" policies were imposed, restaurants, hair salons, retail shops, etc. in other words SMEs, were forced to shut down meaning that, for weeks, their benefits were nil. Moreover, many of them faced bankruptcy, as they were not able to survive weeks closed, and will not be able to confront the recessionary period that has yet to come.

The event industry was also hit hard by the COVID-19 pandemic. Concerts, conferences, weddings, parties, events, brand launches, shows, etc. were forced to cancel. The 2020 Met gala was postponed indefinitely. In the Film Industry the shutdown of 70,000 cinemas in China, around 2,500 in the US and more than 9,000 in the European Union, is inflicting an estimated loss of $5 billion on the global box office; this amount could skyrocket to between $15 billion and $17 billion.[32] The EU film sector is essentially made up of small companies employing creative and technical freelancers, making it particularly vulnerable to the pandemic. The domino effect of the lockdown has triggered the immediate freeze of hundreds of projects in the shooting phase, disrupted cash flows and pushed production companies to the brink of bankruptcy.[33] This problem continues during 2021.

Moreover, due to the nature of the entertainment industry, it is still doubtful if they will be able to receive part of the aids and stimulus package of the different governments. Workforce have been affected without any laws or government regulations for those affected. Sports events, like the Euro 2020 tournament and the Tokyo Olympic games, were cancelled and rescheduled causing several temporary contracts to be halted or suspended.

30   UNESCO, '290 Million Students Out of School Due to COVID-19: UNESCO Releases First Global Numbers and Mobilizes Response' (*UNESCO*, 4 March 2020) <https://en.unesco.org/news/290-million-students-out-school-due-covid-19-unesco-releases-first-global-numbers-and-mobilizes> accessed 24 July 2020.
31   Paul Rigg, '275 Layoffs as University Asks Staff to Make Videos' (*University World News*, 10 February 2021) <www.universityworldnews.com/post.php?story=2021021007111588> accessed 15 March 2021.
32   European Parliament, 'Coronavirus and the European Film Industry' (*European Union*, 2020) <www.europarl.europa.eu/RegData/etudes/BRIE/2020/649406/EPRS_BRI(2020)649406_EN.pdf> accessed 12 December 2020.
33   ibid.

The food sector and the workforce impact

The food sector has been one of the least affected by the pandemic, as their goods are considered a necessity, so that their economic activity did not cease. Moreover, the widespread "panic buying" of citizens (as they feared a shortage of essential goods) has increased the benefits for supermarkets. Nonetheless, one of their weak points has been online shopping, as most of the supermarkets were not prepared for the high amount of orders causing waiting periods of more than two weeks or an order delay.

Some companies have even implemented a bonus for the pandemic, a good example is the chocolate factory "Valor" in Spain who has given employees a 20% extra salary as a production plus for the extremely good financial performance of the company.[34]

Good examples in the Spanish food industry includes: Luis Calvo Sanz (canned tuna producer) added €300 per employee, Grupo Lactalis (milk producers) €500 per employee, La Española and Agro Sevilla (canned olives producers) between €200 to €150 per employee, Juver Alimentación (juices and beverages) €250 per employee, and Nestle Spain €500 per employee.[35] It is obvious that workforce in this sector have been economically benefitted by the crisis without government or laws regulating those extra bonuses.

The fashion sector and the workforce impact

The disruption in global economic activity has forced fashion firms to close their stores and to paralyze their supply chain. This has affected fashion firms enormously for two reasons: their products are seasonal; if they were not able to sell their winter-spring collection, they will have to deal with an overstock problem. As their products are not considered a necessity by the population, they will see a drop in their benefits with the upcoming recession. Losses are expected to be around 30% – 37% in 2020 and, in the luxury sector, the estimations are worse: their losses are expected to be between 35% – 39%.[36] Moreover, we can see a change in the paradigm of the consumer: it is shifting towards a more concerned and sustainable model, so that firms who have a culture which is similar to the new paradigm, can benefit in the future. The "fast fashion" methodology (practiced by the Inditex group firms where new products and collections are constantly being launched to stimulate purchases), has a substantial impact on the

---

34   Herminia Martínez, 'Se extiende la gratificación salarial a los trabajadores por la crisis del Covid-19 (Salary Gratification Is Extended to Workers Due to the Covid-19 Crisis)' (*Alimarket*, 21 April 2020) <www.alimarket.es/alimentacion/noticia/313448/se-extiende-la-gratificacion-salarial-a-los-trabajadores-por-la-crisis-del-covid-19#> accessed 31 July 2020.
35   ibid.
36   Imran Amed and others, 'The State of Fashion 2021: In Search of Promise in Perilous Times' (*McKinsey & Company*, 1 December 2020) <www.mckinsey.com/industries/retail/our-insights/state-of-fashion#> accessed 20 February 2021.

environment.[37] The crisis has witnessed a devastating impact on businesses and jobs in this sector, without proper protection from governments in the form of laws or policies for those affected.

COVID-19 and the workforce impact

As the impact of the virus has different effects depending on the sector that we are analysing, it also happens with the workforce, which leads to the creation of vulnerable groups (women, people with disabilities, racial minorities, people with low education and in low wages jobs) who are especially exposed to the effects of the Pandemic.

Women are essential workers that fight in the frontline (which make up the 70% of the frontline workforce[38]) during the crisis (nurses, cleaners, doctors, drivers). Additionally, women are one of the most affected by the health, economic and social impacts of the crisis. People with disabilities usually felt left behind by the publication of the government measures. The crisis amplifies the threats that children can face (violence, mistreatment, exploitation); in Latin America, about 95% of children enrolled in school are temporarily left without education, as one of the containment measures was to close schools, constituting one of the most serious educational crises which can be linked to the spread of the virus.[39]

In 2019, a McKinsey study found that companies who had a high percentage of gender diversity in executive teams were more likely to have above-average profits, and those who had the highest percentage of ethnic and cultural diversity outperformed those companies who had less percentage by 36%.[40] This is due to the fact that a strong gender-diversity correlation results in an improvement in the organisational health, and a better Corporative Image which increases benefits. A more diverse business team can improve the quality of decision, taking into account

37 Morgan McFall-Johnsen, 'La industria de la moda emite más carbono que los vuelos internacionales y el transporte marítimo juntos: estas son sus mayores consecuencias en el planeta (The Fashion Industry Emits More Carbon than International Flights and Maritime Transport Combined: These Are Its Greatest Consequences on the Planet)' (*BusinessInsider*, 28 October 2019) <https://www.businessinsider.es/impacto-moda-medio-ambiente-terrible-saber-514379> accessed 12 February 2020.

38 The Organisation for Economic Co-operation and Development (OECD), 'Women at the Core of the Fight Against COVID-19 Crisis' (*OECD*, 1 April 2020) 1 <https://read.oecd-ilibrary.org/view/?ref=127_127000-awfnqj80me&title=Women-at-the-core-of-the-fight-against-COVID-19-crisis&_ga=2.22691897.340763577.1622568809-2034336424.1622568809> accessed 12 March 2021.

39 United Nations, 'UN Working to Ensure Vulnerable Groups Not Left Behind in COVID-19 Response' (*Department of Global Communications*, 24 March 2020) <https://www.un.org/en/coronavirus-communications-team/un-working-ensure-vulnerable-groups-not-left-behind-COVID-19> accessed 23 December 2020.

40 Vivian Hunt and others, 'Diversity Wins' (*McKinsey&Company*, May 2020) <www.mckinsey.com/~/media/mckinsey/featured per cent20insights/diversity per cent20and per cent20inclusion/diversity per cent20wins per cent20how per cent20inclusion per cent-20matters/diversity-wins-how-inclusion-matters-vf.pdf> accessed 30 July 2020.

that diversity brings different perspectives towards the same problem due to the cultural background of the workers. It is, therefore, likely to be more innovative, as workers feel empowered to make decisions and express their points of view. If a company develops an Inclusion and Diversity strategy their corporate image will improve. For those reasons, an investment in Inclusion and Diversity can cushion the impact of the crisis, boosting the company and improving their situation.

A good example is Brazil. The great concern in that country is to contain the advance of the pandemic by taking measures not to overburden the health system and, consequently, reduce losses in all sectors of the economy, including the possibility of maintaining employment relationships without causing unemployment. In the field of labour relations, in principle and in accordance with the protection standards to the worker provided for in their Federal Constitution,[41] there would be no basis in the economy to ensure that companies are financially healthy to play their social role of avoiding mass unemployment. Therefore, in the critical moment of the pandemic, due to *force majeure* issues, what should prevail is the harmony and spirit of conciliation between state, company and worker, because the common objective for the entire population, in this state of crisis, is social balance and the maintenance of the economic order, parallel to the fight against the disease. This aspect is what seems to be implicit in Provisional Measure 927,[42] which was urgently edited to contain the progress of the crisis.

According to GlobalData, there are only five sectors of the economy with a steady increase in jobs: Pharma, Medical, Healthcare, Construction and Technology.[43] Our previous analysis clearly shows that there are winners and losers. The impact is alleviated when legislation provides help for those affected. The lack of legislation or government regulations to protect employees/workers from this type of crises is, for them, the difference between life and death. There is a need for legislation that can effectively protect the workforce, including minorities, from crises such as Covid 19; this will not be the first nor the last pandemic in the near future. We also need some worldwide standards on how to behave and how to legislate; each country has acted differently to the same problem (COVID) and the consequences are obvious.

The importance of business digitalisation during COVID-19 times

For the last decade, the business landscape has been experiencing a digital revolution, known as the fourth Industrial Revolution. This has brought us advances in the technological field: It has disrupted the global supply chain, how we make business and how we contact with each other. Terms such as Artificial Intelligence,

---

41 Jadson Azeredo Monteiro, 'A flexibilização das obrigações Trabalhistas frente a pandemia mundial do Coronavírus – Covid-19 (Flexibilization of Workers' Obligations Lieu of the World Pandemic of Coronavirus – COVID-19)' (2020) I *Revista Científica UNIFAGOC* 16.
42 ibid.
43 Pharmaceutical Technology (n 25).

Big Data, Data Scientist, Internet of Things, etc., are gaining more and more popularity and adepts. It makes our production process more efficient, faster and reduces our costs. It has changed our production paradigm from a centralised model to a decentralised and horizontal one.

Following COVID-19's outbreak, this event has accelerated the companies' digital shifts as telework and online shopping, which has become the norm after the quarantine and "stay at home" policies. It is important to know that prior to the spread of the virus, almost 70% of the firms had or were experiencing a digital transformation, but COVID-19 has forced them to accelerate it.[44]

Working from home, has undergone a long legislative evolution and has taken various forms from the early twentieth century to today. Historically, the first form of remote work known by the legal system is that represented by work from home, first governed by different laws worldwide. Such a way of carrying out the work performance, used mostly by entrepreneurs-clients who speculated on an undoubted cost saving both for labour and for maintaining the company premises, has been virtually supplanted by teleworking and, above all, by agile work, a further species of the genus remote work based on the socio-economic panorama of the digital and information revolution. Smart working has seen its own legislative consecration. In Italy, the Law number 81/2017[45] (the so-called autonomous Jobs act) was introduced with the specific objective of facilitating life's reconciliation and working hours, and to increase company's competitiveness.

In Switzerland for example, due to the coronavirus crisis, the number of employees teleworking from home, part-time or for the whole of their working time, has increased enormously.[46] In the absence of specific rules in the common law regime, Eric Cerottini comments about labour contracts and the ordinary provisions of the Code of Obligations on the employment contract and labour legislation that apply in that country.[47] According to him, the parties are advised to provide for an agreement on the organisation and conditions of teleworking. While it offers real opportunities, teleworking from home can also entail risks that should not be underestimated. This involves ensuring the security of data and their communication, as well as preserving the private sphere and the health of the workers concerned. In addition, when the home office is carried out by a

---

44 Smarp, 'How COVID-19 Is Accelerating Digital Transformation in the Workplace' (*Smarp*, 21 April 2020) <https://blog.smarp.com/how-COVID-19-is-accelerating-digital-transformation-in-the-workplace> accessed 18 September 2020.

45 Domenico Iodice and Riccardo Colombani, 'Il lavoro agilenella legge n. 81/2017' (Agile Work in Law No. 81/2017) (ADAPT UP 2017) <https://moodle.adaptland.it/pluginfile.php/29946/mod_resource/content/1/wp_9_2017_iodice_colombani.pdf> accessed 23 February 2021.

46 Jean-Philippe Dunand and Rémy Wyler, 'Quelques implications du coronavirus en droit suisse du travail (Some Implications of the Coronavirus in Swiss Labour Law)' (*Cielo Laboral*, April 2020) <www.cielolaboral.com/wp-content/uploads/2020/04/dunand_wyler_noticias_cielo_n4_2020.pdf> accessed 12 January 2021.

47 Eric Cerottini, *Commentaire du contrat de travail* (*Comments About Labour Contracts*) (Berne, Stämpfli Editions 2013) 12.

frontier worker, the question of possible subjugation to the social security system of the state of residence arises.[48]

Telework, in general, is expected to be maintained for a long period and that is why companies need to have the resources and the infrastructures to allow their workers to efficiently continue their job remotely. During times of crisis, it is important to ensure that workers receive the correct information from their employers. Communication and collaboration must be improved to prevent confusion. A strong and charismatic leadership is needed to guide firms through crises. Furthermore, it is necessary to take place contingency planning for business continuity and such planning must take a full consideration of all possible situations and scenarios to ensure business stability in all circumstances. Building company resiliency is a key aspect of business development.

Germany, for example, took this issue very seriously and introduced new legislation that allows the possibility of video conferencing in two areas. First, for the remainder of 2020, works councils and other bodies of employee representation will be allowed to hold their meetings by video or telephone conference.[49] Second, a further act allows lay judges and parties in labour court proceedings to attend trials from a location other than the courtroom in the event of a nationwide epidemic.[50]

How COVID-19 challenges will help to shape the future workforce

Chief Human Resources Officers' work is, currently, in the business spotlight, as the Pandemic has brought a global disruption of business production. They are going to be key in developing effective strategies for workers to resume the economic activity in a new landscape. Shared workforce resilience, that is working together to keep as many workers healthy, safe and employed as possible during the uncertain times that we are living but having in mind the goal of developing the skills that the workforce of the future will need.[51] They must be developed in the new business paradigm that the Pandemic will bring. This requires the re-education of workers with new skills adapted to the 4th Industrial Revolution we are living in.

The coronavirus (COVID-19) pandemic has resulted in dramatic changes in how people do business and develop relationships with others. In addition to accelerating the shift towards digitalising interactions between firms and customers, social distancing measures have promoted telework as a new paradigm,

48   ibid.
49   Adam Sagan and Christian Schüller, 'COVID-19 and Labour Law in Germany' (2020)11(3) *European Labour Law Journal* 297.
50   ibid.
51   Accenture, 'Creating Shared Workforce Resilience' (*Accenture*, 2020) <www.accenture. com/_acnmedia/PDF-122/Accenture-COVID-19-CHRO-shared-workforce-resilience. pdf#zoom=40> accessed 19 June 2020.

essentially digitalising the relationship between employers and workers. Workers have had to adapt to these changes very rapidly. Without appropriate support of laws, regulations, tools and resources, many people cannot work from home very well and they are not sure if they would be safe after returning back to the working places. This means the pandemic has created an atmosphere of anxiety and uncertainty. These changes and uncertainty have affected workers' mental health. The World Health Organisation found that 45% of health workers are suffering from anxiety in China, while the prevalence of depression in Ethiopia trebled during April 2020.[52]

That is why companies need to move on and provide supportive and confident leadership that let them be informed with clear, transparent and efficient information. Thus, they know what their tasks are. Honest and frequent communication with your workers is a must: Tell them which problems that they are facing so that they feel reassured, engaged, listened to and secure. Offer them the resources and support that they need to work efficiently from home.[53] For a company, it is important to see employees in a human way, not just as mere tools; and this importance accentuates during times of crisis. Understand the private life circumstances of each of your workers: Offer them mental health support, a nanny to take care of their children, health services for their elderlies and tailor their jobs to their different needs. Your workers will appreciate this and, as they feel more motivated and satisfied, they will be more proactive, productive, efficient, and feel empowered to take responsibilities.[54]

What is it clear is that this change cannot be done alone, everyone (from the government, lawmakers, citizens, stakeholders, etc.) must be involved in the process if we want to make a recovery and to develop a resilient future economy. In the US, Federal laws, including the Fair Labour Standards Act and the Family and Medical Leave Act, provide critical worker protections regarding wages and working hours and job-protected leave during the pandemic.[55] Yet, not all countries have had the same approach.

Contingency planning for the firms

Developing a contingency plan quickly is essential if a firm wants to ensure the continuation of the business in the future. This will not only help to tackle the

52   Sarah Kirby, '5 Ways COVID-19 Has Changed Workforce Management' (*World Economic Forum*, 2 June 2020) <www.weforum.org/agenda/2020/06/covid-homeworking-symptom-of-changing-face-of-workforce-management/> accessed 30 August 2020.
53   PricewaterhouseCoopers, 'COVID-19: Workforce Considerations' (*PWC*, 1 May 2020) <https://www.pwc.com/us/en/library/COVID-19/workforce-considerations.html#areas+> accessed 22 November 2020.
54   Accenture (n 51).
55   US Department of Labour, 'Essential Protections During the COVID-19 Pandemic' (*Wage and Hour Division*) <www.dol.gov/agencies/whd/pandemic> accessed 30 November 2020.

impact of COVID-19 in a business and to help them to move on, but it will also let the company to be prepared for future risks so that, if they take place, it will have a plan to put into operation. This will mean that the business can be impacted as little as possible and ensure the continuation of productive activity.

The impact that the virus will have on a business's economic activity will depend on the sector it is in: If the business is within the food industry, then its economic activity will not be as impacted, as it has been considered a "necessary goods" producer and they can continue to develop their activity. Furthermore, the economic activities of businesses in the manufacturing sector and other non-essential sectors have been completely paralysed. This is due to the "stay at home" policies issued by governments worldwide, as well as the lack of preparedness among businesses (for example, in terms of their workforce and resources) to face a global pandemic. Because there is a common mistaken belief that the global pandemics could only occur in science fiction, very few businesses have invested time and resources to prepare a contingency plan for such uncertainties.

To develop an efficient Contingency Plan, the corporation must know its business risk profile. A questionnaire should be carried out by the company: Developing a risk matrix consisting of the likely degree of a risk to the company, how it can affect the business, how it is affecting their environment and how is their production process going to be disrupted. Regarding risk and the impact on your business, the company must take into account that it is essential to minimise the risk of the 4P's. These are: *People*: take into account how the situation might affect every worker's personal life; *Processes*: how it can affect the business production; *Profit*: how to manage to create a profit even in a dangerous situation and to ensure the continuation of the business; and *Partnership*: take into account the different stakeholders that compromise the business and how can they help to minimise the impact.[56]

The creation of a business contingency plan requires time and resources (an investment) but, if done correctly, it could help to mitigate the impact of the risk in a business and even to take advantage of it. The point is to ensure the continuation of the company production under every circumstance so that the relation between the client and the business see the least impact possible.

Back to the "new normality"

It is a fact that COVID-19 will bring us new normality in every aspect of our lives. This Pandemic will bring us a "New Normality", for which firms must adapt if they wish to survive. Before the outburst of the virus, the business environment was experiencing some gradual changes as firms continued to innovate, create

56 International Labour Organization, 'The Six-step COVID-19 Business Continuity Plan for SMEs' (*ILO*, 4 April 2020) <https://www.ilo.org/wcmsp5/groups/public/---ed_dialogue/---act_emp/documents/publication/wcms_740375.pdf> accessed 18 May 2020.

new technology, products, etc., but this event has witnessed a radical change for every firm in every sector. Until a vaccine is developed and provided, we will have to adapt to these new surroundings where masks, social distancing measures, hydrogels, etc., and, in some cases, telework is our new reality.

This new shift will be driven by the digital shift of businesses, offshoring of the firms, changes in the workforce and government interventions in the economy:[57]

- Digital shift: During the pandemic companies have seen a drastic rise in online shopping. This loyalty to e-commerce will stay after the reopening of the economy: more than 55% of consumers are expected to continue shopping online for groceries, and showrooms and Fashion Weeks will remain with online livestream.[58] A complete digitalisation of businesses is essential for its survival.
- Offshoring of the firms: Since COVID-19 exploded in China, a large part of worldwide firms saw their supply chain disrupted, as most of their factories are located there. This situation raised a dilemma in many companies, as they started to relocate their factories outside of China (Samsung was one of them).[59]
- Changes in the workforce: Not only has the environment for workers has changed due to telework, 83% of the employees are willing to work remotely after the pandemic.[60] It has become the new norm, but the skills needed have also changed. With digitalisation and automatisation, many jobs will disappear (mainly those in accommodation, food services, construction, administration, manufacturing) and the skills needed for the jobs of the future are adapting to it (data science and technological skills).
- Government intervention in the economy: Since the start of the pandemic central banks and governments have been developing stimulus packages, fiscal packages, injection of capital in the economy and quarantine measures. The government role in the economy will be a stronger one due to uncertainty, as they will have to act again and to intervene in the economy; nonetheless, this will bring problems to the future of the free trade and free-market economy.
- Lawmakers: It is still uncertain their role on the pandemic. It seems that they are acting slowly or just following and approving government expenses.

57   Marc Bacchetta and others, 'COVID-19 and Global Value Chains' (*World Trade Organization*, 11 January 2021) <www.wto.org/english/res_e/reser_e/ersd202103_e.pdf> accessed 18 April 2021.
58   Amed and others (n 36).
59   Shannon Brandao, 'Yes, Manufacturing Really is Leaving China – And Authorities Are Scrambling to Slow Down the Exodus' (*Arabian Business*, 11 April 2021) <www.arabianbusiness.com/461839-yes-manufacturing-really-is-leaving-china-authorities-are-scrambling-to-slow-down-the-exodus> accessed 13 May 2021.
60   PwC's US Remote Work Survey, 'It's Time to Reimagine Where and How Work Will Get Done' (*PWC*, 12 January 2021) <www.pwc.com/us/en/library/covid-19/us-remote-work-survey.html> accessed 30 April 2021.

There are a few examples worthy of mention. The Brazilian Congress voted for mandatory mask-wearing in public spaces. In many cases, they have also been mobilised for the development of, and to provide oversight of, legislation to deal with the long-term challenges of COVID-19, such as through bringing in economic subsidies to support workers with vulnerable employment.[61] This should not be indented.

What is clear is that the business framework will change, companies will need resilience, imagination and problem-solving skills to adapt to the changes; consequently, the organisation of the firm will also change.

Conclusion

Labour force, workers and employees, and entrepreneurs' disruption of activities has been quite evident during COVID-19 pandemic. Lawmakers, actual laws and governments have tried to catch up but not sufficiently to protect them from layoffs, downsizings, business closures and their inability to receive quick and reliable protection under strong laws, policies and regulations.

This Pandemic has brought us a radical change in the way we work, how we do business and how we create goods. Rapid digitalisation of the business is expected in the following months and a shift in the consumer's paradigm towards online shopping is happening. The way we work has been disrupted by accentuating new measures implemented in our work environment: telework, social-distancing. Further, firms are under the pressure to ensure that their workforce receives the teaching needed to develop the latest skills required for the jobs of the future. An investment in technology and R&D must be carried out by firms if they want to survive in an uncertain business environment. Vulnerable groups must be taken into account and companies must invest in "inclusion and diversity" strategies. Further, interiorizing sustainable and responsible practices in the firms' culture should be executed as soon as possible. They cannot wait for law makers to help them in this process.[62] The idea that you can fight a pandemic by way of legislation is doomed. This virus moves too fast while laws move too slowly in response. Thus, focusing on analysing legislations, regulations and governments' policies has been complicated due to the extremely and extraordinary COVID situation and the different approaches governments and lawmakers have taken. This chapter has provided a vision, perception and analysis with a heavy weight on commercial and business perspectives, focusing on workforce and entrepreneurs.

61 Rebecca Gordon and Nic Cheeseman, 'Legislative Leadership in the Time of COVID-19' (*Westminster Foundation for Democracy*, January 2021) <www.wfd.org/wp-content/uploads/2021/01/Covid-19-legislative-leadership-V5.pdf> accessed 18 February 2021.
62 Charles Hampden-Turner and Fons Trompenaars, *Culture, Crisis and COVID-19: The Great Reset* (Cambridge, Cambridge Scholar Publishing 2021) 68.

This Pandemic will bring us to a "New Normality" and only those who had developed an effective contingency plan, a resilient and imaginative strategy and which is flexible and transparent with their workers and stakeholders, can be expected to survive this crisis and even use it as an opportunity to grow.

Bibliography

Accenture, 'Creating Shared Workforce Resilience' (*Accenture*, 2020) <www.accenture. com/_acnmedia/PDF-122/Accenture-COVID-19-CHRO-shared-workforce-resilience.pdf#zoom=40> accessed 19 June 2020.

Amed I and others, 'The State of Fashion 2021: In Search of Promise in Perilous Times' (*McKinsey & Company*, 1 December 2020) <www.mckinsey.com/industries /retail/our-insights/state-of-fashion#> accessed 20 February 2021.

Bacchetta M and others, 'COVID-19 and Global Value Chains' (*World Trade Organization*, 11 January 2021) <www.wto.org/english/res_e/reser_e/ersd202103_e. pdf> accessed 18 April 2021.

BBC news editor, 'Caída del precio del petróleo: El crudo estadounidense WTI se desploma y se cotiza en negativo por primera vez en la historia (Oil Price Drop: US WTI Crude Slumps and Trades Negative for the First Time in History)' (*BBC News*, 20 April 2020) <www.bbc.com/mundo/noticias-52362339> accessed 19 June 2020.

Bollyky T and Konyndyk J, 'It's Not the WHO's Fault That Trump Didn't Prepare for the Coronavirus' (*The Washington Post*, 14 April 2020) <www.washingtonpost. com/outlook/2020/04/14/trump-who-coronavirus-response/> accessed 31 March 2020.

Brandao S, 'Yes, Manufacturing Really is Leaving China – And Authorities Are Scrambling to Slow Down the Exodus' (*Arabian Business*, 11 April 2021) <www.arabianbusiness.com/461839-yes-manufacturing-really-is-leaving-china-authorities-are-scrambling-to-slow-down-the-exodus> accessed 13 May 2021.

Cerottini E, *Commentaire du contrat de travail (Comments about Labour Contracts)* (Berne, Stämpfli Editions 2013).

Chen ZJ, 'Economic Watch: Europe Prepares to Reopen Tourism Sector, but Unlikely to Reach Pre-pandemic Level Soon' (*Xinhua*, 8 May 2021) <www.xinhuanet.com/ english/2021-05/08/c_139932689.htm> accessed 10 May 2021.

Dimson J and others, 'COVID-19 and European Small and Medium-Size Enterprises: How They Are Weathering the storm' (*McKinsey & Company*, 22 October 2020) <www.mckinsey.com/industries/public-and-social-sector/our-insights/covid-19-and-european-small-and-medium-size-enterprises-how-they-are-weathering-the-storm> accessed 12 December 2020.

Dunand J-P and Wyler R, 'Quelques implications du coronavirus en droit suisse du travail (Some Implications of the Coronavirus in Swiss Labour Law)' (*Cielo Laboral*, April 2020) <www.cielolaboral.com/wp-content/uploads/2020/04/ dunand_wyler_noticias_cielo_n4_2020.pdf> accessed 12 January 2021.

El Independiente, 'Las "caceroladas" contra Sánchez se extienden desde Madrid a otras ciudades (The Caceroladas Against Sánchez Extent from Madrid to Other Cities)' (*El Independiente*, 18 May 2020) <www.elindependiente.com/ politica/2020/05/18/las-caceroladas-contra-sanchez-se-extienden-desde-madrid-a-otras-ciudades/> accessed 23 July 2020.

European Central Bank, 'Monetary Policy Decisions' (*European Central Bank*, 4 June 2020) <www.ecb.europa.eu/press/pr/date/2020/html/ecb.mp200604~a307d3429c.en.html> accessed 30 August 2020.

European Central Bank, 'Pandemic Emergency Purchase Programme' (*ECB*) <www.ecb.europa.eu/mopo/implement/pepp/html/index.en.html> accessed 10 December 2020.

European Parliament, 'Coronavirus and the European Film Industry' (*European Union*, 2020) <www.europarl.europa.eu/RegData/etudes/BRIE/2020/649406/EPRS_BRI(2020)649406_EN.pdf> accessed 12 December 2020.

Eurostat, 'Unemployment Statistics' (*Eurostat Statistics Explained*, March 2021) <https://ec.europa.eu/eurostat/statistics-explained/index.php?title=Unemployment_statistics#Unemployment_in_the_EU_and_the_euro_area> accessed 10 May 2021.

Gordon R and Cheeseman N, 'Legislative Leadership in the Time of COVID-19' (*Westminster Foundation for Democracy*, January 2021) <www.wfd.org/wp-content/uploads/2021/01/Covid-19-legislative-leadership-V5.pdf> accessed 18 February 2021.

Hampden-Turner C and Trompenaars F, *Culture, Crisis and COVID-19: The Great Reset* (Cambridge, Cambridge Scholar Publishing 2021).

Hunt V and others, 'Diversity Wins' (*McKinsey & Company*, May 2020) <www.mckinsey.com/~/media/mckinsey/featured per cent20insights/diversity per cent20and per cent20inclusion/diversity per cent20wins per cent20how per cent20inclusion per cent20matters/diversity-wins-how-inclusion-matters-vf.pdf> accessed 30 July 2020.

Instituto Nacional de Estadística, 'Cuenta satélite de turismo en España 2019 (Satellite Tourism Account in Spain 2019)' (*INE*, 11 December 2020) <www.ine.es/dyngs/INEbase/es/operacion.htm?c=estadistica_C&cid=1254736169169&menu=ultiDatos&idp=1254735576863> accessed 10 May 2021.

International Labour Organization, 'The Six-Step COVID-19 Business Continuity Plan for SMEs' (*ILO*, 4 April 2020) <www.ilo.org/wcmsp5/groups/public/-ed_dialogue/-act_emp/documents/publication/wcms_740375.pdf> accessed 18 May 2020.

Iodice D and Colombani R, *Il lavoro agilenella legge n. 81/2017 (Agile Work in Law No. 81/2017)* (ADAPT UP 2017) <https://moodle.adaptland.it/pluginfile.php/29946/mod_resource/content/1/wp_9_2017_iodice_colombani.pdf> accessed 23 February 2021.

Kirby S, '5 Ways COVID-19 Has Changed Workforce Management' (*World Economic Forum*, 2 June 2020) <www.weforum.org/agenda/2020/06/covid-homeworking-symptom-of-changing-face-of-workforce-management/> accessed 30 August 2020.

Lynn S, 'China's Role in Global Generic Pharmaceutical Supply Chain' (*GLG*, 4 February 2020) <https://glginsights.com/articles/chinas-role-in-global-generic-pharmaceutical-supply-chain/> accessed 3 March 2020.

Mann T and Sider A, 'Hotels Seek $150 Billion in Aid as Travel Plummets' (*The Wall Street Journal*, 17 March 2020) <www.wsj.com/articles/hotels-seek-150-billion-in-aid-as-travel-plummets-11584486738> accessed 23 June 2020.

Martínez H, 'Se extiende la gratificación salarial a los trabajadores por la crisis del Covid-19 (Salary Gratification Is Extended to Workers Due to the Covid-19 Crisis)' (*Alimarket*, 21 April 2020) <www.alimarket.es/alimentacion/noticia/313448/se-extiende-la-gratificacion-salarial-a-los-trabajadores-por-la-crisis-del-covid-19#> accessed 31 July 2020.

McFall-Johnsen M, 'La industria de la moda emite más carbono que los vuelos internacionales y el transporte marítimo juntos: estas son sus mayores consecuencias en el planeta (The Fashion Industry Emits More Carbon than
International Flights and Maritime Transport Combined: These Are Its Greatest
Consequences on the Planet)' (*Business Insider*, 28 October 2019)' <www.business
insider.es/impacto-moda-medio-ambiente-terrible-saber-514379> accessed 12
February 2020.

Minder R, 'Counting Bodies and Pointing Fingers as Spain Tallies Coronavirus Dead'
(*The New York Times*, 16 April 2020, Updated 16 November 2020) <www.nytimes.
com/2020/04/16/world/europe/coronoavirus-spain-death-toll.html> accessed
10 December 2020.

Ministerio de Industria, Comercio y Turismo, 'Marco Estratégico en Política de Pyme
2030 (Strategic SME's Political Framework 2030)' (*Ministry of Industry, Commerce and Tourism*, April 2019) <https://industria.gob.es/es-es/Servicios/Mar-
coEstrategicoPYME/Presentacion_Estrategia_PYME.pdf> accessed 23 May 2020.

Nhamo G and others, *Counting the Cost of COVID-19 on the Global Tourism Industry*
(Cham, Switzerland, Springer Nature 2020).

Nhamo JA, 'A flexibilização das obrigações Trabalhistas frente a pandemia mundial do Coronavírus – Covid-19 (Flexibilization of Workers' Obligations Lieu of
the World Pandemic of Coronavirus – COVID-19)' (2020) I *Revista Científica
UNIFAGOC* 16.

Nicola M and others, 'The COVID-19 Pandemic Has Resulted in Over 4.3 Million
Confirmed Cases and Over 290' (2020)78 *IJS* 189 <https://reader.elsevier.com/
reader/sd/pii/S1743919120303162?token=72AF42040776348CA53570BA50
511A24CD086B1976C8F6044EA281969FF9F878D87FD8EE6F106444A5AD-
85D0D4D1AA49> accessed 13 July 2020.

The Organisation for Economic Co-operation and Development (OECD),
'Women at the Core of the Fight Against COVID-19 Crisis' (*OECD*, 1
April 2020) 1 <https://read.oecd-ilibrary.org/view/?ref=127_127000-awfnqj80
me&title=Women-at-the-core-of-the-fight-against-COVID-19-crisis&_
ga=2.22691897.340763577.1622568809-2034336424.1622568809> accessed
12 March 2021.

Ozili P and Arun T, 'Spillover of COVID-19: Impact on the Global Economy'
(*Research Gate*, 2020) <www.researchgate.net/publication/340236487_
Spillover_of_COVID-19_impact_on_the_Global_Economy> accessed 18 May 2020.

Pérez BJ and Falótico JA, 'Various Perspectives of Labour and Human Resources
Challenges and Changes Due to Automation and Artificial Intelligence' (2019)20
AISJ 112 <www.academicus.edu.al/nr20/Academicus-MMXIX-20-106-118.pdf>
accessed 23 January 2021.

Pharmaceutical Technology, 'Pharma Jobs Index Vs Other Sectors (Last 12 Months)'
(*Global Data Jobs Analytics Database*, May 2021)accessed 12 May 2021.

PricewaterhouseCoopers, 'COVID-19: Workforce Considerations' (*PWC*, 1
May 2020) <www.pwc.com/us/en/library/COVID-19/workforce-considerations.
html#areas+> accessed 22 November 2020.

PwC's US Remote Work Survey, 'It's Time to Reimagine Where and How Work Will
Get Done' (*PWC*, 12 January 2021) <www.pwc.com/us/en/library/covid-19/
us-remote-work-survey.html> accessed 30 April 2021.

Rappeport A and Chokshi N, 'Crippled Airline Industry to Get $25 Billion Bail-out, Part of It as Loans' (*The New York Times*, 17 March 2021) <www.nytimes.com/2020/04/14/business/coronavirus-airlines-bailout-treasury-department.html> accessed 23 February 2021.

Rigg P, '275 Layoffs as University Asks Staff to Make Videos' (*University World News*, 10 February 2021) <www.universityworldnews.com/post.php?story=2021021007111588> accessed 15 March 2021.

Sagan A and Schüller C, 'COVID-19 and Labour Law in Germany' (2020)11(3) *European Labour Law Journal* 297.

Silver C and Hyman AD, 'COVID-19: A Case Study of Government Failure' (*CATO Institute*, 15 September 2020) <www.cato.org/pandemics-policy/covid-19-case-study-government-failure> accessed 15 December 2020.

Smarp, 'How COVID-19 Is Accelerating Digital Transformation in the Workplace' (*Smarp*, 21 April 2020) <https://blog.smarp.com/how-COVID-19-is-accelerating-digital-transformation-in-the-workplace> accessed 18 September 2020.

Tan G, 'Hilton Draws Down $1.75 Billion Credit Line to Ease Virus Hit' (*Bloomberg*, 11 March 2020) <www.bloomberg.com/news/articles/2020-03-11/hilton-to-draw-down-part-of-1-75-billion-line-as-virus-spreads> accessed 12 June 2020.

Tooze A, 'The Eurozone's "Whatever It Takes" Mantra Has a Problem' (*Financial Times*, London, 3 April 2020) 34.

UNESCO, '290 Million Students Out of School Due to COVID-19: UNESCO Releases First Global Numbers and Mobilizes Response' (*UNESCO*, 4 March 2020) <https://en.unesco.org/news/290-million-students-out-school-due-covid-19-unesco-releases-first-global-numbers-and-mobilizes> accessed 24 July 2020.

United Nations, 'UN Working to Ensure Vulnerable Groups Not Left Behind in COVID-19 Response' (*Department of Global Communications*, 24 March 2020) <www.un.org/en/un-coronavirus-communications-team/un-working-ensure-vulnerable-groups-not-left-behind-COVID-19> accessed 23 December 2020.

US Department of Labour, 'Essential Protections During the COVID-19 Pandemic' (*Wage and Hour Division*) <www.dol.gov/agencies/whd/pandemic> accessed 30 November 2020.

World Bank Group, 'Global Economic Prospect, January 2021' (*World Bank*, January 2021) <https://openknowledge.worldbank.org/bitstream/handle/10986/34710/9781464816123.pdf> accessed 12 February 2021.

Part IV

Conclusion

10 Reflections on COVID-19

Luo Li, Carlos Espaliú Berdud, Steve Foster and Ben Stanford

Introduction

During the time that this chapter and edited collection has been written, many countries in Europe are gradually lifting lockdown restrictions from the third wave of COVID-19.[1] The United Kingdom (UK) also announced its next step of the lifting policy on 17 May, in which two households or six people maximum could meet indoors.[2] The announcement of the planned lifting policy shows the UK government's confidence in controlling the spread of COVID-19, largely because many people have received the first or second dose of the COVID-19 vaccination. However, it does not mean the whole world would return to normal very soon. Looking at the data announced by the World Health Organization (WHO), there were in total more than 3.2 million deaths because of COVID in the whole world by 11 May 2021.[3] More importantly, the death figure and confirmed cases were still increasing every single day.[4] According to the Our World in Data, built by Oxford University and an educational charity, only a very few countries achieved a high vaccination dose rate.[5] In other words, the rest of the world is still suffering. It can be seen that many developing and least developed countries are still in a critical condition of national emergency because of COVID-19 or its variants, as well as a lack of sufficient vaccination doses. For example, 'the recent surge in cases in India, Nepal and Japan is changing the picture'.[6] India is currently suffering the second wave of COVID-19, which has

---

1   BBC, 'Covid: Is Europe Lifting Lockdown Restrictions?' (*BBC News*, 30 April 2021) <www.bbc.co.uk/news/explainers-53640249> accessed 11 May 2021.

2   Emma Harrison and Joseph Lee, 'Lockdown: Boris Johnson to Announce 17 May Changes for England' (*BBC News*, 10 May 2021) <www.bbc.co.uk/news/uk-57050860> accessed 11 May 2021.

3   WHO, 'WHO Coronavirus (COVID-19) Dashboard' (*WHO*, 11 May 2021) <https://covid19.who.int/> accessed 11 May 2021.

4   1 See the latest daily figure about deaths and confirmed cases at The Visual and Data Journalism Team, 'Covid Map: Coronavirus Cases, Deaths, Vaccinations by Country' (*BBC News*, 10 May 2021) <www.bbc.co.uk/news/world-51235105> accessed 11 May 2021.

5   ibid.

6   ibid.

DOI: 10.4324/9781003176848-15

been called "devastating": the confirmed case figures rose sharply from 11,000 cases in February, to 89,800 in just two months.[7]

Although the original idea from President Biden, who calls for pharmaceutical companies to waive vaccine patents,[8] would perhaps be welcome by many developing countries – as they argued this would help with developing countries' efficient response to COVID-19 without a restriction of patent issue[9] – the reality seems to be more complicated. The pharmaceutical companies warned that Biden's call would significantly and negatively affect the vaccine production process, resulting in further issues including counterfeiting vaccines and a slowdown in the production due to a competition of limited ingredients for vaccine production.[10] There is a debate on whether the waiver of intellectual property (IP) is a one-off solution and some people argue that perhaps IP is the least concern compared with issues such as production facilities and infrastructure, whereas others look at it more positively.[11] While it is not known whether any WTO members would agree with a waiver of IP, and what kind of waiver they would prefer if the answer is yes, it is accepted that the pandemic situation would continue for a considerable time. This is because that not only would it take some time to get most of the world immunised through vaccination, but also that it depends on what extent the existing vaccines would still be working for all current COVID variants or potentially new variants. The Indian COVID variant has already been found in the UK with an increased tendency.[12] Although scientists say, 'the vaccines are likely to remain effective against the Indian variant,[13] and can 'limit

7   Vikas Pandey and Shadab Nazmi, 'Covid-19 in India: Why Second Coronavirus Wave Is Devastating' (*BBC News*, 21 April 2021) <www.bbc.co.uk/news/world-asia-india-56811315> accessed 11 May 2021.

8   Dan Diamond and others, 'Biden Commits to Waiving Vaccine Patents, Driving Wedge with Pharmaceutical Companies' (*The Washington Post*, 6 May 2021) <www.washingtonpost.com/health/2021/05/05/biden-waives-vaccine-patents/> accessed 11 May 2021.

9   India and South Africa, Waiver from Certain Provisions of the TRIPS Agreement for the Prevention, Containment and Treatment of COVID-19 (2020) WTO IP/C/W/669 <https://docs.wto.org/dol2fe/Pages/SS/directdoc.aspx?filename=q:/IP/C/W669.pdf&Open=True> accessed 13 May 2021.

10 Diamond and others (n 8).

11 Ann Danaiya Usher, 'South Africa and India Push for COVID-19 Patents Ban' (2020)396 *World Report* 10265 <www.thelancet.com/journals/lancet/article/PIIS0140-6736(20)32581-2/fulltext> accessed 11 May 2021; Enrico Bonadio and Filippo Fontanelli, 'Push for COVID-19 Vaccine Patent Waiver Isn't a Panacea: But It Could Nudge Companies to Share' (*The Conversation*, 12 May 2021) <https://theconversation.com/push-for-covid-19-vaccine-patent-waiver-isnt-a-panacea-but-it-could-nudge-companies-to-share-160802?utm_source=linkedin&utm_medium=bylinelinkedinbutton> accessed 13 May 2021.

12 Jim Reed, 'PM: India Coronavirus Variant Must Be "Handled Carefully"' (*BBC News*, 7 May 2021) <www.bbc.co.uk/news/health-57016110> accessed 11 May 2021.

13 Gayathri Vaidyanathan, 'Coronavirus Variants Are Spreading in India – What Scientists Know so Far' (*Nature*, 11 May 2021) <www.nature.com/articles/d41586-021-01274-7> accessed 13 May 2021.

severe disease',[14] 'the surge in cases in India and the scenes witnessed there is of grave concern internationally'.[15]

The whole world has suffered from the coronavirus pandemic for more than one year since it first appeared. If human beings ideally thought this pandemic would end last summer naturally, the evidence of COVID suffering at present shows us how far that was from the correct perception or direction. If COVID and its variants exist in the future, it is necessary for us to have a realistic perception of the post-pandemic situation. This will allow us to review and consider a long-term responding strategy and reflect it in our existing laws, regulations and policies so as to accommodate extreme situations such as the pandemic. Therefore, this chapter concludes with reflections by the co-editors. We give the audience a general perception through gathering the research findings by chapter contributors and explain why these findings, and perhaps solutions, are helpful for the rest of the world. The chapter also considers the future direction of laws in responding to the crisis in the area of information protection, creative industry and business.

Where we were?

If returning to the beginning of 2020 and looking back over the last ten to twenty years, the areas of information, creative industry and business have been massively influenced by globalisation and digitalisation. Therefore, a variety of legal considerations and reforms at both national and international levels are reflected by these two streams.

Globalisation

The term "globalisation" has been applied since the 1970s. Following technological changes and improvement, the worldwide globalisation process became faster, and more and more countries became involved in this globalisation party in pursuing either national or mutual interests. Early in 2000, the International Monetary Fund (IMF) defined globalisation as 'the increasing integration of economies around the world, particularly through trade and financial flows. The term sometimes also refers to the movement of people (labour) and knowledge (technology) across international borders'.[16] The IMF identifies four aspects of globalisation, which are, respectively, trade, capital/investment movements, migration and movement of people, and spread of knowledge and technology.[17] After the Second World War, the whole world is relatively peaceful and the

---

14 ibid.
15 ibid.
16 IMF, 'Globalization: Threat or Opportunity?' (*IMF*, 12 April 2000) <www.imf.org/external/np/exr/ib/2000/041200to.htm#II> accessed 14 May 2021.
17 ibid.

international relationships among most countries aimed towards collaboration rather than opposition. This gives globalisation a friendly international environment and an opportunity to grow without disruption. There is no doubt that these four aspects of globalisation allowed most countries in the world to be engaged: Most enterprises/companies and most individuals are involved and also benefit from it. It is also accepted that a variety of legal issues and challenges arise because of the globalised market and global trade.

Although there is a debate on whether globalisation brings better than worse conditions,[18] and some talk about winners or losers in globalisation,[19] before the pandemic most thought globalisation is irreversible (or at least difficult to do so even if there is an opinion about de-globalisation). Relevant legal debate and legal concerns mainly concentrate on how the laws could maximise its roles in maintaining a smooth delivery of commercial and trade activities across the borders, and how the laws could encourage the development of more soft infrastructure for markets as well as maintaining the hard infrastructure.[20] A series of considerations arise including harmonisation of national laws of different countries via bilateral, regional and international treaties, legal reforms of national laws and regulations to reduce obstacles for an active economy, fair trade and economy efficiency; in addition to mapping issues to maximise protection of right holders and main stakeholders.[21]

Digitalisation

There is no firm and clear definition of the term "digitalisation". The term "digitalisation" is different from that of "digitalise". The term "digitalise" means 'to change something such as a document to a digital form (= a form that can be

18 Sylvanus Kwaku Afesorgbor and Binyam Afewerk Demena, 'Globalization May Actually Be Better for the Environment' (*The Conversation*, 24 April 2018) <https://theconversation.com/globalization-may-actually-be-better-for-the-environment-95406> accessed 25 May 2021; Nikil Saval, 'Globalisation: The Rise and Fall of an Idea That Swept the World' (*The Guardian*, 14 July 2017) <www.theguardian.com/world/2017/jul/14/globalisation-the-rise-and-fall-of-an-idea-that-swept-the-world> accessed 25 May 2021.
19 The World Bank, 'The Winners and Losers of Globalization: Finding a Path to Shared Prosperity' (*The World Bank*, 25 October 2013) <www.worldbank.org/en/news/feature/2013/10/25/The-Winners-and-Losers-of-Globalization-Finding-a-Path-to-Shared-Prosperity> accessed 25 May 2021.
20 Fiona MacMillan, 'Making Corporate Power Global' (1999)5(1) *International Trade Law & Regulation* 3–9. Mohamed Wahab, 'Globalisation and ODR: Dynamics of Change in E-Commerce Dispute Settlement' (2004)12(1) *International Journal of Law & Information Technology* 123–52; Alireza Naghavi and Giovanni Prarolo, 'Harmonisation and Globalisation of Intellectual Property Culture' (2018)41(7) *The World Economy* 1847–66.
21 David W Maher, 'The UDRP: The Globalization of Trademark Rights' (2002)33(8) *International Review of Intellectual Property and Competition Law* 924–40; Jurgita Malinauskaite, 'Harmonisation in Competition Law in the Context of Globalisation' (2010)21(3) *European Business Law Review* 369–97.

stored and read by computers)',[22] whereas the term "digitalisation" is defined by some scholars as 'the way in which many domains of social life are restructured around digital communication and media infrastructures'.[23] It is 'the use of digital technologies to change a business model and provide new revenue and value-producing opportunities . . . the process of moving to a digital business'.[24] Digitalisation is also 'The adoption of digital technologies to modify a business model. The aim is to create a value from the use of new, advanced technologies by exploiting digital network dynamics and the giant digital flow of information.'[25] With the support of the powerful internet platform and the advanced technologies, nearly every industry or sector goes into a digital-engaged business model, although many maintain a traditional manner of producing, selling and distributing. In fact, the appearance of any new technology would lead to law reforms to meet the challenges brought by that technology. The digitalisation process would perhaps lead to even radical changes, especially in the information and creative industry. Therefore, those legal concerns in the digitalisation context are quite prominent and concentrated in how and to what extent a piece of information can and should be protected in aspects of data protection and data privacy. This is because digitalisation results in an easy way of copying and leaking as well as abuse by enterprises and individuals.

Besides, since many data, technologies, know-how and other creations are not tangible assets, how to ensure effective protection and guarantee of right holders' interest in these intangible assets in this digital world raises much discussion.[26] In fact, globalisation and digitalisation are inter-related factors that need to be considered in both the law design and reform. Globalisation requires a faster and more efficient business model, whereas digitalisation gives governments and enterprises an alternative to achieve such requirements with technology as an assistant. Meanwhile, digitalisation could well help a stronger and deeper globalisation network framework. 'Globalization is not moving into reverse. Instead digital flows are soaring – transmitting information, ideas, and innovation around the world and broadening participation in the global economy.'[27]

---

22 The definition of the term "digitalise" can be seen at Cambridge Dictionary <https://dictionary.cambridge.org/dictionary/english/digitalize> accessed 14 May 2021.
23 Jason Bloomberg, 'Digitization, Digitalization, And Digital Transformation: Confuse Them at Your Peril' (*Forbes*, 29 April 2018) <www.forbes.com/sites/jasonbloomberg/2018/04/29/digitization-digitalization-and-digital-transformation-confuse-them-at-your-peril/?sh=1ec127262f2c> accessed 14 May 2021.
24 ibid.
25 Veronica Scuotto and others, 'The Shift Towards a Digital Business Model: A Strategic Decision for the Female Entrepreneur' in Tomos F and others (eds), *Women Entrepreneurs and Strategic Decision Making in the Global Economy* (Hershey, IGI Global 2019) 142–43.
26 Marilena Garis, 'Meeting the Challenges of Digitalisation' (2010)199 *Managing Intellectual Property* 88–90; Niva Elkin-Koren, 'Affordances of Freedom: Theorizing the Rights of Users in the Digital Era' (2012)6 *Jerusalem Review of Legal Studies* 96–109.
27 James Manyika and others, 'Digital Globalisation: The New Era of Global Flows' (*In Brief*, 2016) <www.mckinsey.com/~/media/mckinsey/business%20functions/mckinsey%20

Nevertheless, it is noticeable that whether we are talking of globalisation or digitalisation, they follow a willingness of human beings and are human-made results. Although globalisation and digitalisation bring many challenges and issues, they do not try to turn the existing business models overnight but allow traditional and new models to exist at the same time and gradually change or replace the traditional ones. They do not, therefore, fundamentally change most of the existing values and human beings know they are moving in a direction that they can anticipate to some extent. Therefore, even when the laws are changing or reforming, the existing legal frameworks are always following pre-existed principles or foundations but mapping the man-made issues and modifying the laws and regulations in that particular sector gradually. Thus, even if laws have rules responding to emergencies, the laws are given a pre-requisite condition based on past experiences: Normally in short periods of time in a limited geographical region in a specific industry or sector. Human beings naturally dislike the combined existence of a present with uncertainties and an unpredictable future. The laws were, thus, confident and consistent until the pandemic arrived.

Where we are during the pandemic?

The continuous widespread of COVID-19 since the beginning of 2020, and a variety of coronavirus variants, significantly affects not only the health of human beings, but has destroyed, or is destroying, business in many sectors as well as raising many challenges and issues due to the contingency plans implemented by the governments in response to the COVID-19 outbreak. The recurrent coronavirus outbreak and subsequent responding measures, such as re-lockdown and restriction policies, massively disrupts the smooth delivery of trade and business continuity, temporarily disconnecting worldwide supply chains and resulting in remaining stagnant globalisation progress or even a return to de-globalisation. All of them tell us a reality: We are not returning to normal, but we are turning to a new normality. However, most laws designed in the normal age seem to lack sufficient flexibility and confidence to respond to such extreme situations and its subsequent effects. More importantly, those issues that were not sufficiently focused in the past, because of heavier attention on economic factors, are prominent during the pandemic, which pushes us to consider a law with more vision.

It is recognised universally that no matter what reform there is, there is a need for some legal reform. A high-standard law reform would 'enhance justice and legal efficiency and contribute to socio-economic development'.[28] Law reform is different from law revision or consolidations, which is 'normally used to refer to statutory amendments that make no change at all to the substance of the

---

digital/our%20insights/digital%20globalization%20the%20new%20era%20of%20global%20flows/mgi-digital-globalization-full-report.pdf> accessed 25 May 2021.
28   Commonwealth Secretariat, *Changing the Law: A Practical Guide to Law Reform* (London, Commonwealth Secretariat 2017) 3.

law'.[29] Law reform refers to change to the substance of the law, whereas law revision and consolidation only refer to form changed (statutory amendment but no substance of the law).[30] However, whether it is law reform or even a birth of a new law, it is a reflection of the contemporary needs of the economy, politics and social concerns in a certain period of time. To some extent, it must be accepted that every law has its limitation in both flexibility and vision, since the law itself is a result of that particular age and tries to fit most needs in that particular period of time.

Nevertheless, while certain needs become a priority or get more attention, it seems to be unavoidable that the laws would be more engaged to focus on those needs. For the last decades, globalisation and digitalisation are the main themes, and how to maintain an active economy and achieve a successful and smooth business transformation in the post-globalisation and digitalisation era is the main discussion point in both the international and national level, and from a governmental, academic and social-economic perspective. Therefore, law reforms including the appearance of new laws in the commercial context focus more on the economy and private interest, and on the protection of rights holders in information, creative industry and business areas.[31] Although there are legal and public interest concerns in using information, sustainability in-laws, and guarantees of other stakeholders' rights,[32] the law's reaction is lagging behind and resistant, compared with economic needs. Therefore, while the law overlooks a large section of the public, it is easy to explain why the law is not able to cope with the pandemic issues (since the COVID-19 pandemic crisis influences a wider interest of the public).

The pandemic shows the weakness of the laws in dealing with unpredictable events in the commercial law context, even though they were strong in covering normal unexpected ones. Understandably, legislation-designers would not warmly support the mapping of those extreme events, like the COVID-19 pandemic, that perhaps would happen once in a hundred years, or even a longer period of time. Nevertheless, legislators may ignore the results that extreme events bring: radical changes in aspects of economy, politics, society and value. Legislators may also not realise that extreme events can have a long-term impact instead of a short-term breakout. That ignorance and un-realisation together form a fixed logic in designing and reforming our laws. Therefore, this results

---

29 ibid 12.

30 ibid.

31 Esther H Lim and Mai-Trang D Dang, 'IP Rights and DRM: The Copyright Holder's Guide to Navigating DRM Technology Through Hostile Territory' (2007)21(1) *World Intellectual Property Report* 22–26; Rita Cheung, 'Shareholders' Personal Rights Under the Articles – Clarity and Confusion' (2011)3 *Journal of Business Law* 290–98.

32 Nick Scharf, 'Digital Rights Management and Fair Use' (2010)1(2) *European Journal of Law and Technology* <https://ejlt.org/index.php/ejlt/article/view/22/51> accessed 25 May 2021; Catherine Wilson, 'Blockchain and Sustainability' (2020)44(4) *Company Secretary's Review* 57–58.

in having a strong initiative to resolve legal issues that are prominent at present and foreseen in a very short period of time, but reluctant to take time to be engaged in mapping and exploring those regarded as being not urgent at present. These, being triggered only in some special situations, need more effort and time in order to see a positive result. The problem is this would lead laws to have less capacity to respond to uncertainties, while their internal frameworks have restricted such possibilities. Even some legal rules are defined as non-exhaustive in nature, whereas legal interpretation and legal practice try to give more detailed examples that narrows down their non-exhaustive scope.

Furthermore, legal interpretations and legal practice are based on past experiences, which normally exclude those extreme situations. Therefore, we can see laws are rushed and unprepared for the pandemic situation. That is why it is necessary to review the existing laws and consider a more flexible approach or add a separate special regulation to cover extreme situations such as a pandemic. In addition, when the extreme situation is no longer a one-off and short-term event, but has become a normal one, simply adding separate special regulations responding to temporarily extreme situations is not suitable any longer. Moreover, the subsequent long-term impacts that would fundamentally change the business models and lifestyles, such as the new full-digitalisation era, also require laws to have sufficient flexibility to cover such changes. In this case, a multi-compatible law is necessary. Obviously, existing laws need significant changes to fit this purpose. In fact, not only the laws, but governments, enterprises and individuals all need a more flexible and compatible strategy to respond to such extreme events and their possible subsequent impact.

Besides, the COVID-19 crisis shows that the current laws do not consider wider stakeholders' interests effectively, or at least do not treat them as equally to so-called main right holders. In a commercial context, enterprises and those individuals who create and control intellectual assets or/and control the enterprises, are recognised as main players in massive innovation, creation and other commercial activities. Therefore, although there is some discussion about a wider stakeholder's interest in a commercial law area,[33] these voices are covered by: concerns on how laws could protect enterprises' business and reinforce its governance, how laws could guarantee innovator/creators' rights of control in their intellectual assets and guarantee their rights in the commercial activities so as to maintain a continually active economy and non-disruptive development. In this case, there is a tendency to maximise protection to the main right holders, with a deficiency in exploring to what extent a wider stakeholders' interest should be guaranteed. This can be wider public users who obtain information (including creations and innovations) from the information holder; or employees or other

---

33   Chrispas Nyombi and others, 'Shareholder Primacy and Stakeholders' Interests in the Aftermath of a Takeover: A Review of Empirical Evidence' (2015)2 *International Business Law Journal* 161–86; Robert Burrell, 'Defending the Public Interest' (2000)22(9) *European Intellectual Property Review* 394–404.

stakeholders in a company/enterprise whose interest seems to be more suitable for a long-term development strategy of the company/enterprise than that of the main shareholders. Unfortunately, existing laws do not have a clear answer and have chosen to silent until the pandemic pushed us to see.

In addition, the pandemic indicates that whatever the economy, societies, industries or the laws, sustainability should always be a desired goal. The term "sustainability" is defined by the Cambridge Dictionary as 'the quality of being able to continue over a period of time'.[34] In the legal context, the term "sustainability" refers to 'Ability to continue an activity in the long term'.[35] Sustainability is not a new topic, rather it has been discussed, argued and debated for decades. The United Nations adopted seventeen sustainable development goals (SDGs) in 2015, sharing a 'vision of humanity and a social contract between the world's leaders and the people'.[36] This Agenda for Sustainable Development embraces all member states and forms a blueprint to 'wipe out poverty, fight inequality and tackle climate change over the next 15 years'.[37] In a legal context, the term "sustainability" links more with environmental law at first, but later the concept of sustainability has been extended to a much wider scope and is argued as a fundamental principle being equivalent to justice, freedom and equality.[38] The issue of sustainability has been discussed in wider legal aspects of corporate governance,[39] legal strategy and concerns for business,[40] and employment.[41] Nevertheless, it is

---

34 'Sustainability' (*Cambridge Dictionary*) <https://dictionary.cambridge.org/dictionary/english/sustainability> accessed 17 May 2021.

35 'Sustainability' (*The Law Dictionary*) <https://thelawdictionary.org/sustainability/> accessed 18 May 2021.

36 United Nations, 'Sustainable Development Goals Kick Off with Start of New Year' (*UN Sustainable Development Goals*) <www.un.org/sustainabledevelopment/blog/2015/12/sustainable-development-goals-kick-off-with-start-of-new-year/> accessed 18 May 2021.

37 ibid.

38 Klaus Bosselmann, *The Principle of Sustainability: Transforming Law and Governance* (New York, Routledge 2016) 57–73.

39 Valeria Naciti and others, 'Corporate Governance and Sustainability: A Review of the Existing Literature' (2021) *Journal of Management and Governance* (*SpingerLink*, 3 January 2021) <https://link.springer.com/article/10.1007/s10997-020-09554-6> accessed 18 May 2021.

40 Roberto Hernández-Chea and others, 'Integrating Intellectual Property and Sustainable Business Models: The SBM-IP Canvas' (*MDPI*, 26 October 2020) <www.mdpi.com/2071-1050/12/21/8871/htm> accessed 25 May 2021; Karen Fong, 'Sustainability and IP: A Match Made in Heaven?' (2016) *In-House Lawyer* 87–88; Fabian Klein, 'GREEN IP – A Look at How Sustainability Influences IP and How IP Can Help in Achieving Sustainability' (*Ashurst*, 30 April 2020) <www.ashurst.com/en/news-and-insights/legal-updates/a-look-at-how-sustainability-influences-ip-and-how-ip-can-help-in-achieving-sustainability/> accessed 18 May 2021.

41 Tonia Novitz, 'The Paradigm of Sustainability in a European Social Context: Collective Participation in Protection of Future Interests?' (2015)31(3) *International Journal of Comparative Labour Law and Industrial Relations* 243–62; Inger Marie Hagen, 'Sustainable Decisions and Social Dialogue: Some Significant Developments in Norway' (2011)8(2–3) *European Company Law* 83–87.

concerning that sustainability is not treated with the same status as those universally recognised principles, and therefore many discussions about sustainability still remain at a literal level rather than substantially incorporated into a wider legal framework. The COVID-19 crisis highlights the insufficiency to sustainability in the laws and this lack of sustainability consideration will lead the laws toward a short-term vision rather than a long-term development strategy.

Where we will be at post-pandemic age?

We are indeed in the post-COVID period and many experts call it a "new normal" and claim this "new normal" situation will become normality. Considering what COVID-19 brings has been fundamental and radical, and has combined both short-term and long-term changes/impacts, it is necessary to understand what this new normality will be and then what kind of laws are needed in response.

Scientists have warned the world before that human beings would suffer a pandemic of some kind, although they could not predict the time of when it would happen and what kind of infectious diseases it would be.[42] Although many of us use the phrase "new normal" or "new normality" to describe the post-pandemic period, it is difficult to describe exactly what the "new normal" will be. This is because, on the one hand, human beings have not actually experienced any pandemic in the past 70 years, and there are too many uncertainties to be able to foresee exactly what a stable post-pandemic period will look like. 'The language of a "new normal" is being deployed almost as a way to quell any uncertainty ushered in by the coronavirus.'[43] On the other hand, it seems unclear that what the word "normal" points at – is it the pandemic itself, or does it mean the ways that we approach and deal with the present and foreseen reality. Furthermore, while the COVID-19 pandemic brings a so-called "new normality" – such as the way of working and living different from that we did before the COVID pandemic – other viruses resulting in a pandemic of another kind may bring us a different "new normality".

However, over the past year and a half, we have seen some trends on what has been changed and whether such changes would remain in the post-pandemic period. First, our way of working has been fundamentally shifted from physical office hours to a situation of working at home. Although some countries have a high vaccine dose rate and therefore there is an expectation that we are able to be back to offices working very soon, many companies have noticed the benefits with the new model of working. Hence, some types of work may be permanently shifted to an online model, require new skills and capabilities, or even be replaced

42   Mattea Bubalo and others, 'Are Pandemics the New Normal?' (*BBC News*, 4 January 2021) <www.bbc.co.uk/news/av/world-55415763> accessed 19 May 2021.
43   Chime Asonye, 'There's Nothing New About the "New Normal": Here's Why' (*World Economic Forum*, 5 June 2020) <www.weforum.org/agenda/2020/06/theres-nothing-new-about-this-new-normal-heres-why/> accessed 19 May 2021.

or disappear due to digitalisation or automation. After all, no corporations would like to take more risks in hiring human employees if the pandemic happened again, and a digitalised system and automation infrastructure is much easier to operate and manage, being more efficient and minimising the risk, damage and profit loss in extreme situation like the pandemic. Nevertheless, such a shift would fundamentally influence a large number of the workforce and related legal rights. For some types of jobs relating to key workers, it is as well consider comprehensive well-beings policies and rules and guarantee these benefits through the law.

Secondly, the governments' contingency plans to respond to the pandemic reflect a de-socialisation nature. While the whole world has been in a deepensocialised and connected age, it is very difficult to move in the opposite direction. Digital solutions became the sole approach to support and maintain the socialisation nature in our economy, politics, society and culture. In this case, 'people's relationship with technology will deepen as larger segments of the population come to rely more on digital connections for work, education, health care, daily commercial transactions and essential social interactions'.[44] If we were halfway to a digitalisation world before the pandemic, COVID-19 is the power to accelerate the achievement of the full digitalisation environment. This requires all parties including individuals, enterprises, governments and other organisations to be ready for a digital-everything world. Therefore, a series of legal challenges would arise. A wider scope of concern will be how will the law have flexibility to respond to the full digitalisation world, or how would the law be shifted by digitalisation. Some detailed concerns would be how to guarantee information holders' rights and regulate their responsibilities in misinformation, issues on privacy and data security in digitalisation, how to use the technology of digitalisation to enhance justice and equality of laws, and in what way can the law balance the short-term interest of individuals and long-term interest of a wider public.

Finally, the pandemic will make all of us re-evaluate what is important to us. There is an opinion that ' "new normal" can be a stepping stone to a "new future", with benefits for other health issues, and far beyond the response to COVID-19'.[45] The "new normal" pushes us to think about who we want to be and what we really need. Appreciation perhaps would be the keyword toward that new future, and sustainability would be the best reflection to appreciation. After the loss of lives, lockdown and social distance policies, we will appreciate what we still have at present, and, more importantly, we may want to protect those things and guarantee that our next generations can still enjoy them. Therefore,

---

44 Janna Anderson and others, 'Experts Say the "New Normal" in 2025 Will Be Far More Tech-Driven, Presenting More Big Challenges' (*Pew Research Centre*, 18 February 2021) <www.pewresearch.org/internet/2021/02/18/experts-say-the-new-normal-in-2025-will-be-far-more-tech-driven-presenting-more-big-challenges/> accessed 19 May 2021.

45 Takeshi Kasai, 'From the "New Normal" to a "New Future": A Sustainable Response to COVID-19' (*WHO*, 13 October 2020) <www.who.int/westernpacific/news/commentaries/detail-hq/from-the-new-normal-to-a-new-future-a-sustainable-response-to-covid-19> accessed 19 May 2021.

making things sustainable would no longer have a literal meaning but should be operational as an urgent mission. Whether it is corporate governance, industry/business models, other commercial activities, or the laws that regulate these activities, they all should be considered from a sustainable perspective with long-term strategies.

Conclusion: a law with vision?

We are in a changing world and change always brings uncertainties. The COVID-19 pandemic accelerated the changes and has enlarged our attention to those uncertainties in a short time. It also makes us re-evaluate the past and consider what we would like to correct in the near future. In this case, a law, being as 'the resolution of social problems, the regulation of human relationships, and the educative or ideological function',[46] is a wonderful instrument to deal with the issues at present and a foreseen future. From a macro perspective, through massive systematic regulations and frameworks, and binding all people of the human-being community, laws maintain a stable and safe 'public order, political order, social order, economic order, international order, and moral order'.[47] From a micro perspective, laws protect our safety, guarantee our rights, identify accepted and forbidden behaviours in the processes of business transactions and other commercial activities, as well as preventing abuse of rights to assist public justice, equality and freedom. Before the pandemic, we saw that we were working hard to make laws flexible as well, to fit the changed social and commercial problems, to try to fix the issues that troubled us because of cutting-edge and developing technologies and to achieve a certain control of uncertainties.

Nevertheless, the COVID-19 pandemic tells us our vision to laws is still incomplete. While this health crisis unpredictably caused chaos to the global world's economic, public and social order, deepening the complication to the international and political order, it has triggered a moral order to some extent. We realise what little work we have done before and what a long way there is to go in constructing the legal framework and governance. Hence, it is time to re-consider what laws we need in the "new normal" era or to face future uncertainties.

We believe we need laws with a wide vision and there are three elements to target this vision: balance, sustainability and flexibility. To some extent, these three elements are interactive and inter-connected with each other. A balanced, sustainable and flexible law is able to better shape all relevant stakeholders/parties' interests rather than giving bias to a certain group. Although the laws may seem a compromise in a short-term view, they would be a substantial success from a long-term perspective. A well balanced, sustainable and flexible law is able to deal with routine activities in the normal time as well as a capability to cover

---

46 Martin Partington, *Introduction to the English Legal System 2019–2020* (14th edn, Oxford, OUP 2019) 8.

47 ibid.

uncertainties beyond our control and predictions. This includes extreme situations and other unpredictable events. In other words, such a law can harmonise well and is suitable for a variety of situations. If we could agree universally that this is what we need to respond to future uncertainties such as a pandemic, then the next question is how we could achieve this goal. This is not an easy-answered question. However, some strategies perhaps could be considered: We need to be more brave and open-minded, consider the big picture and take the initiative in pursuing long-term goals and benefits when designing the legal framework and legal regulations. In this case, we may note that even if some laws have a strong private law feature, it is still worth having a perspective of a wider interest of the public. It is also perhaps worth us having a more tolerant and positive attitude to those cutting-edge technologies and the uncertainties that they bring. This will bring a more creative and innovative initiative to the transformations of laws, affected by these new things and changes.

Besides, we need to take a Three-C Strategy: communication, coordination and cooperation. The COVID-19 pandemic shows that no single country can escape from all uncertainties and extreme situations. Although laws show a distinctive nature of territorial, good communication would always make us know and understand better the laws within different cultures, and legal systems. Then, good coordination could build up a good foundation to smoothly implement and harmonise laws within different areas, linking with maximised interest parties. Finally, stronger cooperation would bring us greater safeguarding capabilities to respond to any disaster-scaled unknown. The territorial nature of laws should not be utilised to disrupt or disconnect such cooperation. Instead, laws should give such space for us to form stronger cooperation relations among all levels – whether that be different stakeholders in a legal context, or different countries at an international level. Fighting against uncertainties such as the pandemic is not simply a law mission, we all need to make efforts.

We never know the future, but we can be the future.

Bibliography

Afesorgbor SK and Demena BA, 'Globalization May Actually Be Better for the Environment' (*The Conversation*, 24 April 2018) <https://theconversation.com/globalization-may-actually-be-better-for-the-environment-95406> accessed 25 May 2021.

Anderson J and others, 'Experts Say the "New Normal" in 2025 Will Be Far More Tech-Driven, Presenting More Big Challenges' (*Pew Research Centre*, 18 February 2021) <www.pewresearch.org/internet/2021/02/18/experts-say-the-new-normal-in-2025-will-be-far-more-tech-driven-presenting-more-big-challenges/> accessed 19 May 2021.

Asonye C, 'There's Nothing New About the "New Normal": Here's Why' (*World Economic Forum*, 5 June 2020) <www.weforum.org/agenda/2020/06/theres-nothing-new-about-this-new-normal-heres-why/> accessed 19 May 2021.

BBC, 'Covid: Is Europe Lifting Lockdown Restrictions?' (*BBC News*, 30 April 2021) <www.bbc.co.uk/news/explainers-53640249> accessed 11 May 2021.

Bloomberg J, 'Digitization, Digitalization, And Digital Transformation: Confuse Them At Your Peril' (*Forbes*, 29 April 2018) <www.forbes.com/sites/jason bloomberg/2018/04/29/digitization-digitalization-and-digital-transformation-confuse-them-at-your-peril/?sh=1ec127262f2c> accessed 14 May 2021.

Bonadio E and Fontanelli F, 'Push for COVID-19 Vaccine Patent Waiver Isn't a Panacea: But It Could Nudge Companies to Share' (*The Conversation*, 12 May 2021) <https://theconversation.com/push-for-covid-19-vaccine-patent-waiver-isnt-a-panacea-but-it-could-nudge-companies-to-share-160802?utm_source=linkedin&utm_medium=bylinelinkedinbutton> accessed 13 May 2021.

Bosselmann K, *The Principle of Sustainability: Transforming Law and Governance* (New York, Routledge 2016) 57–73.

Bubalo M and others, 'Are Pandemics the New Normal?' (*BBC News*, 4 January 2021) <www.bbc.co.uk/news/av/world-55415763> accessed 19 May 2021.

Burrell R, 'Defending the Public Interest' (2000)22(9) *European Intellectual Property Review* 394–404.

Cambridge Dictionary <https://dictionary.cambridge.org/dictionary/english/digitalize> accessed 14 May 2021.

Cheung R, 'Shareholders' Personal Rights Under the Articles – Clarity and Confusion' (2011)3 *Journal of Business Law* 290–98.

Commonwealth Secretariat, *Changing the Law: A Practical Guide to Law Reform* (London, Commonwealth Secretariat 2017) 3.

Diamond D and others, 'Biden Commits to Waiving Vaccine Patents, Driving Wedge with Pharmaceutical Companies' (*The Washington Post*, 6 May 2021) <www.washingtonpost.com/health/2021/05/05/biden-waives-vaccine-patents/> accessed 11 May 2021.

Fong K, 'Sustainability and IP: A Match Made in Heaven?' (2016) *In-House Lawyer* 87–88.

Garis M, 'Meeting the Challenges of Digitalisation' (2010)199 *Managing Intellectual Property* 88–90.

Hagen IM, 'Sustainable Decisions and Social Dialogue: Some Significant Developments in Norway' (2011)8(2–3) *European Company Law* 83–87.

Harrison E and Lee J, 'Lockdown: Boris Johnson to Announce 17 May Changes for England' (*BBC News*, 10 May 2021) <www.bbc.co.uk/news/uk-57050860> accessed 11 May 2021.

Hernández-Chea R and others, 'Integrating Intellectual Property and Sustainable Business Models: The SBM-IP Canvas' (*MDPI*, 26 October 2020) <www.mdpi.com/2071-1050/12/21/8871/htm> accessed 25 May 2021.

IMF, 'Globalization: Threat or Opportunity?' (*IMF*, 12 April 2000) <www.imf.org/external/np/exr/ib/2000/041200to.htm#II> accessed 14 May 2021.

India and South Africa, Waiver from Certain Provisions of the TRIPS Agreement for the Prevention, Containment and Treatment of COVID-19 (2020) WTO IP/C/W/669 <https://docs.wto.org/dol2fe/Pages/SS/directdoc.aspx?filename=q:/IP/C/W669.pdf&Open=True> accessed 13 May 2021.

Kasai T, 'From the "New Normal" to a "New Future": A Sustainable Response to COVID-19' (*WHO*, 13 October 2020) <www.who.int/westernpacific/news/commentaries/detail-hq/from-the-new-normal-to-a-new-future-a-sustainable-response-to-covid-19> accessed 19 May 2021.

Klein F, 'GREEN IP – A Look at How Sustainability Influences IP and How IP Can Help In Achieving Sustainability' (*Ashurst*, 30 April 2020) <www.ashurst.com/en/news-and-insights/legal-updates/a-look-at-how-sustainability-influences-ip-and-how-ip-can-help-in-achieving-sustainability/> accessed 18 May 2021.

Lim EH and Dang MD, 'IP Rights and DRM: The Copyright Holder's Guide to Navigating DRM Technology Through Hostile Territory' (2007)21(1) *World Intellectual Property Report* 22–26.

MacMillan F, 'Making Corporate Power Global' (1999)5(1) *International Trade Law & Regulation* 3–9.

Maher DW, 'The UDRP: The Globalization of Trademark Rights' (2002)33(8) *International Review of Intellectual Property and Competition Law* 924–40.

Malinauskaite J, 'Harmonisation in Competition Law in the Context of Globalisation' (2010)21(3) *European Business Law Review* 369–97.

Manyika J and others, 'Digital Globalisation: The New Era of Global Flows' (2016) <www.mckinsey.com/~/media/mckinsey/business%20functions/mckinsey%20 digital/our%20insights/digital%20globalization%20the%20new%20era%20of%20 global%20flows/mgi-digital-globalization-full-report.pdf> accessed 25 May 2021.

Mohamed W, 'Globalisation and ODR: Dynamics of Change in E-Commerce Dispute Settlement' (2004)12(1) *International Journal of Law & Information Technology* 123–52.

Naciti V and others, 'Corporate Governance and Sustainability: A Review of The Existing Literature' (2021) *Journal of Management and Governance* (*Spinger-Link*, 3 January 2021) <https://link.springer.com/article/10.1007/s10997-020-09554-6> accessed 18 May 2021.

Naghavi A and Prarolo G, 'Harmonisation and Globalisation of Intellectual Property Culture' (2018)41(7) *The World Economy* 1847–66.

Niva Elkin-Koren, 'Affordances of Freedom: Theorizing the Rights of Users in the Digital Era' (2012)6 *Jerusalem Review of Legal Studies* 96–109.

Novitz T, 'The Paradigm of Sustainability in a European Social Context: Collective Participation in Protection of Future Interests?' (2015)31(3) *International Journal of Comparative Labour Law and Industrial Relations* 243–62.

Nyombi C and others, 'Shareholder Primacy and Stakeholders' Interests in the Aftermath of a Takeover: A Review of Empirical Evidence' (2015)2 *International Business Law Journal* 161–86.

Pandey V and Nazmi S, 'Covid-19 in India: Why Second Coronavirus Wave Is Devastating' (*BBC News*, 21 April 2021) <www.bbc.co.uk/news/world-asia-india-56811315> accessed 11 May 2021.

Partington M, *Introduction to the English Legal System 2019–2020* (14th edn, Oxford, OUP 2019) 8.

Reed J, 'PM: India Coronavirus Variant Must Be "Handled Carefully"' (*BBC News*, 7 May 2021) <www.bbc.co.uk/news/health-57016110> accessed 11 May 2021.

Saval N, 'Globalisation: The Rise and Fall of an Idea That Swept the World' (*The Guardian*, 14 July 2017) <www.theguardian.com/world/2017/jul/14/globalisation-the-rise-and-fall-of-an-idea-that-swept-the-world> accessed 25 May 2021.

Scharf N, 'Digital Rights Management and Fair Use' (2010)1(2) *European Journal of Law and Technology* <https://ejlt.org/index.php/ejlt/article/view/22/51> accessed 25 May 2021.

Scuotto V and others, 'The Shift Towards a Digital Business Model: A Strategic Decision for the Female Entrepreneur' in Tomos F and others (eds), *Women Entrepreneurs and Strategic Decision Making in the Global Economy* (Hershey, IGI Global 2019) 142–43.

'Sustainability' (*Cambridge Dictionary*) <https://dictionary.cambridge.org/dictionary/english/sustainability> accessed 17 May 2021.

'Sustainability' (*The Law Dictionary*) <https://thelawdictionary.org/sustainability/> accessed 18 May 2021.

United Nations, 'Sustainable Development Goals Kick Off with Start of New Year' (*UN Sustainable Development Goals*) <www.un.org/sustainabledevelopment/blog/2015/12/sustainable-development-goals-kick-off-with-start-of-new-year/> accessed 18 May 2021.

Usher DA, 'South Africa and India Push for COVID-19 Patents Ban' (2020)396 *World Report* 10265 <www.thelancet.com/journals/lancet/article/PIIS0140-6736(20)32581-2/fulltext> accessed 11 May 2021.

Vaidyanathan G, 'Coronavirus Variants Are Spreading in India – What Scientists Know so Far' (*Nature*, 11 May 2021) <www.nature.com/articles/d41586-021-01274-7> accessed 13 May 2021.

The Visual and Data Journalism Team, 'Covid Map: Coronavirus Cases, Deaths, Vaccinations by Country' (*BBC News*, 10 May 2021) <www.bbc.co.uk/news/world-51235105> accessed 11 May 2021.

WHO, 'WHO Coronavirus (COVID-19) Dashboard' (*WHO*, 11 May 2021) <https://covid19.who.int/> accessed 11 May 2021.

Wilson C, 'Blockchain and Sustainability' (2020)44(4) *Company Secretary's Review* 57–58.

The World Bank, 'The Winners and Losers of Globalization: Finding a Path to Shared Prosperity' (*The World Bank*, 25 October 2013) <www.worldbank.org/en/news/feature/2013/10/25/The-Winners-and-Losers-of-Globalization-Finding-a-Path-to-Shared-Prosperity> accessed 25 May 2021.

Index

Note: Page numbers in *italics* indicate a figure on the corresponding page. Page numbers followed by "n" indicate a note.

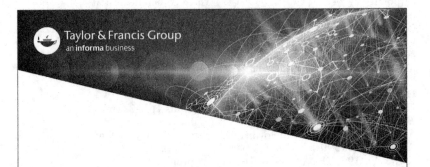

Printed in the United States
by Baker & Taylor Publisher Services